**...FOR DUMMIES** ™

## COMPUTER BOOK SERIES FROM IDG

# References for the Rest of Us

Are you intimidated and confused by computers? Do you find that traditional manuals are overloaded with technical details you'll never use? Do your friends and family always call you to fix simple problems on their PCs? Then the *". . . For Dummies"*™ computer book series from IDG is for you.

*". . . For Dummies"* books are written for those frustrated computer users who know they aren't really dumb but find that PC hardware, software, and indeed the unique vocabulary of computing make them feel helpless. *". . . For Dummies"* books use a lighthearted approach, a down-to-earth style, and even cartoons and humorous icons to diffuse computer novices' fears and build their confidence. Lighthearted but not lightweight, these books are a perfect survival guide for anyone forced to use a computer.

Already, hundreds of thousands of satisfied readers agree. They have made *". . . For Dummies"* books the #1 introductory-level computer book series and have written asking for more. So if you're looking for the most fun and easy way to learn about computers, look to *". . . For Dummies"* books to give you a helping hand.

## IDG BOOKS

# UNIX
## FOR
## DUMMIES™

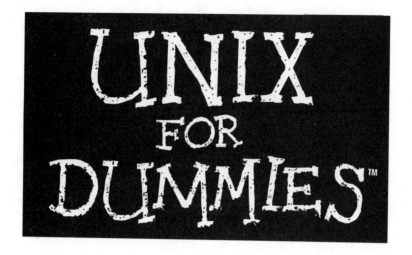

# by John R. Levine and Margaret Levine Young

**IDG BOOKS**

IDG Books Worldwide, Inc.
An International Data Group Company

San Mateo, California ✦ Indianapolis, Indiana ✦ Boston, Massachusetts

# UNIX For Dummies

Published by
**IDG Books Worldwide, Inc.**
An International Data Group Company
155 Bovet Road, Suite 310
San Mateo, CA 94402

Library of Congress Catalog Card No.: 92-75795

ISBN 1-878058-58-4

Printed in the United States of America

10 9 8 7 6 5 4 3 2 1

Distributed in the United States by IDG Books Worldwide, Inc.

Distributed in Canada by Macmillan of Canada, a Division of Canada Publishing Corporation; by Woodslane Pty. Ltd. in Australia and New Zealand; and by Computer Bookshops in the U.K. and Ireland.

For information on translations and availability in other countries, contact Marc Jeffrey Mikulich, Foreign Rights Manager, at IDG Books Worldwide; FAX NUMBER 415-358-1260.

For sales inquiries and special prices for bulk quantities, write to the address above or call IDG Books Worldwide at 415-312-0600.

# Acknowledgments

The authors would like to thank Lydia Spitzer, Jordan Young, and Meg Young for putting up with us while we wrote this book. It probably isn't always easy to live with such smart-alecks.

Also, thanks to Steve Dyer, for help with the GUI screen images and network examples.

(The publisher would like to give special thanks to Patrick J. McGovern, without whom this book would not have been possible.)

# *About IDG Books Worldwide*

Welcome to the world of IDG Books Worldwide.

IDG Books Worldwide, Inc., is a division of International Data Group (IDG), the world's largest publisher of computer-related information and the leading global provider of information services on information technology. IDG publishes over 190 computer publications in 61 countries. Thirty million people read one or more IDG publications each month.

If you use personal computers, IDG Books is committed to publishing quality books that meet your needs. We rely on our extensive network of publications, including such leading periodicals as *Macworld, InfoWorld, PC World, Computerworld, Publish, Network World,* and *SunWorld,* to help us make informed and timely decisions in creating useful computer books that meet your needs.

Every IDG book strives to bring extra value and skill-building instruction to the reader. Our books are written by experts, with the backing of IDG periodicals, and with careful thought devoted to issues such as audience, interior design, use of icons, and illustrations. Our editorial staff is a careful mix of high-tech journalists and experienced book people. Our close contact with the makers of computer products helps ensure accuracy and thorough coverage. Our heavy use of personal computers at every step in production means we can deliver books in the most timely manner.

We are delivering books of high quality at competitive prices on topics customers want. At IDG, we believe in quality, and we have been delivering quality for over 25 years. You'll find no better book on a subject than an IDG book.

John Kilcullen
President and C.E.O.
IDG Books Worldwide, Inc.

IDG Books Worldwide, Inc. is a division of International Data Group. The officers are Patrick J. McGovern, Founder and Board Chairman; Walter Boyd, President; Robert A. Farmer, Vice Chairman. International Data Group's publications include: **ARGENTINA's** Computerworld Argentina, InfoWorld Argentina; **ASIA's** Computerworld Hong Kong, PC World Hong Kong, Computerworld Southeast Asia, PC World Malaysia, PC World Malaysia; **AUSTRALIA's** Computerworld Australia, Australian PC World, Australian Macworld, Network World, Reseller, IDG Sources; **AUSTRIA's** Computerwelt Oesterreich, PC Test; **BRAZIL's** Computerworld, Mundo IBM, Mundo Unix, PC World, Publish; **BULGARIA's** Computerworld Bulgaria, Ediworld, PC World Bulgaria; **CANADA's** Direct Access, Graduate Computerworld, InfoCanada, Network World Canada; **CHILE's** Computerworld, Informatica; **COLUMBIA's** Computerworld Columbia; **CZECH REPUBLIC's** Computerworld Elektronika, PC World; **DENMARK's** CAD/CAM WORLD, Communications World, Computerworld Danmark, Computerworld Focus, Computerworld Uddannelse, Lotus World, Macintosh Produktkatalog, Macworld Danmark, PC World Danmark, PC World Produktguide, Windows World; **EQUADOR's** PC World Ecuador; **EGYPT's** Computerworld Middle East, PC World Middle East; **FINLAND's** MikroPC, Tietoviikko, Tietoverkko; **FRANCE's** Distributique, GOLDEN MAC, InfoPC, Languages & Systems, Le Guide du Monde Informatique, Le Monde Informatique, Telecoms & Reseaux; **GERMANY's** Computerwoche, Computerwoche Focus, Computerwoche Extra, Computerwoche Karriere, edv aspekte, Information Management, Macwelt, Netzwelt, PC Welt, PC Woche, Publish, Unit; **HUNGARY's** Alaplap, Computerworld SZT, PC World, ; **INDIA's** Computers & Communications; **ISRAEL's** Computerworld Israel, PC World Israel; **ITALY's** Computerworld Italia, Lotus Magazine, Macworld Italia, Networking Italia, PC World Italia; **JAPAN's** Computerworld Japan, Macworld Japan, SunWorld Japan; **KENYA's** East African Computer News; **KOREA's** Computerworld Korea, Macworld Korea, PC World Korea; **MEXICO's** Compu Edicion, Compu Manufactura, Computacion/Punto de Venta, Computerworld Mexico, MacWorld, Mundo Unix, PC World, Windows; **THE NETHERLANDS'** Computer! Totaal, LAN Magazine, MacWorld Magazine; **NEW ZEALAND's** Computer Listings, Computerworld New Zealand, New Zealand PC World; **NIGERIA's** PC World Africa; **NORWAY's** Computerworld Norge, C/World, Lotusworld Norge, Macworld Norge, Networld, PC World Ekspress, PC World Norge, PC World's Product Guide, Publish World, Student Data, Unix World, Windowsworld, IDG Direct Response; **PANAMA's** PC World Panama; **PERU's** Computerworld Peru, PC World; **PEOPLES REPUBLIC OF CHINA's** China Computerworld, PC World China, Electronics International, China Network World; **IDG HIGH TECH BEIJING's** New Product World; **IDG SHENZHEN's** Computer News Digest; **PHILLIPPINES'** Computerworld, PC World; **POLAND's** Computerworld Poland, PC World/Komputer; **PORTUGAL's** MacIn; **RUSSIA's** Computerworld-Moscow, Mir-PC, Sety; **SLOVENIA's** Monitor Magazine; **SOUTH AFRICA's** Computing S.A.; **SPAIN's** Amiga World, Computerworld Espana, Communicaciones World, Macworld Espana, NeXTWORLD, PC World Espana, Publish, Sunworld; **SWEDEN's** Attack, ComputerSweden, Corporate Computing, Lokala Natverk/LAN, Lotus World, MAC&PC, Macworld, Mikrodatorn, PC World, Publishing & Design (CAP), Datalngenjoren, Maxi Data, Windows World; **SWITZERLAND's** Computerworld Schweiz, Macworld Schweiz, PC & Workstation; **TAIWAN's** Computerworld Taiwan, Global Computer Express, PC World Taiwan; **THAILAND's** Thai Computerworld; **TURKEY's** Computerworld Monitor, Macworld Turkiye, PC World Turkiye; **UNITED KINGDOM's** Lotus Magazine, Macworld, Sunworld; **UNITED STATES'** AmigaWorld, Cable in the Classroom, CD Review, CIO, Computerworld, Desktop Video World, DOS Resource Guide, Electronic News, Federal Computer Week, Federal Integrator, GamePro, inCider/A+, IDG Books, InfoWorld, InfoWorld Direct, Laser Event, Macworld, Multimedia World, Network World, NeXTWORLD, PC Games, PC World, PC Letter, Publish, Sumeria, SunWorld, SWATPro, Video Event, Video Toaster World; **VENEZUELA's** Computerworld Venezuela, MicroComputerworld Venezuela; **VIETNAM's** PC World Vietnam

 The text in this book is printed on recycled paper.

# About the authors

John Levine and Margaret Levine Young were members of a computer club in high school (this was before high school students, or even high schools, *had* computers). They came in contact with Theodor H. Nelson, the author of *Computer Lib* and the inventor of hypertext, who fostered the idea that computers should not be taken seriously. He showed them that everyone can understand and use computers.

John wrote his first program in 1967 on an IBM 1130 (a computer roughly as powerful as your typical modern digital wristwatch — only more difficult to use). His first exposure to UNIX was while hanging out with friends in Princeton in 1974; he became an official UNIX system administrator at Yale in 1975. John began working part-time for Interactive Systems, the first commercial UNIX company, in 1977 and has been in and out of the UNIX biz ever since. He used to spend most of his time writing software, but now he mostly writes books because it's more fun. He also teaches some computer courses and publishes and edits an incredibly technoid magazine called *The Journal of C Language Translation*. He has a B.A. and a Ph.D. in computer science from Yale University.

Margy has been using small computers since the 1970s. She graduated from UNIX on a PDP/11 to Apple DOS on an Apple II to MS-DOS and UNIX on a variety of machines. She has done all kinds of jobs that involve explaining to people that computers aren't as mysterious as they might think, including managing the use of PCs at Columbia Pictures, teaching scientists and engineers what computers are good for, and writing computer manuals. She has been president of NYPC, the New York PC Users' Group.

Margy has written several computer books, including *Understanding Javelin PLUS* (John also wrote part of it) and *The Complete Guide to PC-File*. She has a degree in computer science from Yale University.

# Credits

**Publisher**
David W. Solomon

**Acquisitions Editor**
Janna Custer

**Managing Editor**
Mary Bednarek

**Project Editors**
Rebecca Whitney
Diane Graves Steele

**Editor**
Alice Martina Smith

**Technical Reviewer**
Linda Slovick

**Production Manager**
Beth J. Baker

**Production Coordinator**
Cindy L. Phipps

**Production Assistant**
Mary A. Breidenbach

**Proofreader**
Sandy Grieshop

**Book Design and Production**
Peppy White
Francette M. Ytsma
Tracy Strub
*(University Graphics, Palo Alto, California)*

# Contents at a Glance

# Cartoons at a Glance

## By Rich Tennant

page 127

page 7

page 199

page 289

page 71

page 37

page 326

page 109

page xxvi

page 247

# Table of Contents

• • • • • • • • • • • • • • • • • • • • • • • • • • • • • • • • • • • • • • • • •

# Introduction

● ● ● ● ● ● ● ● ● ● ● ● ● ● ● ● ● ● ● ● ● ● ● ● ● ● ● ● ● ● ● ● ● ● ● ● ● ● ● ● ● ● ●

*W*elcome to *UNIX for Dummies!* There are lots of books about UNIX, but most of them assume that you have a degree in computer science, would love to learn every strange and useless command UNIX has to offer, and enjoy memorizing unpronounceable commands and options. This book is different.

Instead, this book describes what you really do with UNIX — how to get started, what commands you really need, and when to give up and go for help. And we describe it all in plain, old English.

## About This Book

This book is designed to be used when you can't figure out what to do next. We don't flatter ourselves that you are interested enough in UNIX to sit down and read the whole thing. When you run into a problem using UNIX ("I thought I typed a command that would copy a file, but it didn't respond with any message..."), just dip into the book long enough to solve your problem.

We have included sections about these kinds of things:

- ✔ Typing commands
- ✔ Copying, renaming, or deleting files
- ✔ Printing files
- ✔ Finding where your file went
- ✔ UNIX commands for people who know DOS

## How to Use This Book

Use this book as a reference. Look up your topic or command in the table of contents or the index; they refer to the part of the book in which we describe what to do and perhaps define a few terms, if absolutely necessary.

When you have to type something, it appears in the book like this:

```
cryptic UNIX command to type
```

Type it just as it appears. Use the same capitalization we do — UNIX cares deeply about CAPITAL and small letters. Then press Enter or Return. The book tells you what should happen when you give each command and what your options are. Sometimes part of the command is in *italics*; the italicized stuff is a sample name, and you have to substitute the actual name of the file, computer, or person affected.

Some chapters list error messages you might run into in addition to common user mistakes. You might want to peruse the latter (see Chapter 25) to avoid these mistakes before they happen.

# Who Are You?

In writing this book, we have assumed these things about you:

- You have a UNIX computer or terminal.
- You want to get some work done with it.
- Someone has set it up so that, if you turn it on (in many cases, it's left on all the time), you are talking to UNIX.
- You are not interested in becoming the world's next great UNIX expert.

# How This Book Is Organized

This books has eight parts. The parts stand on their own — you can begin reading wherever you want. This section lists the parts of the book and what they contain:

## Part I: Before the Beginning

This part tells you how to get started with UNIX, including figuring out which kind of UNIX you are using. (You need to know this information later because commands can differ from one type of UNIX to another.) You learn how to log in, type UNIX commands, and ask for help.

## *Part II: Some Basic Stuff about Programs, Files, and Directories*

Like most computer systems, UNIX stores information in files. This part explains how to deal with files — creating, copying, and getting rid of them. It also talks about directories so that you can keep your files organized.

## *Part III: A Quick Tour In and Near Your Computer*

While you are using UNIX, you are also using the computer. This section tells you what you need to know about the machine and the equipment attached to it, and how to care for it.

## *Part IV: Of Mice and Computers*

Many UNIX users must deal with a GUI — a graphical user interface. This part explains the purpose of GUIs and introduces the most common ones: OPEN LOOK, Motif, and the plain X Windows System.

## *Part V: Getting Things Done*

This part talks about getting some work done in UNIX. It also gives step-by-step instructions for using the three most common text editors to create and change text files, how to run several programs at a time (to get confused several times as fast), and a Rosetta stone to help DOS users figure out how to use UNIX.

## *Part VI: The World Outside the UNIX Biosphere*

Most UNIX systems are connected to networks; this part prepares you for the world of communications, including instructions for sending and receiving electronic mail.

## Part VII: Help!

If disaster strikes, check this part of the book. It includes information about what to do if something bad happens, what to do about backups, and a list of common UNIX error messages.

## Part VIII: The Part of Tens

This part is a random assortment of other tidbits about UNIX, including common mistakes, how to find lost files, and how to get on-line help — all organized in convenient 10-item lists, sort of. This part also lists most UNIX commands, including those you use all the time, frequently, rarely, and commands you might see UNIX experts type if you look over a UNIX wizard's shoulder. If you are smart, you will never try to read the UNIX reference manuals, which are written in a strange dialect of neo-Bulgarian. Use this part of *UNIX for Dummies* instead.

# Icons Used in This Book

This symbol lets you know that some particularly nerdy, technoid information is coming up, giving you the opportunity to skip it.

This symbol indicates that a nifty little shortcut or time-saver is explained.

Watch out below — time to duck and cover!

This part applies only if your computer is on a network. If it is not, you can skip to the next section.

This symbol reminds you about something presented in an earlier section of the book or something you need to remember to do.

# *What Now?* _____

That's all you need to know to get started. Whenever you hit a snag in UNIX, just look up the problem in the table of contents or index of this book. You will have the problem solved in a flash — or you will know to find some expert help.

Because UNIX was not designed to be particularly easy to use, don't feed bad if you have to look up a number of topics before you feel comfortable using the computer. Most computer users, after all, never have to face anything as daunting as UNIX (point this out to your DOS and Macintosh user friends)!

# Part I

---

# Before
# the Beginning

**The 5th Wave    By Rich Tennant**

THAT'S RIGHT, THE UPPER CASE BUTTON WORKS ON-SCREEN, BUT THEY'RE NOT COMING OUT ON THE DANG PRINTER! HOLD? SURE, I'LL HOLD.

Poet e.e. cummings makes his last service call.

## In this part...

OK, so now you're a UNIX user. This means that you have been inducted, kicking and screaming, into a fraternity of hard-bitten, humorless nerds with a religious dedication to a 20-year old computer system written by the same people who came up with direct-distance dialing. What? You don't feel religious or dedicated? We can't blame you.

If you're like most new UNIX users, a zealot came by, connected your terminal or workstation, gave you five minutes of incomprehensible advice, demonstrated a few not very exciting games (I mean, since when can you play solitaire better with a $10,000 workstation than with a $1.29 deck of cards?) and disappeared. Now you're on your own.

Since you're here anyway, let's talk about the absolute minimum you need in order to get your UNIX system's attention, persuade it that you are allowed to use it, and maybe even accomplish something useful.

# Chapter 1
# Start 'Er Up, UNIX!

## Turning Your Computer On and Off

If you think that turning your computer on and off is easy, you may be wrong. Because UNIX runs on so many almost-but-not-quite-compatible computers — all of which work somewhat differently — you first must figure out which kind of UNIX computer you have before you can turn it on.

### A dumb terminal

The simplest way to hook up to a UNIX system is with what's known (sneeringly) as a *dumb terminal*. You can identify a dumb terminal by a complete absence of mice and floppy disks and all that other stuff that causes confusion in a more advanced computer. There's a lot to be said for dumb terminals: they're simple and reliable. With UNIX, you can do hundreds, if not thousands, of things wrong to totally scramble a more advanced machine; these same boo-boos make no difference to a dumb terminal.

Turning a dumb terminal on is easy. You find the power switch (probably on the back) and flip it on. Because there are no pesky disks and stuff, you can turn it on or off whenever you want and not break anything. People make long, sort of theological arguments about whether to leave the picture tube on all the time. Personally, we turn off our terminals overnight and don't worry about them at other times.

After you turn on the terminal, you use it to communicate with the computer that is running UNIX. If it is wired directly to the computer, UNIX asks you to log in before you can do anything else (see the section "Hey, UNIX! I Want to Log In" later in this chapter). If not, you may have to do some additional steps to call the computer or otherwise connect to it.

## If a train stops at a train station, what happens at a workstation?

A *workstation* is a computer with a big screen, a mouse, and a keyboard. You may say, "I have a PC with a big screen, a mouse, and a keyboard. Is it really a workstation?" Although UNIX zealots get into long arguments over this question, for our purposes, we'll say that it is.

Turning on a workstation is easy enough: You reach around the back and turn on the switch. Cryptic things that appear on the screen tell you that UNIX is going through the long and not-at-all-interesting process of starting up. Starting up can take anywhere from 10 seconds to 10 minutes, depending on the version of UNIX, number of disks, phase of the moon, and so on. Sooner or later, UNIX demands that you log in. To find out how, skip to the section "Yo, UNIX!" later in this chapter.

Turning off a workstation is a more difficult problem. Workstations are jealous of their prerogatives and will punish you if you don't turn them off in exactly the right way. Their favorite punishment is to throw away all the files related to whatever you were just working on. The exact procedure varies from one model of workstation to another, so you have to ask a local guru for advice. Typically, you enter a command along these lines:

```
shutdown +3
```

This command tells the workstation to shut down in three minutes. With some versions of UNIX, that would be too easy. The version we use most often uses this command:

```
init 5
```

The workstation then spends a while putting a program to bed or whatever else it does to make it feel important because it knows that you're waiting there, tapping your feet. Eventually, it tells you that it's done; at that point, turn it off right away before it gets any more smart ideas.

An approved method for avoiding the hassle of remembering how to turn off
your workstation is never to shut off your computer (although you can switch
the screen off). That's what we do.

## X marks the terminal

An *X terminal* is similar to an extremely stripped-down workstation that can run
only one program — the one that makes X Windows work. (See Chapter 21,
"When X Goes Bad," to find out what X Windows are — or don't. It's all the same
to us.) Turning an X terminal on and off is pretty much like turning a regular
dumb terminal on and off. Because the X terminal doesn't run programs, turning
it off doesn't cause the horrible problems that turning off a workstation can
cause.

## The PC masquerade ball

Because PCs are so cheap these days, it is common to press a PC into duty as a
terminal. You run a *terminal emulator* program on the PC, and suddenly your
mild-mannered PC turns into a super UNIX terminal. (Truthfully, it's more the
other way around: You make a perfectly good PC that can run Leisure Suit Larry
and other business productivity-type applications act like a dumb terminal that
can't do much of anything on its own.)

When you finish with UNIX, you leave the terminal emulator, usually by pressing
Alt-X or some equally arcane combination of keys (consult your local guru:
there's no standardization). Like Cinderella at the stroke of midnight, the
terminal-emulating PC turns back into a real PC. To turn it off, you wait for the
PC's disks to stop running (carefully scrutinize the front panel until all the little
red or green lights go out) and then reach around and turn off the big, red
switch. If you don't wait for the lights to go out, you're liable to lose some files.

# Hey, UNIX! I Want to Log In

Whether you use a terminal or a workstation, you have to get the attention of
UNIX. You can tell when you have its attention because it demands that you
identify yourself by logging in. If you use a workstation, when UNIX is done load-
ing itself, it is immediately ready for you to log in (skip ahead to the section
"Logging In: U(NIX) Can Call Me Al"). But you terminal users (X or otherwise)
may not be so lucky.

If you're lucky, your terminal is attached directly to the main computer so that it immediately displays a friendly invitation to start work, something like this:

```
ttyS034 login:
```

Well, maybe the invitation isn't that friendly. By the way, the ttyS034 is the name UNIX gives to your terminal. Why doesn't it use something easier to remember, like Fred or Muffy? Beats us!

This catchy phrase tells you that you have UNIX's attention and that it is all ears (metaphorically speaking) for you to log in. You can skip the next section and go directly to the section "Logging In: U(NIX) Can Call Me Al."

If your UNIX system displays a terminal name, make a note of it. You don't care what your terminal's name is, but, if something gets screwed up and you have to ask an expert for help, we can promise you that the first thing the guru will ask is, "What's your terminal name?" If you don't know, the guru may make a variety of nerd-type disparaging comments. But, if you can say, "A-OK, Roger. That's terminal tty125," your guru will assume that you are a with-it kind of user and maybe even try to help you.

# *Yo, UNIX!*

If you're using a PC with a modem, you probably will have to tell the modem to call the UNIX system. All terminal emulators have a way to make the call with two or three keystrokes, but all these ways are different, of course. (Are you surprised?) You have to ask your local guru for info.

After your terminal is attached to the computer, turned on, and otherwise completely ready to do some work, UNIX, as often as not, doesn't admit that you're there. It just sits there and doesn't say anything. In this way, UNIX resembles a recalcitrant child — firm but kind discipline is needed here.

The most common ways to get UNIX's attention are shown in this list:

✔ Press the Return or Enter key. (We call it the Enter key in this book, if you don't mind.) Try it two or three times if it doesn't work the first time. If you're feeling grouchy, try it 20 or 30 times and use a catchy cha-cha or conga rhythm. It doesn't hurt anything and is an excellent way to relieve stress.

✔ Try other attention-getting keystrokes. Ctrl-C (hold down the Ctrl key, sometimes labeled Control, and press C) is a good one. So is Ctrl-Z. Repeat to taste.

> ✔ If you're attached to UNIX through a modem, you may have to do some
> speed matching (described in a minute). You do this by pressing the Break
> key a few times. If you're using a terminal emulator, the Break key may be
> disguised as Alt-B or some other hard-to-find combination. Ask your guru.

Two modems can talk to each other in about 14,000 different ways, and they
have easy-to-remember names, like B212, V.32, and V.22bis (*bis* is French for
"and a half." Really.). After you call the UNIX system's modem with your modem, the two modems know perfectly well which way they're communicating,
but UNIX sometimes doesn't know. Every modem made since about 1983 an-
nounces the method it's using when it makes the connection. Because the
corresponding piece of UNIX code dates from about 1975, though, UNIX ignores
the modem's announcement and guesses, probably incorrectly, at what's being
used.

If you see something like ~xxx~~r.!" on-screen, you need to try *speed matching*. Every time you press Break (or the terminal emulator's version of Break),
UNIX makes a different guess at the way its modem is working. If it guesses
right, you see the login prompt; if it guesses wrong, you see another bunch of
~xxx~~~@(r)!" or you see nothing. If UNIX guessed wrong, press Break again.
Break cycles through all the speeds; if you miss it the first time, you keep break-
ing until the right speed comes around again.

After a while, you will learn exactly how many Returns, Enters, Breaks, and
whatnots your terminal needs in order to get UNIX's attention. It will become
second nature to type them, and you won't even notice what a nerd you look
like while you do it. There's no way around that last part, unfortunately.

# Logging In: U (NIX) Can Call Me Al

Every UNIX user has a user name and a password. Your system administrator
assigns you a user name and a password. You can and should change your
password, but you're stuck with your user name.

Before you can start work, you must prove your *bona fides* by logging in, that is,
by typing your user name and password. How hard can it be to type two words?
Really, now. The problem is this: Because of a peculiarity of human brain wiring, you will find that you can't enter your user name and password without
making a typing mistake. It doesn't matter whether your user name is *al* — you
will type *Al, la, a;L,* and every other possible combination.

UNIX always considers upper- and lowercase letters to be different: If your user name (sometimes also called your login name) is egbert, you must type it exactly that way. Don't type *Egbert, EGBERT,* or anything else. Yes, we know that your name is *Egbert* and not *egbert,* but your computer doesn't know that. UNIX user names almost always are written entirely in lowercase. Pretend that you're a disciple of e. e. cummings.

When you type your user name and password and make a mistake, you may be tempted to backspace over your mistake. If only life were that easy. Guess how you backspace over typing errors when you type your user name and password? You use the # key, of course! (We're sure that it made sense in 1975.) Some — but not all — versions of UNIX have changed so that you can use Backspace or Delete; you may have to experiment. If you want UNIX to ignore everything you have typed, press @, unless your version of UNIX has changed the command key to Ctrl-U (for *untype,* presumably — doubleplusungood). So, Egbert (as you typed your user name), you may have typed something like this:

```
ttyS034 login: Eg##egberq#t
```

Finish entering your user name by pressing Enter or Return.

After you type your user name, UNIX asks you to enter your password, which you type the same way and end by pressing Enter (or Return, but we call it Enter). Because your password is secret, it doesn't appear on-screen as you type it. How can you tell whether you've typed it correctly? You can't! If UNIX agrees that you've typed your user name and password acceptably, it displays a variety of uninteresting legal notices and a message from your system administrator (usually `delete some files, the disk is full`) and passes you on to the shell, which you learn about in Chapter 2.

If UNIX did not like either your user name or password, UNIX says `Login incorrect` and tells you to start over with your user name.

In the interest of security, UNIX asks you for a password even if you type your user name wrong. This arrangement confuses the bad guys but not nearly as much as it confuses regular users. So, if UNIX rejects your password even though you're sure that you typed it correctly, maybe you typed your user name wrong.

## Password Smarts

Like every UNIX user, you should have a password. You can get along without a password only under these circumstances:

✔ You keep the computer in a locked room to which you have the only key.

✔ You don't mind whether unruly 14-year-olds borrow your account and randomly insert dirty knock-knock jokes in the report you're supposed to give to your boss tomorrow.

The choice of your password deserves some thought. You want something easy for you to remember but difficult for other people to guess. Here are some bad choices for passwords: single letters or digits, your name, the name of your spouse or significant other, your kid's name, your cat's name, or anything less than six letters long. (Bad guys can try every possible five-letter password in just a few hours.)

Good choices include something like your college roommate's name misspelled and backward. Throw in a digit or two or some punctuation, and capitalize a few letters to add confusion so that you end up with something like yeLLas12. Another good idea is to use a pair of words, like *fat;Head*. Password names have no character limit, but often only the first eight matter.

You can change your password whenever you're logged in, by using the passwd program. It asks you to enter your old password to prove that you're still who you were when you logged in (computers are notoriously skeptical). Then the passwd program asks you to enter your new password twice, to make sure that you type it, if not correctly, at least consistently. None of the three passwords you type appears on-screen, of course. We tell you how to run the passwd program in Chapter 2.

Some system administrators do something called *password aging*; this strategy makes you change your password at least once a month. Some administrators put rules in the passwd program that try to enforce which passwords are permissible, and some even assign passwords chosen randomly. This idea is terrible because the only way you can remember a password you didn't choose is to write it on a Post-it note and stick it on your terminal, which defeats the purpose of having passwords.

In any event, be sure that no one but you knows your password. Change your password whenever you think that someone else might know it. UNIX stores passwords in a scrambled form so that even the system administrator can't find out what yours is. If you forget your password, the administrator can give you a new one, but she can't tell you what your old one was.

If you really want to be paranoid about passwords, don't use a password that appears in any dictionary. Some truly fiendish system-breaker may decide to use UNIX's password-encryption program to encrypt every last word in a dictionary and then compare every encrypted word to your password — another thing to keep you awake at night.

# Ciao, UNIX!

Logging out is easy — at least compared to logging in. You usually can type `logout`. Depending on which shell you're using (a wart we worry about in Chapter 2), you might have to type `exit` instead. In many cases, you can press Ctrl-D to log out.

You will know that you have logged out successfully because UNIX either invites the next sucker to log in or hangs up the phone.

# Chapter 2

# What Is UNIX, Anyway?

• • • • • • • • • • • • • • • • • • • • • • • • • • • • • • • • • • • • • • • • • • •

## In This Chapter

▶ Why you care: some boring UNIX history

▶ How to tell which version of UNIX you have

▶ How to use the UNIX shell

▶ Shell traps and pitfalls

• • • • • • • • • • • • • • • • • • • • • • • • • • • • • • • • • • • • • • • • • • •

*T*his entire chapter tells you how to figure out which kind of UNIX system you have gotten involved with. If you *really* don't think that you care, skip this chapter. As you read the rest of this book and run into places where you need to know which kind of UNIX or shell you are using, you can always come back here.

## Why Do We Ask Such Dumb Questions?

"What is UNIX?" UNIX is UNIX, right? Not entirely. UNIX has been evolving feverishly for 20 years, sort of like bacteria in a cesspool — only not so attractive. As a result, there have been many different varieties of UNIX along the way. They all share numerous characteristics, but (we bet this doesn't surprise you) they differ just enough that even experienced users are tripped up by the differences between versions.

## Let a Hundred Flowers Blossom

Indulge us while we tell a historical parable. (If you're not into this, skip to the following sections that list the various major UNIX versions.) Imagine, for the moment, that UNIX is a kind of automobile rather than a computer system. In the early days, every UNIX system was distributed with a complete set of source code and development tools. If UNIX had been a car, this distribution method would have been the same as every car being supplied with a complete set of blueprints, wrenches, arc-welders, and other car-building tools. Now imagine that nearly all these cars were sold to engineering schools. You might expect that the students would get to work on their cars and, soon enough, no two cars would be the same. That's pretty much what happened to UNIX.

Bell Labs released the earliest editions of UNIX only to colleges and universities (because Bell Labs was The Phone Company at that time, it wasn't supposed to be in the software business); from that seed, a variety of more-or-less scruffy mutants sprang up and different people modified and extended different versions of UNIX.

Although about 75 percent of the important stuff is the same on all UNIX systems, it helps to know which kind of UNIX you're using, for two reasons. You can tell which of several alternatives applies to you. You can impress your friends by saying things like "HP-UX is a pretty good implementation of BSD, although it's not as featureful as SunOS." It doesn't matter whether you know what it means — your friends will be amazed and speechless.

Throughout this book, we note when a command or feature being discussed differs among the three major versions of UNIX. We won't waste your time with a family tree of UNIX systems. The following sections describe the three most common kinds of systems, with a note about a fourth.

The two main versions of UNIX are BSD UNIX and System V. Although they differ in lots of little ways, the easiest way to tell which one you're using is to see how you print something. If the printing command is `lp`, you have System V; if it's `lpr`, you have BSD. (If the command is `print`, you cannot be using UNIX: nothing in UNIX is that easy.) The other two versions we will describe are OSF/1 and XENIX.

# Berkeley (with an e) UNIX: The Techno-UNIX

One of the schools that received an early copy of UNIX was the University of California at Berkeley. Then it received some government money (your tax dollars at play) and added every bell and whistle it could think of to its version of UNIX. No student's career was complete without adding a small feature to Berkeley UNIX; you can still see on every part of BSD UNIX the greasy fingerprints of a generation of students, particularly a guy named Bill, whom you will hear more about later.

When word got out about all the swell stuff Berkeley had done, the Berkeley people made an official Berkeley Software Distribution version of their hacked-up UNIX code (code-named BSD UNIX). As Berkeley kept making changes, it gave numbers to its versions. The most widely used versions of BSD UNIX are versions 4.2 and 4.3. Berkeley promises that 4.4 will be the last version. We can only hope.

Berkeley graduates fanned out across the country, working for and even starting new computer companies. Most of these companies sell some descendant of BSD UNIX. Many of the founders of Sun Microsystems came from Berkeley; Sun markets SunOS and Solaris. Hewlett-Packard has HP-UX, Digital Equipment has Ultrix, and IBM has AIX (a mixture of BSD UNIX and too much other stuff to contemplate).

Most workstations run some version of BSD UNIX.

## V for victory

Meanwhile, back at The Phone Company, legions of programmers were making different changes to UNIX. They gave their versions of UNIX Roman numerals — which are classier than plain ol' digits. Their current version of UNIX is known as System V.

There are many versions of System V; these subversions are known as System V Release 1 — or SVR1 — and SVR2, SVR3, SVR3.2, and SVR4. The latest version is SVR4.2. (Where *do* they get these numbers?)

Most non-workstation versions of UNIX are based on System V or occasionally its predecessor, System III. (What happened to System IV? Not ready for prime time, we guess.)

After sniping at each others for years, the BSD and System V camps decided to bury the hatchet and combine all the features of BSD and System V into the latest version of System V — SVR4, which has so many goodies that it's only slightly smaller than a blimp and is widely regarded as a godsend to the makers of the large disks needed to hold it all. If your system runs SVR4, you have to pay attention to the hints about both BSD *and* System V.

*Helpful advice to Sun users:* Although Sun changed the name of its software from SunOS to Solaris, it didn't change the way it worked (at least in Solaris 1.0, which is still a BSD-flavored UNIX). So, if you use Solaris 1.0, follow instructions for BSD UNIX. Solaris 2.0 is based on SVR4, however, so you have to worry about both BSD and System V. Is this clear? We're still confused about it.

## *To ensure mystification, we introduce OSF/1*

When System V and BSD UNIX merged to form SVR4, many UNIX vendors were concerned that, with only one version of UNIX, there would be insufficient market confusion. They started the Open Software Foundation, which makes yet another kind of UNIX: OSF/1. OSF/1 is mostly BSD but includes a goulash of some System V, a little of this, and a little of that. Although Digital Equipment Corporation is the primary company that ships OSF/1, IBM's AIX also is related to OSF/1.

If you use OSF/1, pay attention to the BSD advice in this book and you should be OK.

## *XENIX: the antique that refuses to die*

A few older versions of UNIX just won't die. The most notable version is XENIX, originally from Microsoft Corporation and later sold by the Santa Cruz Organization (SCO), a Microsoft affiliate.

XENIX is considered to be hopelessly obsolete. On one hand, it occupies much less disk space than do more modern versions of UNIX; on the other hand, it runs much faster. (To be fair, it's missing some of the more modern versions' zoomy features, but not many you would be likely to notice.)

XENIX is based on one of the ancestors of System V, and SCO, the largest XENIX vendor, added many System V features to later versions of XENIX, so most System V advice applies to XENIX.

# *How Can You Tell?*

When you log in to your UNIX system, a variety of copyright notices usually flash by, with an identification of the kind of UNIX you are accessing. Carefully scrutinize the information on the screen and you may be able to tell which version you have.

If you can't tell which UNIX you have, break down, grovel, and ask your local UNIX expert. When you figure out which kind of UNIX you are running, write it down on the Cheat Sheet in the front of this book. You never know when you might need to know that stuff.

If you're using a dumb terminal or an X terminal (or a PC acting like a terminal), the kind of UNIX you're using depends on the maker of the main computer you're attached to — not on the maker of the terminal. Generally, you see the identification of the main computer in a message it sends to the terminal just before or just after you log in.

# Cracking the Shell

Now that you have figured out which general variety of UNIX you have, you must figure out one other vital consideration: which shell you're using. You might say, "I don't want to use *any* shell; I just want to get some work done," but the shell is the only way to get to where you want to be.

The guts of UNIX are buried deep in the bowels of the computer. They don't deign to deal with such insignificant details as determining what users might want to do. That nasty business is delegated to a category of programs known as shells. A *shell* is a program that waits for you to type a command and then executes it. From the UNIX point of view, a shell is nothing special, other than the first program UNIX runs after you log in. Because you can designate any old program to run when you log in, any fool can write a shell — indeed, many have done so. About a dozen UNIX shells are floating around, all slightly incompatible with each other (you probably guessed that).

Fortunately, all the popular shells fall into two groups: the Bourne (or Korn) shell and the C shell. If you can figure out which of the two categories your shell is in, you can get some work done. (You're getting close!)

If you use a GUI (see Chapter 10), you see windows and icons after you log in, not a boring little UNIX prompt. But you still have to use a UNIX shell from time to time, usually to perform housekeeping tasks. Usually, when the GUI starts up, one of the windows looks like a little terminal with a shell prompt, so you can type your shell commands there.

## You can disregard this discussion about the true nature of shells

What UNIX calls a shell, many other people — especially DOS users — call a command processor. What DOS users call a shell is a fancy graphical program that is supposed to make the computer easier to use by displaying cute little icons for programs and files and other such user-friendly goodies.

The people who wrote UNIX didn't go for all this wimpy, fru-fru, hand-holding stuff, so their idea of a shell was a program in which you could type zq to run a program called zq. (These guys were notoriously lazy typists.) User-friendly shells are available for UNIX, but they're not widely used, and we don't mention them again in this book.

If a Windows or Macintosh fanatic says rude things about the UNIX shell, you can respond that, although UNIX might be somewhat challenging to use, as a UNIX user, at least you're not a wimp.

You can easily tell which kind of shell you're using. If UNIX displays a $ after you log in, you have the Bourne shell; if UNIX displays a %, you're using the C shell. Traditionally, System V systems use the Bourne shell, and BSD systems use the C shell. These days, however, because all versions of UNIX come with both shells, you get whichever one your system administrator likes better. Preferences in command languages are similar to preferences in underwear: People like what they like, so you get what you get.

After you have determined whether you have a Bourne shell ($) or a C shell (%), note this fact on your Cheat Sheet.

## The Bourne shell

The most widely used UNIX shell is the Bourne shell, named after Steve Bourne, who originally wrote it. The Bourne shell is on all UNIX systems. It prompts you with $, after which you type a command and press Enter (or Return). Like all UNIX programs, the Bourne shell itself is a program, and its program name is sh. Clever, eh?

There are a few alternative versions of the original Bourne shell, most notably the Bourne Again shell (also called bash). This version of the Bourne shell is used in many places because of its price — it's free. Some people claim that it's still overpriced, but we won't get into that. The bash program is enough like the original Bourne shell that anything we say about the Bourne shell applies also to bash.

## The Korn-on-the-cob shell

After the Bourne shell was in common use for a couple of years, it became apparent to many people that it was so simple and coherent that a single person could understand all its features and use them all effectively. Fortunately, this shameful situation was remedied by someone who added about a thousand new features to the Bourne shell and ended up with the Korn shell (called ksh and named after the guy who added all the new stuff). Only people who write *shell scripts* (sequences of shell commands saved in a file) are interested in most of the new features, so you can probably consider the Korn shell to be the same as the Bourne shell.

## She sells C shells

No, the C shell wasn't written by someone named C; it was written by Bill, the guy we mentioned earlier. (He sells C shells by the C shore? Probably.) We would discuss our opinion of the C shell at length, except that Bill is 6'4", in excellent physical shape, and knows where we live. The C shell's name is csh.

## Who says the C shell isn't user-friendly?

If you use the C shell, be aware that some punctuation characters do special and fairly useful things.

An exclamation point ( ! ) tells the C shell to repeat a command. Two of them ( ! ! ) means to repeat the last command you typed. One exclamation point followed by the first few characters of a command means to repeat the last command that started with those characters. Type this line, for example:

```
!cp
```

to repeat the last cp command you gave. This is great for lazy typists.

You can use carets (^) also to tell the C shell to repeat a command with some change. If you type this line:

```
^old^new
```

the C shell repeats the last command and substitutes new for old wherever it appears in what you typed. The C shell also uses colons ( : ) and slashes (/) to perform truly confusing editing of previous commands, which we don't get into here.

The most notable difference between the C shell and the other leading shell brands is that the C shell has many more magic characters (characters that do something special when you type them). Fortunately, unless you use a lot of commands with names like ed!3x, this isn't a problem.

There are many versions of the C shell; most of them differ in which bugs are fixed and which are still there. You might run into a program called tcsh, a slightly extended C shell.

# *Are There Any Good Programs On?*

You may be wondering why we refer sometimes to commands and sometimes to programs. What's the difference?

A command is something you type that tells UNIX (the shell, actually) what to do. A program is a file that contains executable code. The confusion comes because, in UNIX, to run a program, you just type its name. (In old-fashioned operating systems, you usually typed something like RUN BUDGET_ANALYSIS to run a program called BUDGET_ANALYSIS.)

When you type a command, such as ls or cp or emacs (a text editor we talk about in Chapter 12), the shell looks at it carefully. There are some commands the shell knows how to do by itself, including cd and exit. If the command isn't one the shell can do by itself, it looks around for a program of the same name.

DOS users may recognize the way this works: Commands DOS can do itself are called internal commands and commands that require running another program are called external commands. Internal commands are also called built-in commands.

# Finally! You're Ready to Work

We wrap up this chapter with a little advice about hand-to-hand combat with the shell. There are many commands you can give to your shell. Every shell has about a dozen built-in commands, most of which aren't very useful in day-to-day use. All the other commands are the names of other programs. The fact that every UNIX system has hundreds of programs lying around translates into hundreds of possible shell commands.

One nice thing about UNIX shells is that, within a given shell, the way you type commands is completely consistent. If you want to edit a file called my-calendar, for example, and use an editor called e, you type this line:

```
$ e my-calendar
```

As always, press Enter at the end of the line to tell the shell you have finished. The shell runs the e editor, which does whatever it does. When you finish, you return to the shell, where you can issue another command.

Whenever you see a UNIX prompt (either $ or %), a shell is running, waiting to do your bidding. Throughout this book, we usually refer to the entire package — UNIX plus shell — as UNIX so that we don't confuse things. We say, "Use the ls command to get UNIX to display a list of files" rather than "Use the ls command to get the shell to get UNIX to display a list of files." OK?

Now you know which kind of UNIX you are using, which shell you are using, and why you care. Let's look at a few UNIX (or shell) commands you can use to begin getting something done.

## Ending command lines without hard feelings

Remember to end every command line by pressing Enter. UNIX is pretty dumb; in most cases, your pressing Enter is the only way UNIX can tell that you have finished doing something.

With a few programs, notably the text editors vi and emacs, you don't need to press Enter anywhere; we point out those exceptions. Everywhere else, remember to press the Enter key at the end of every line.

# We could tell you the password, but then we'd have to kill you

When you logged in, you probably hated your password because someone else picked it. Hating your password is a good reason to change it. Another reason you might want to change it is that, to get this far, you enlisted the aid of some sort of expert and had to reveal your password. This section shows how to change your password: Use the passwd command.

This is easy stuff. Just type the following line:

```
passwd
```

As always, press Enter after typing the command. The passwd command asks you to type your current password to make sure that you are really you. (If it didn't do this, whenever you wandered off to get some more coffee, someone could sneak over to your desk and change your password. Not good.) Type your current password and press Enter. The password doesn't appear on-screen as you type (security reasons — sorry).

Then passwd asks for your new password. (Chapter 1 gave you lots of sage advice about how to choose a password.) You have to type the new password twice so that passwd is sure that you typed it correctly. Assuming that you type the new password twice in the same way, passwd changes your password. The next time you log in, you are expected to know it.

If you forget your password, there is no way to retrieve it, not even by your system manager. The manager can assign you a new one, though, and you can change it again, preferably to something more memorable than the one you forgot.

# Gimme a list of my files

This section discusses a command you use a lot: the ls command, which lists your files. Chapter 3 talks more about files, directories, and other stuff ls helps you with; for now, here's ls Lesson 1. Type the following line (we're not telling you to press Enter anymore because we know that you have the hang of it):

```
ls
```

The ls command lists the names of the files in your home directory. (Chapter 3 talks about home directories.)

## Oops!

If you are a world-class typist, you can skip this section. If you make thousands of typos a day, as we do, pay close attention. If you type something wrong, you can probably press the Backspace key to back up and retype it. If that doesn't work, though, all is not lost. Try the Delete key, the # key (Shift-3), or Ctrl-H (hold down the Ctrl key and press H). One of these combinations should work to back you up.

To give up and start the entire line over again (not usually necessary with nice, short commands, such as ls), press Ctrl-U. If that doesn't work, press @ (Shift-2).

## Play it again, Sam

Sometimes, you may want to issue the same command again (it was so much fun the first time). To do this, type the following:

```
!!
```

This command works only in the C shell. If you use the Bourne shell, you are out of luck and must type your command over again. In the Korn shell, you can type this line to reissue a command:

```
r
```

## Don't turn off the computer if you make a typo!

To repeat something we have hinted at, if you make a mistake and all is not going well, do not turn off the computer, unplug it, or otherwise get unnecessarily rough. PC users get used to just turning the darned thing off if things aren't going well, but UNIX computers don't respond well to this approach.

Instead, suggest politely to UNIX that it stop doing whatever it is you don't like. To stop a command, press the Ctrl-C key or the Delete key (if you have it).

If the situation is out of control, UNIX is running a program you don't want, and you can't get it to stop, you can use some Advanced and Obscure Techniques to wrestle extremely recalcitrant programs into line. See Chapter 21 if you're desperate.

# *Everything you wanted to know about typing commands (but were afraid to ask)*

This list shows a wrap-up of what to do when UNIX displays a prompt (either $ or %) and you want to type a command:

- ✔ As you type, a cursor moves along to indicate where you are. The cursor looks like an underline or a box.

- ✔ If you make a typing mistake, press Backspace (or try Delete, #, or Ctrl-H).

- ✔ To cancel the entire command before you press Enter or Return, press Ctrl-U (or try @).

- ✔ When you finish typing a command, press Enter. (If you don't, UNIX — and you — will wait forever.)

- ✔ If you issue a command that UNIX (actually, the shell) doesn't know, you see a message like this:

  ```
  blurfle: Command not found.
  ```

  This message means that you typed the command wrong, you typed a command UNIX doesn't know (maybe a command from some other computer crept in), or someone hasn't told UNIX the right places to look for your programs.

- ✔ Don't stick extra spaces in the middle of commands, as in `pass wd`. Type the command exactly as `we show it`. On the other hand, *do* type a space after the name of the command but before any additional information you have to type on the line (more about that subject in Chapter 3). Also, do not capitalize except where you know the command has a capital letter.

- ✔ You know that a command resembles a sentence, but you don't end it with a period. UNIX doesn't like the period, and UNIX is extremely unforgiving.

TIP

# The UNIX cast of special characters

One of the more exciting aspects of typing shell commands is that many characters are special. They have special meanings to UNIX; the next few chapters discuss some of them. Special characters include the ones in this list:

```
?      <      >      '
*      !      \      "
#      |      @      $
```

Spaces also are considered special because they separate words in a command. If you want to put special characters in a command, you must quote them. You quote stuff by putting quotation marks around it. Suppose that you have a file called c* (not a great idea, but sometimes you get these things by mistake). You can edit it by typing the following line:

```
e "c*"
```

You can use either single or double quotation marks as long as you're consistent. You can even quote single quotes with double quotes, and quote double quotes with single quotes. Is that clear? Never mind.

# Chapter 3
# Pleading for Help

● ● ● ● ● ● ● ● ● ● ● ● ● ● ● ● ● ● ● ● ● ● ● ● ● ● ● ● ● ● ● ● ● ● ● ● ● ● ● ● ● ●

## In This Chapter
▶ When to plead for help
▶ Whom to ask
▶ How to ask
▶ Bribes and inducements

● ● ● ● ● ● ● ● ● ● ● ● ● ● ● ● ● ● ● ● ● ● ● ● ● ● ● ● ● ● ● ● ● ● ● ● ● ● ● ● ● ●

## Arrghh! This Will Never Work!

Sooner or later, you run into a problem you can't solve on your own. If the time from when you start work until you give up is greater than 15 seconds, you have already beaten the averages.

You need to ask for help. In a perfect world, you pick up the phone, call someone, and describe what's wrong; the person tells you exactly the right thing to do. Of course, in that perfect world, there is also an Easter bunny. In the real world, the people you can call range from those who don't want to help you to those who couldn't help you even if they wanted to.

You can get some help as long as you carefully consider whom you ask for help and how you ask for it.

## A Taxonomy of Possibly Helpful People

There are two general categories of people you can ask for help: normal people and abnormal people. The latter category is divided into Wizards (people who know more about UNIX than is healthy) and System Administrators (people whose job it is to keep the computer working).

## Getting help from normal people

Usually, the best person to ask for help is some other, slightly more experienced user. There are several reasons for this approach: These people probably learned about this stuff just last week, so they're proud to show it off. They aren't so expert that they answer all your questions in incomprehensible gobbledygook. Statistically, there are many more normal users than wizards and system administrators, so they are much easier to find.

## Getting help from UNIX wizards

No, a UNIX wizard is not a guy who has a pointy hat and who, for surgical reasons, cannot reproduce. It's someone who knows a heck of a lot about UNIX and has spent so long learning it that he (they're almost all male) has long since forgotten that not everyone knows this stuff.

Here are some of the pros and cons of asking a wizard for help:

*Pro:* A true UNIX wizard can answer any question about UNIX that you can possibly ask.

*Con:* The wizard is really busy and probably doesn't want to answer your question.

*Con:* Even if the wizard does answer your question, you may not understand the answer.

## Getting help from system administrators

The system administrator is the person in charge of your UNIX system. UNIX systems generally are complicated enough that someone must have the formal job of assigning user names and making sure that printers print, networks network, modems mo and dem, and so forth. Traditionally, all system administrators have been wizards also (they had to be). The demand for system administrators has increased and (strange but true) the job of managing UNIX systems has gotten easier; the typical system administrator, however, doesn't know much about UNIX other than what's required to do administrative work. Not to belittle them: they surely know more than your average user does.

One thing all system administrators have in common is that they're extremely overworked. They have way too many systems to manage, no time to manage them, no budget, and so on. You can be sure that system administrators, no matter how nice they are in real life, will welcome your entreaties for help with about as much enthusiasm as they would greet a case of athlete's foot. But there are a few problems that only your system administrator can solve.

Every UNIX system has one user known as the *superuser.* (For historical reasons, the superuser's name is *root,* presumably because one of the original UNIX guys loved fine food and was a fan of Waverly Root, the food writer.) There are some jobs that only the superuser can do, such as adding and deleting users, installing new software, and rearranging disks to give you more disk space. Because the system administrator should be the only person who knows the password for the superuser, there's no one else to ask for help for these types of tasks. The system administrator is most likely to know the correct answer to other questions also, such as the version of the operating system you're using (sometimes essential for tracking down problems) and network-configuration questions. This information often changes weekly, and a user with last week's answer may inadvertently be lying to you.

Here are some pros and cons of asking the system administrator for help:

*Pro:* He or she is well informed about system configuration...

*Con:* ...but overworked and will not welcome your question.

## Getting help from help desks and the like

If you work for a large organization, it may have a help desk staffed by people whose job it is to answer questions from people within the organization. What the heck, give it a try. The quality of the help varies; if nothing else, these help sources have heard a lot of questions. Even an answer of "We have no idea how to solve your problem, but Mary in Purchasing had the same problem last week," can lead you in useful directions.

## Getting electronic help

Most UNIX systems are attached to computer networks, which means that you might be able to direct an electronic question to thousands of other people out there. It's worth learning how to use electronic mail because often you can get help faster from someone on the network thousands of miles away than you can get it from someone down the hall. See Chapter 18 for more details about using electronic mail.

# Phrasing Your Plea

No matter who you ask, there are better and worse ways to ask for help. This section can steer you through some of these thorny areas.

## Ask nicely

We hope that asking nicely is an obvious tip, but we know from bitter experience that it's not. Remember that no one really has to help you, despite what their job description says. And answers can range from the brutally short ("Type `kill -9 `ps | grep 123 | cut -f1`` and don't ask me why") to the truly useful answer. So, be nice. And say "thank you" afterward, like your mother told you.

## I'm running FrameMaker 11.72 on ttyS034, and it just weirded out when I pressed F7

The more concretely you can phrase your question, the more likely you are to get useful help. If something didn't work the way you expected, what were you doing just before it screwed up? Remember the exact commands you typed and what messages were spat back. Did you do something different from the way you did it before? Did you use different files or programs? A different terminal? Do you know your terminal name? (See Chapter 1.) Do you know the names of the files and programs involved? If the answer to that last one is No, expect to encounter considerable rolling of eyes and deep, heartfelt sighs.

## Don't ask the same question three times

Nothing wears out your welcome faster than asking the same question (or what seems to be the same question to the person you're asking) over and over again. You probably will find that, even after someone gives you a nice, clear answer you understand so that you can fix your problem and forge ahead, if you're not careful, you will forget what the answer was. The next time you run into the same problem, you won't remember what to do. Then you not only will ask the same question again, but also be beet red from embarrassment.

Don't let this happen to you! Many people find it helpful to write things down, preferably in a little notebook with something like "Jeff's Compleat Compendium of UNIX Hints and Tricks" written on the cover. (If your name isn't Jeff, feel free to adjust the title as necessary. Ours is called "Stupid UNIX Tricks.") In fact, we have found that, after you write down an answer or a hint, you never have to look it up because the act of writing it down is enough to commit it to memory.

Do write down solutions to your problems — unless you are absolutely, 100 percent sure that either you will never, never, run into that problem again or you have memorized the answer for all time. Then write it down anyway.

## *"Nothing changed, but...."*

Never say this. There's nothing as exasperating to a UNIX wizard — or even to a genuinely helpful normal person — as someone who comes up and says "Nothing changed, but now the `furble` command doesn't work anymore." Something must have changed. Different file? Terminal? Program? It's possible that your system administrator changed something behind your back, but it's far more likely that something you did which seemed unimportant is indeed the problem.

Think of this as your key to power: If you screwed it up, you can probably fix it yourself! On the other hand, if it's broken, you may well have broken it.

## *Don't leap to confusions*

Beware of the situation in which you think you're three-quarters of the way to solving a problem but you're heading down the wrong road. For example, one time we wanted to print a file with line numbers down the left side of the page. We had just learned about a UNIX program called `sed` (sort of a Swiss army-knife program for pushing around text in files) and decided that it was the natural way to print line numbers. We asked our local wizard how to get `sed` to insert line numbers, and he told us. It turns out that `sed` isn't very good at numbers, but if you stand on your head, hold your breath, whistle Dixie, and recite the Declaration of Independence in Bulgarian, you can, indeed, get `sed` to put line numbers in a file. (We exaggerate here, but not much.) So, with a couple of hours' effort, we managed to get the job done.

What we didn't know, and what the wizard didn't tell us because we didn't ask, is that *another* program called `nl` does nothing but add line numbers to a file — no cleverness required — and we could have finished the entire job in two minutes. Oops.

When you ask for help, do yourself a favor and ask the question to which you really want the answer.

# *The Care and Feeding of UNIX Wizards*

Your local helpful people (normal, wizardly, or even system-administratorish) are more likely to view your entreaties with favor if you make it worth their while. Cash is a little tacky, but you can express your appreciation in many other appropriate ways:

- Food is the most reliable bribe, discussed in greater detail later in this chapter.
- Flowers, silly little statuettes for the desk, novelty Post-its, or other such items remind the guru of what a fine and appreciative user you are.

- ✔ If you're an attractive member of the opposite sex, a nice hug or kiss on the cheek is sometimes appropriate, although the extremely nerdy are likely to overreact and respond with a sincere proposal of marriage. Use your discretion.

- ✔ It is always appropriate, of course, to write an enthusiastic memo to the person's boss and exclaim what wonderful help you received. This method is *not* appropriate when giving help is not what the person is supposed to be doing. ("She's far too knowledgeable to be wasting her time talking to mere users.")

# Nerds and Food

There is a widely held stereotype that technical types eat only the type of food found in vending machines, particularly soda pop. In some cases, this is still true, but don't count on it. With the graying of the baby boomers, people who used to live on Jolt cola (the brand that "has all the sugar and twice the caffeine") often find that it now causes a variety of physical symptoms we don't need to describe in detail; they have switched to Perrier because it makes their kidneys feel better. An entire new generation of UNIX nerds are into granola and tofu. Know your nerd.

A thank-you gift with a personal touch is always appreciated (brownies or cookies, for example). Some people can't tell real homemade cookies from the kind made from a tube of dough you buy at the store, cut into little slices, and bake (which is much easier than making them from scratch).

If you use store-bought dough, be sure to remove the plastic before slicing it; otherwise, it's a dead giveaway. Some people won't notice, but don't count on it.

## Pizza

The most appreciated food item for most UNIX technical types is pizza, particularly when it arrives at lunchtime on a day when the guru otherwise would have to go out for lunch in 34-degree weather when it's raining slush. With pizza delivery now available in all parts of the world, you don't have to go out in the slush either; just remember to make a phone call or two at 11:30 a.m.

The selection of pizza toppings is important. Some younger UNIX wizard types have a blanket policy of never eating anything green, which rules out otherwise all-star ingredients such as bell peppers and broccoli. Some highly educated technical types, particularly graduates of technical schools in such places as Berkeley, California, and Cambridge, Massachusetts, have had their consciousness raised and don't eat any pizza unless the cheese comes from a free-will cooperative dairy owned by the cows themselves. On the other hand, we have known some strict vegetarians who, for the purposes of pizza design, have declared pepperoni an honorary vegetable. Your best bet, at least until you get to know your pizza lovers' tastes, is to order several different kinds of pizzas. The concept of too much pizza is unknown in technical circles, so let your wallet be your guide.

## Chinese food

A possible alternative to pizza is Chinese food, another category that meets the criteria of food you can get delivered in 34-degree weather. But be careful: Many technical schools are surrounded by Chinese restaurants, and a typical M.I.T. graduate knows an astonishing amount about Oriental cuisine and has little patience with third-rate Chinese food. Chinese food as a bribe or thank-you offering is a good idea only if it's really good; in this sense, pizza is much more reliable. It is possible to ruin a pizza by putting sauerkraut on it, something we discovered at a pizza joint, high in the Rocky Mountains, that was run by someone named Heidi (not an auspicious name for a pizza maker); other than that, though, pizza is foolproof.

# Part II
# Some Basic Stuff About Programs, Files, and Directories

The 5th Wave          By Rich Tennant

"OOPS, I FORGOT TO LOG OFF AGAIN."

## In this part...

**U**NIX, like other computer systems, keeps your information in things called files. When you work with UNIX, you frequently need to make new files, rename existing ones, make copies of particular interesting files, or get rid of files that have outlived their usefulness.

This section talks about files: what they are, what you can do with them, how to create them, and how to blow them away.

# Chapter 4

# Files for Fun and Profit

• • • • • • • • • • • • • • • • • • • • • • • • • • • • • • • • • • • • • • • • • • • •

## In This Chapter

▶ Listing information about files

▶ Duplicating a file

▶ Erasing a file

▶ Renaming a file

▶ Looking at what's in a file

▶ Printing a text file

• • • • • • • • • • • • • • • • • • • • • • • • • • • • • • • • • • • • • • • • • • • •

*A* *file* is a bunch of information stored together, like a letter to your mom or a database of customer invoices. Every file has a name. You will end up with tons of them.

This chapter explains how to work with files, including getting rid of the ones you no longer want.

As a reminder, you must log in before you can do any of the nifty things we talk about in this chapter (see Chapter 1). When you see the UNIX prompt (% or $), you are ready to rock and roll.

## What Files Do You Have?

To see a list of your files (actually, a list of the files in the working directory, which we talk about in Chapter 5), type the following (as always, press Enter at the end of the command line):

```
ls
```

This command stands for *list,* but could the lazy typists who wrote UNIX have used the other two letters? No-o-o.... This command lists all the files in your working directory (Chapter 5 discusses directories and how to make lots of them). The ls command just shows the names of the files in alphabetical order. For more information about each file, you can type this line:

```
ls -l
```

The `-l` is called a *switch,* or *option.* That's the letter *l,* not the digit *1.* Even though these characters look nearly the same, the computer insists on treating them completely differently. In this case, `-l` tells `ls` to display the long format of the listing, which is to say, an entire line of information about each file, like this:

```
-rwxr-xr-x   1   staff   john    14632   Dec 14   12:15   budget
drw-rw-rw-   3   staff   john    128     Apr 3    10:34   Letters
-rw-rw-rw-   2   staff   margy   25785   Jul 5    18:12   chocolate.cake.recipe
```

You can ignore the first half of each line, which tells who can do what to this file and who owns it (security stuff, described in Chapter 28). The second half of the line tells the size of the file in bytes (characters), the date and time the file was last changed, and its filename.

## To switch or not to switch?

Lots of UNIX commands have options (also called switches because you switch the options on and off by typing or not typing them when you type the command). Options make commands both more versatile and more confusing. When you type a command with one or more options, keep these rules handy:

✔ Leave a space after the command name (the command `ls`, for example) and before the option (the `-l` part).

✔ Type a hyphen as the first character of the option (`-l`, for example).

✔ Type a space after the option if you want to type more information on the command line after the option.

## Making a long listing stop and start when you're ready

If you have a lot of files, the `ls` listing may fly right off the top of your screen. If you have this problem, type the following line:

```
ls | more
```

The vertical bar is called a *pipe* (we talk more about the pipe in Chapter 6). The `| more` option after the basic `ls` command tells UNIX to stop listing information to the screen just before the first file disappears from view. Press the spacebar to see the next screenful of filenames.

# Copying Files: Send In the Clones

You can make an exact duplicate of a file. To do this, you must know the name of the file you want to copy, and you must create a new name to give to the copy. If a file contains your January budget (called `budget.jan`, for example) and you want to make a copy of it to use for the February budget (to be called `budget.feb`, for example), type this line:

```
cp budget.jan budget.feb
```

The lazy typists strike again. Be sure to leave spaces after the `cp` command and between the exiting and new filenames. This command doesn't change the existing file (`budget.jan`); it just creates a new file with a new name.

## A good way to lose some work

What if a file named `budget.feb` *already* exists? Tough cookies: UNIX blows it away and replaces it with a copy of `budget.jan`. It truly is an excellent idea to use the `ls` command first to make sure that you don't already have a file with the new name you have chosen.

In UNIX System V Release 4, you can use the `-i` switch to ask `cp` to inform you whether a file with the new name already exists. If it does, the `-i` switch asks you whether to proceed. If you have this version of UNIX, type `cp -i` rather than just `cp` to use this nifty little feature.

If all goes well and `cp` works correctly, it doesn't give you any message. Blessed silence on the part of UNIX usually means that all is well. You should use the `ls` command to check that the new file really does exist, just in case.

## What's in a name?

When you create a file, you give it a name. UNIX has rules about what makes a good filename:

> ✔ Filenames can be pretty long; they're not limited to eight characters and a three-character extension, like some operating systems we could name. On older versions of UNIX, the limit is 14 characters for a filename; newer ones have no character limit, so you can call a file
> `Some_notes_I_plan_to_get_around_to_typing_up_eventually_if_I_live_that_long`.

✔ Don't use weird characters that mean something special to UNIX or some shell you might encounter. Stay away from the following characters when you name files:

| | | |
|---|---|---|
| / | ! | @ |
| # | $ | ^ |
| & | * | - |
| ( | ) | + |
| ' | " | \ |
| \| | ? | |

Stick primarily to letters and numbers.

✔ Don't put spaces in a filename. Although some programs let you put them in, they cause nothing but trouble because other programs simply cannot believe that a filename might contain a space. So, don't borrow trouble. Most UNIX people use periods to string together words to make filenames such as budget.jan.94 or pumpkin.soup. Underscores and hyphens work too.

✔ UNIX considers uppercase and lowercase letters to be completely different. Budget, budget, BUDGET, and BuDgEt all are different filenames.

# Nuking Files Back to the Stone Age

You can also get rid of files by using the command that the lazy typists call rm. To erase (delete, remove — it's all the same thing) a file, type the following line:

```
rm budget.feb
```

If all goes well, UNIX reports nothing and you see another prompt. Use ls to see whether the rm command worked and the file is gone. If you want to get rid of a bunch of files, you can list all their names in the same rm command, separated by spaces.

Watch out! Under most circumstances, there is no way to get a file back after you delete it.

To be safe, you can use the -i option to ask rm to ask you to confirm deletion of the file. This is a particularly good idea if you use wildcard characters to delete a group of files at a time (see Chapter 6).

## *Big, big trouble*

If you delete something really, really important and will be called on to perform ritual seppuku if you can't get it back, don't give up hope. Your local UNIX guru probably makes things called *backups* on some regular basis. Backups contain copies of some or all the files on the UNIX system. Your files may be among those on the backup. Go to the guru on bended knee and ask whether the file can be restored. If the file wasn't backed up recently, you may get an older version of it, but hey — it's better than the alternative.

Even before you get yourself into this kind of pickle, you may want to ask your UNIX expert to confirm that regular backups are made. Make sure that your important files are included in the backups. If no one is making regular backups, panic. This is not a safe situation. See Chapters 7 and 22.

## *Good housekeeping*

You should get rid of files you no longer use, for several reasons:

- ✔ It gets confusing when you have all kinds of files lying around, and it's hard to remember which ones are important.
- ✔ The useless files take up disk space. Whoever is in charge of your UNIX system probably will bother you regularly to "take out the garbage," that is, to get rid of unnecessary files and free up some disk space.

On the other hand, it can be a good idea to make extra copies of files. If you have been working on a report for three weeks, it isn't a bad idea to make an extra copy every day or so. That way, if you make some revisions that, in hindsight, were stupid, you can always go back to a previous revision.

# *What's in a Name (Reprise)*

Having given a file a name, you may want to change it later. Maybe you spelled it wrong in the first place. In any case, you can rename a file by using the `mv` (lazy typist-ese for *move*) command.

Suppose that you made a file called `bugdet.march`. Oops, dratted fingers.... Type the following line to correct the error in the filename:

```
mv bugdet.march budget.march
```

After mv, you type the current name of the file and then the name you want to change it to. Note that it can be harder to retype the same typo than to type the name correctly!

Because you can't have two files with the same name in the same directory, if a file already has the name you want to use, mv thoughtfully blows it away (probably not what you want to do). Type carefully. SVR4 users can use mv -i (like cp -i) to prevent inadvertent file clobbering.

# Looking at the Guts of a File

We have been slicing and dicing files for a while now, but you still haven't seen what's inside one. There are two basic types of files:

- ✔ Files which contain text that UNIX can display nicely on-screen
- ✔ Files which contain special codes that look like monkeys have been at the keyboard when you display the files on-screen

The first type of files are called *text files;* spreadsheet files, database files, program files, and just about everything else comprise the second type. Text editors make text files, as do a few other programs.

To display a text file, type the following line:

```
cat eggplant.recipe
```

The cat stands for *catalog,* or maybe *catenate* — who knows? We're surprised that the lazy typists didn't call it something like q. If you try to use cat with a file that doesn't contain text, your screen looks like a truck ran over it — but you won't hurt anything. Sometimes the garbage in the file can put your terminal in a strange mode in which characters you type don't appear or appear as strange Greek squiggles. See Chapter 21 to learn how to un-strange your terminal.

If the file is long, the listing goes whizzing by. (You learn how to look at the file one screen at a time in Chapter 6.) To see just the first ten lines of the file with BSD versions of UNIX, you can type this line:

```
head eggplant.recipe
```

# *Is This a Printout I See Before Me?*

If a file looks OK on-screen by using the `cat` command, try printing it. If you use UNIX System V, type the following line:

```
lp eggplant.recipe
```

If you use BSD UNIX, type the following:

```
lpr eggplant.recipe
```

Assuming that you have a printer and that it's hooked up, turned on, and has paper, and your user name is set up to use it, the `eggplant.recipe` file prints. If it doesn't, see Chapter 9 to straighten things out. If your computer is blessed with a network, the printed copy may come out down the hall or on another floor. In one inexplicable case, when users in New York printed any file, the copies ended up on a printer somewhere in Japan. If your printer isn't attached directly to your computer, you probably will have to ask for advice about where to pick up the printout. If you can print files on more than one printer, see the section "Printers, printers, everywhere" in Chapter 9 to learn how to choose a printer.

# Chapter 5

# Directories for Fun and Profit

• • • • • • • • • • • • • • • • • • • • • • • • • • • • • • • • • • • • • • • • • • • • • • • • • • • •

## In This Chapter

▶ Defining a directory

▶ Getting to the right directory

▶ Defining a home directory

▶ Making a new directory

▶ Erasing a directory

▶ Renaming a directory

▶ Moving a file from one directory to another

▶ Organizing your files

▶ Finding files

• • • • • • • • • • • • • • • • • • • • • • • • • • • • • • • • • • • • • • • • • • • • • • • • • • • •

*A*fter you begin working with UNIX, you will make more and more files. You will have files with important memos to co-workers and customers, programs that analyze productivity and costs, recipes for pumpkin soup, and programs that play battleship. All of this is very important stuff, so you don't want to lose anything. This chapter explains how to organize your UNIX files in directories and how to find things after you have done so.

## Good News for DOS Users

We have good news about UNIX for you experienced DOS users. UNIX works almost exactly the same as DOS does when it comes to directories and files. Actually, it's the other way around — a guy named Mark added directories to DOS back in 1982, and ripped off, er, emulated, the way UNIX did things — with a few confusing changes, of course.

Briefly, DOS users should know the following things about UNIX directories:

- ✔ All those backslashes (\) you learned to type in DOS turn into regular slashes (/) in UNIX. Mark decided that DOS slashes should lean backward because DOS already used forward slashes for command-line switches. The reason was that the original version of DOS was a clone of the earlier CP/M, which borrowed its slash syntax from a 1960s vintage time-sharing system for the DEC PDP-10. But we digress.

- ✔ The UNIX cd (change directory) command works (more or less) like the DOS CD command; remember not to capitalize it.

- ✔ The UNIX command for making a directory is mkdir rather than the DOS MD command; to remove a directory in UNIX, you use the rmdir command rather than the DOS RD command. (Where were the lazy typists when we needed them?) These two commands also work like the DOS versions. Don't capitalize them, either.

- ✔ As always, UNIX believes that capital and small letters have nothing to do with each other. They are completely different, so be sure to use the correct capitalization when you type directory names and filenames.

- ✔ If you really like DOS commands and want to make UNIX understand them, you can make shell scripts (the UNIX equivalent of DOS batch files) that let you type DIR or COPY while you are using UNIX. (Chapter 14 tells you how to make shell scripts.) Or, if you absolutely fall in love with UNIX commands (who doesn't!), you can make DOS batch files on your PC so that you can type ls and cp while you are using the PC.

If you understand directories and paths intuitively from your vast experience with PCs, skip forward to the sidebar titled "Getting the big picture."

# *What Is a Directory?*

A *directory,* for the rest of you non-DOS people, is a group of files, or a work area. (Macintosh users may recognize this as a "folder.") You give a directory a name, such as Budget or Letters or Games or Harold. You can put as many files as you want in a directory.

The good thing about directories (also sometimes called *subdirectories*, for no good reason) is that you can use them to keep together groups of related files. If you make a directory for all your budget files, those are the only files you see while you are working in that directory. Directories make it easy to concentrate on what you are doing so that you're not distracted by the zillions of other files on the disk.

You can make directories, move files into them, rename directories, and get rid of them. This chapter describes the commands that do each of these stunts.

# Divide and Conquer

Interestingly, a directory can contain other directories. You might have a directory called Budget, for example, for your departmental budget. The Budget directory might contain several other directories (also called subdirectories) such as Year1993, Year1994, and Estimates. If a directory contains so many files that you can't find things, you should create some subdirectories to divide things up.

Files and directories are stored on disks. Every disk has a main directory that contains everything on the disk. This directory is called the *root directory*. The designers of UNIX were thinking of trees here, not turnips. They imagined an upside-down tree with the root at the top and the branches reaching downward, like the picture in Figure 5-1. This arrangement of directories is called a *tree-structured directory*.

Strangely, you don't type `root` when you are talking about the root directory. Rather, you type /. Just like that: A single slash means "root" in UNIX-ese.

## Paths to power

Unfortunately, UNIX never shows you the directory structure as a nice picture, like Figure 5-1. That would be too easy. Rather, to tell UNIX which file you want to use, you type its pathname. The *pathname* is the step-by-step map UNIX

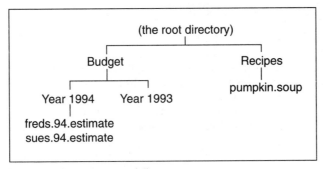

**Figure 5-1:** A tree-structured directory.

follows to get to the file, starting at the root. The pathname for the file named
`freds.94.estimate` in Figure 5-1, for example, contains these steps:

| | |
|---|---|
| `/` | The root, where you start |
| `Budget` | The name of the first directory you move to on your way to the file |
| `/` | Confusingly, this slash doesn't refer to another root: it's just the character used to separate one name from the next in the pathname |
| `Year1994` | The next directory on your way to the file |
| `/` | Another separator character |
| `freds.94.estimate` | The filename you want |

When you type this pathname, you string it all together, with no spaces, like
this:

```
/Budget/Year1994/freds.94.estimate
```

Luckily, you don't have to type big, long pathnames like this one very often
because it's devilishly hard to get all that right on the first try!

## Family matters

You can also think of the tree structure of directories as a family tree. In this
way of thinking, the `Year1994` directory is a *child* of the `Budget` directory, and
the `Budget` directory is the *parent* of the `Year1994` directory. You will see these
terms sometimes if you read more about UNIX.

## Names for directories

Choose names for directories in the same way you choose names for files:
Avoid funky characters and spaces, don't make the name so long that you will
never type it correctly, and so on. Some people capitalize the first letter of directory names so that they can tell what's a directory and what's a file. When
you use `ls` to list the contents of a directory, the command lists both filenames
and the names of subdirectories. When you use capitalization to distinguish
between directory names and file names, you can quickly tell which are which.

## Getting the big picture

If you have a UNIX workstation that's all your own, most of or all the files on its hard disk are yours. If you have a terminal and share a UNIX computer with others, the computer's hard disk has files that belong to all the users. As you can imagine, we are talking about oodles of files. To keep the files — and the users! — organized, there are lots of different directories.

There are lots of directories for the UNIX program files themselves, program files for other programs,

and other stuff you definitely are not interested in. The files that belong to users (such as yourself) usually are stored in one area. A directory called `/usr` (or sometimes `/home`) contains one subdirectory for every user. If your user name is `bclinton`, for example, the `/usr` directory contains a subdirectory called `bclinton` that contains your files.

# There's No Place Like Home

Every user has a *home directory* (sweet, isn't it?) in which you store your personal stuff, mail, and so on. When you log in, UNIX starts you working in your home directory, where you work until you move somewhere else. Your home directory is your subdirectory in the `/usr` directory, so Bill C.'s home directory is `/usr/bclinton`.

Because most UNIX systems involve lots of people sharing disk space and files, UNIX has a security system to prevent people from reading each other's private mail or blowing away each other's work (accidentally, of course). Chapter 28 talks about the security system. In your home directory, you usually have the right to create, edit, and delete all the files and subdirectories. You can't do this in someone else's home directory unless they give you permission.

## I've been working in the directory

Whenever you use UNIX, the directory you are working in is the *working directory*. Some people call it the current directory, which makes sense too.

When you first log in, your home directory is your working directory. Although you start in your home directory, you can move around. If you move to the `/Budget` directory, for example, the `/Budget` directory becomes the working directory. (Your home directory is still your home directory — it never moves.)

If you forget where you are in the directory structure, you can ask UNIX. Type the following line to ask UNIX where you are:

```
pwd
```

This line is short for *print working directory*. UNIX doesn't print the information on paper, it just displays it on your screen. For example, you see the following:

```
/Budget/Year1994
```

When you use the `ls` command (or most other UNIX commands), UNIX assumes that you want to work with just the files in the working directory. The `ls` command lists just the files in the working directory unless you tell it to look somewhere else.

To move to another directory to do some work (if you are tired of working on the budget and want to get back to that recipe for pumpkin soup, for example), you can change directories. To move from anywhere in the `/Budget` directory to the `/Recipes` directory, type the following line:

```
cd /Recipes
```

Remember that `cd` is the change *directory* command. After the `cd` (and a space), you type the directory you want to go to. You can tell UNIX in two ways exactly which directory you want:

✔ Type a *full pathname*, or *absolute pathname* (the pathname starting at the root, as you did earlier)

✔ Type a *relative pathname* (the pathname starting from where you are now)

This is confusing, we know, but UNIX has to know exactly which directory you want before it makes the move. Because there can be more than one directory called `Recipes` on the disk, UNIX has to know which one you want.

When you type a full pathname starting at the root directory, the pathname starts with a `/`. When you type a relative pathname starting at the current working directory, the pathname doesn't start with `/`. That's how UNIX (and you) can tell which kind of path it is.

If you are in the `/Budget` directory (on the `/Budget` branch of the directory tree) and want to go to the `Year1994` subdirectory (a branchlet off the main `/Budget` branch), for example, just type `cd Year1994`. To go to a different branch, or to move upward toward the root, you must use the slashes. To move from the `/Budget/Year1994` branchlet back to the main `/Budget` branch, type `cd /Budget`. To move from the `/Budget` branch to the `/Recipes` branch, for example, type `cd /Recipes`.

## I want to go back to Kansas

If you move to another directory (/Oz, for example) and want to get back to your home directory (/Kansas, that is), you can do so as easily as clicking the heels of your ruby slippers together three times (or were they glass slippers?). Just type this line:

```
cd
```

When you don't tell UNIX where you want to go, it assumes that you want to go home.

If you try to move to a directory that doesn't exist or if you incorrectly type the directory name or pathname, UNIX says:

```
Dudegt: No such file or directory
```

(or whatever directory name you typed).

# Putting Your Ducks in a Row

As with everything else in life (if we may be so bold as to suggest it), it pays to be organized when you are naming files and putting them in directories. If you don't have at least a little organization, you will never find anything. Think about which types of files you will make and use: word processing files? spreadsheet files? Then make a directory for every type of file or for every project you are working on. This section shows you how.

## Making directories

Before you make a directory, be sure that you make it in the right place. Remember that you type the following line to display your working directory (that is, the current directory):

```
pwd
```

The most likely place to make a subdirectory is in your home directory. If you're not there already, type this line to go back home:

```
cd
```

When you create a directory, you give it a name. To create a directory called Temp to hold temporary files, type this line:

```
mkdir Temp
```

Most people have a directory called Temp to hold files temporarily. These files can be the ones you need to keep just long enough to print, to copy to a floppy disk or tape, or whatever. Anyway, you have one now too. To confirm that the Temp directory is there, type this line:

```
ls
```

You can even go in there and look around:

```
cd Temp
ls
```

When you create a directory, it starts out empty (there are no files in it).

Most people have directories with names something like the following:

Mail    For electronic mail (see Chapter 16).

Docs    For miscellaneous documents, memos, and letters.

Temp    For files you don't plan to keep. Use Temp to store files you plan to throw away soon. If you put them in some other directory and don't erase them when you finish with them, you may forget what they are and be reluctant to delete them later. Directories commonly fill up with junk in this way. Make it a rule that any files left in the Temp directory are considered deletable.

bin     For programs that you use but that aren't stored in a central place. You system administrator may have already made you your own bin directory. (See Chapter 14 for information about the bin directory and making your own programs.)

You can also make one or more directories to contain actual work.

### Dot and Dot Dot

There are two funny pseudodirectory names you can use — especially with the cd and ls commands. One is . (a single dot), which stands for the current directory. You type the following line, for example, to tell UNIX to list the files in the current directory:

```
ls .
```

This is pretty pointless, of course, because typing the following line does exactly the same thing:

```
ls
```

OK, forget about . (the single dot). But .. (the double dot, or dot dot) can be useful. It stands for the parent directory of the current working directory. The *parent* directory is the one in which the working directory is a subdirectory. It is one level up the tree from where you are now. If you are in the directory /usr/home/bclinton/Budget, for example, the .. (dot dot, or parent) directory is /usr/home/bclinton.

Suppose that you type the following:

```
ls ..
```

You see a list of the files in the parent directory of where you are now. This can save you some serious typing (and the associated errors).

## Neat operations you can perform on directories

After you have some directories, you may want to change their names or get rid of them. You may also want to move a file from one directory to another. Let's try that first.

### Transplanting files

Chapter 4 described the use of the mv command to rename a file. You can use the same command to move files from one directory to another. To get the mv command to move files rather than just rename them, you tell the mv command two things:

- ✔ The name of the file you want to move
- ✔ The name of the path where you want to put it

You can rename the file at the same time you move it, but let's keep things (comparatively) simple. Suppose that you put the file allens.94.estimates into the /Budget/Year1993 directory rather than in /Budget/Year1994. The easiest way to move it is to go first to the directory in which it is located. In this example, you type the following line:

```
cd /Budget/Year1993
```

Use ls to make sure that the file is in the current directory. After you are sure that the file is there, you can move it to the directory you want by typing the following line:

```
mv allens.94.estimates /Budget/Year1994
```

Be sure to type one space after mv and one space between the name of the file and the place you want to move it. If you use ls again, you discover that the file is no longer in the working directory (Year1993). You should change to the directory to which you moved the file and use ls to make sure that the file is there. Make one typing mistake in a mv command and you can move a valuable file to some unexpected place.

### Amputating unnecessary directories

You can use the rmdir command to remove a directory, but what about the files in the directory? Are they left hanging in the air with the ground blown out from under them? Nope; you must either get rid of the files in the directory (delete them) or move them elsewhere before you can hack away at the directory.

To erase a directory, do the following:

1. Use the rm command to delete any files you don't want to keep. (See Chapter 4 for the gory details of using the rm command.)

2. If you want to keep any of the files, move them somewhere else by using the mv command (as explained in the preceding section).

3. Move to some other directory when the directory you want to delete is empty. UNIX doesn't let you delete the current working directory. The easiest thing to do is to move to the working directory's parent directory:

   cd ..

4. Remove the directory by typing the following line:

   rmdir *OldStuff*

   Replace *OldStuff* with the name of the directory you want to ax.

5. Use ls to confirm that the directory is gone.

You can delete a directory and all the files in it, or even a directory and all the subdirectories and files in them, but this is pretty dangerous stuff. You usually are better off sifting through the files and deleting or moving them in smaller groups.

### Renaming a directory

If you have used DOS, you will be thrilled to learn that in UNIX you can rename a directory after you create it. (DOS doesn't let you do this.) Again, the mv command comes to the rescue.

To rename a directory, you tell mv the current directory name and the new directory name. Go to the parent directory of the directory you want to rename and then type the mv command. To rename the /Budget directory as /Finance, for example, go to the / directory (type cd  /) and then type this line:

```
mv Budget Finance
```

Remember to make sure first that a directory with that name isn't already there. If it is, UNIX moves the first-named directory to become a subdirectory of the existing directory. In other words, if a /Finance directory is already there, /Budget moves to become /Finance/Budget. Could be handy, if that's what you have in mind. Then again, it could drive you out of your mind if that's not what you expected.

# Lost: The File I Need for My Presentation in Half an Hour

The good thing about directories is that you can use them to keep all your files in tidy, related groups. The problem with directories is that sometimes files end up in the wrong directory and can be hard to find. (Files frequently seem to grow little legs and wander off on their own, like toddlers in a shopping mall.) This section shows some ways to find a wayward file, assuming that you know the file's name.

## Beating the bushes

The first approach to finding a lost file is to use the brute-force method. Starting in your home directory, use ls to search through each of your directories. In every directory, type the following line:

```
ls important.file
```

Obviously, replace important.file with the name of the file you are looking for. If the file is in the current directory, ls lists it. If the file isn't there, ls complains that it can't find it. This approach can take a while if you have a lot of directories; an additional drawback is that you won't find the missing file if it has wandered off to someone else's directory.

## *Getting smart*

If you know — or think you know — that your file is nearby, you can use * (asterisk) wildcards in directory names. (Wildcards are covered in Chapter 6. They let you work with lots of files or directories at a time.) To find important.file in any of the subdirectories in the working directory, type this line:

```
ls */important.file
```

This technique doesn't work if you have directories within directories: it looks only one level down. To look everywhere, either everywhere in your own directory structure or everywhere on the entire computer, use the find command. The find command is tricky but endlessly useful; we talk more about it in Chapter 26. To use it to find important.file in any of your directories, go to your home directory and then type this line:

```
find . -name important.file -print
```

Remember to replace important.file with the name of the file you are looking for. Be sure to type these components when you use the find command:

- ✔ A space after the find command
- ✔ A dot (to tell find to start looking in the working directory)
- ✔ Another space
- ✔ -name (to tell find that you know the file's name)
- ✔ Another space
- ✔ The name of the file you are looking for
- ✔ Another space
- ✔ -print (to tell find to print the full pathname of the file it finds; if you don't include this option, find doesn't say anything even if it finds the file)

This find command starts in the working directory (because of the dot you typed in the command) and searches for the file in not only the working directory but also all its subdirectories (and sub-subdirectories, ad infinitum).

If the find command doesn't work and you think that the file might be in some other user's directory, type the same find command and replace the . (dot) with a / (slash). This version tells find to starting looking in the root directory and to search every directory on the disk. As you can imagine, this process can take some time, so try other things first.

## Desperately seeking a filename

If you don't know the name of the file you have lost but you do know a word or phrase the file contains (preferably a phrase not contained in dozens of other files), you can use the `grep` command to find it (see Chapter 26).

### Links to shadow files

You may run into a situation in which a file seems to be in several directories at one time (Twilight Zone music here, please). DOS users know that this is patently absurd. Surprise! In UNIX, you *can* have a file in several places at the same time. It can even have several different names. It can be mighty useful, in fact, for a file to be in, for ex-

ample, the home directories of several people at one time so that they all can easily share it.

To achieve this magical feat, you use *links*. We discuss links in Chapter 26. In the meantime, don't panic if you see a file lurking around in one place when you're sure that it belongs somewhere else.

# Chapter 6
# Cute UNIX Tricks

● ● ● ● ● ● ● ● ● ● ● ● ● ● ● ● ● ● ● ● ● ● ● ● ● ● ● ● ● ● ● ● ● ● ● ● ● ● ● ● ●

## In This Chapter

▶ Using redirection

▶ Viewing a file one screen at a time

▶ Printing the output of any command

▶ Working with groups of files

● ● ● ● ● ● ● ● ● ● ● ● ● ● ● ● ● ● ● ● ● ● ● ● ● ● ● ● ● ● ● ● ● ● ● ● ● ● ● ● ●

*N*ow you know how to work with files and how to type some commands to UNIX (you type them to the shell, as you know, but let's not get bogged down in that here). UNIX has a clever way to increase the power of its commands: *redirection.* This chapter shows you how to use redirection and how to use wildcards to work with groups of files.

## This Output Is Going to Havana: Redirection

When you use a UNIX command like 1s, the result (or *output*) of the command is displayed on-screen. The standard place, in fact, for the output of most UNIX commands is the screen. There is even a name for this: *standard output.* As you can imagine, there is also *standard input,* usually the keyboard. You type a command; if it needs more input, you type that too. The result is output displayed on-screen — all very natural.

You can pervert this natural order by *redirecting* the input or output of a program. A better word is *hijacking.* You say to UNIX, "Don't display this output on-screen — instead, put it somewhere else." Or, "The input for this program is not coming from the keyboard this time — look for it somewhere else."

The "somewhere else" can be any of these sources:

- ✔ **A file.** You can store the output of ls (your directory listing) in a file, for example.
- ✔ **The printer.** Useful only for output; getting input from a printer is a losing battle.
- ✔ **Another program.**

Bunches of UNIX programs are designed primarily to use input from a source other than the keyboard and to output stuff to somewhere other than the screen. These kinds of programs are called *filters.* Readers old enough to remember what cigarettes are may recall that the really advanced ones had a filter between the cigarette and your mouth to make the smoke smoother, mellower, and more sophisticated. UNIX filters work in much the same way, except that they usually aren't made of asbestos.

The only exception to this redirection business is with programs, like text editors and spreadsheets, that take over the entire screen. Although you can redirect their output to the printer, for example, you won't like the results (nor will your co-workers, as they wait for a pile of your garbage pages to come out of the printer). Full-screen programs write all sorts of special glop (they give instructions) to the screen to control where stuff is displayed, what color to use, and so forth. These instructions don't work on the printer because printers use their own, different kind of glop. The short form of this tip is that *redirection and editors don't mix.*

## Grabbing output

So, how do you use this neat redirection stuff, you ask? Naturally, UNIX does it with funny characters. The two characters ‹ and › are used for redirecting input and output to and from files and to the printer. Another character (|) is used to redirect the output of one program to the input of another program.

To redirect (or *snag,* in technical parlance) the output of a command, use ›. Think of this symbol as a tiny funnel *into which* the output is pouring (hey, we use any gimmick we can to remember which funny character is which). To make a file called list.of.files that contains your directory listing, for example, type this line:

```
ls > list.of.files
```

UNIX creates a new file, called list.of.files in this case, and puts the output of the ls command into it.

If list.of.files already exists, UNIX blows away the old version of the file.

If you don't want to erase the existing file, you can tell UNIX to add this new
information to the end of it (*append* the new information to the existing information). To do this, type the following line:

```
ls >> list.of.files
```

The double >> symbol makes the command append the output of ls to the
list.of.files file, if it already exists. If list.of.files doesn't exist already,
ls creates it.

If you use > (single-angle) redirection, it blows away any previous contents of
the file into which you redirect the output. For this reason, >> (double-angle)
redirection is much safer. Some (but not all, of course) versions of the C shell
check to see whether the file already exists and refuse to let you wreck an existing file with redirection. If your C shell works like this, to overwrite the file, use
rm to get rid of the old version.

## Redirecting input

Redirecting input is less often useful than redirecting output, and we can't think
of a single, simple example in which you would want to use it. Suffice it to say
that you redirect input just like you redirect output, but you use the < character
rather than the > character.

# Gurgle, Gurgle: Running Data Through Pipes

It can be really useful to redirect the output of one program so that it becomes
the input of another program. This process is the electronic equivalent of
whisper-down-the-lane, with each program doing something to the information
being whispered.

To play whisper-down-the-lane with UNIX, you use a *pipe*. The symbol for a pipe
is a vertical bar ( | ). Search your keyboard for this character. It's often on the
same key with \ (the backslash). Sometimes the keytop shows the vertical bar
with a gap in the middle, but the gap doesn't matter. If you type two commands
separated by a | , you tell UNIX to use the output of the first command as input
for the second command.

## Gimme just a little at a time

When you have many files in a directory, the output of the `ls` command can go whizzing by too fast to read, which makes it impossible to see the files at the beginning of the list before they disappear off the top of the screen. A UNIX program called `more` solves this problem. The `more` program displays on the screen the input you give it, but it pauses as soon as it fills the screen and waits for you to press a key to continue. To display your list of files one screenful at a time, type this line:

```
ls | more
```

This line tells the `ls` command to send the file listing to the `more` command. The `more` command then displays the listing. You can think of the information from the `ls` command gurgling down through the little pipe to the `more` command (we think of it this way).

## The `cat` and the fiddle, er, file

As explained in Chapter 4, you can use the `cat` command to display the contents of a text file. If the text file is too long to fit on-screen, however, the beginning of the file disappears too fast to see. You can display a long file on-screen one screenful at a time in these two ways:

✔ Redirect the output of the `cat` command to `more` by typing the following line (assuming, of course, that the file is called `really.long.file`):

```
cat really.long.file | more
```

✔ Just use the `more` command by typing this line:

```
more really.long.file
```

If you use the `more` command without a pipe (without the |), `more` takes the file you suggest and displays it on-screen a page at a time.

## Sorting, sort of

A program called `sort` sorts a file line-by-line in alphabetical order. It alphabetizes all the lines according to the first letter or letters in each line. Each line in the file is unaffected — only the order of the lines changes.

Suppose that you have a file called `bonus.recipients` that looks like this:

```
Meg Young
Shelly Horwitz
Tyler Rioff
Eliot Mooiweer
Elana Kleiman
Kate Henoch
Timothy Kenny
Emily Miller
Alexander Milona
Becky Pittore
Gabrielle Zandi
```

To sort it line by line in alphabetical order, type the following:

```
sort bonus.recipients
```

The result looks like this:

```
Alexander Milona
Becky Pittore
Elana Kleiman
Eliot Mooiweer
Emily Miller
Gabrielle Zandi
Kate Henoch
Meg Young
Shelly Horwitz
Timothy Kenny
Tyler Rioff
```

You can also sort the output of a command, like this:

```
ls | sort
```

Because `ls` displays filenames in alphabetical order anyway, this last example doesn't do you much good. But if you want the filenames in *reverse* alphabetical order (we're stretching for an example here), you can use the `-r` option with the `sort` command, like this:

```
ls | sort -r
```

If you are sorting numbers, be sure to tell UNIX. Otherwise, UNIX sorts the numbers alphabetically (the sort of imbecilic and useless trick only a computer would do). To sort numbers, use the -n option:

```
sort -n order.numbers
```

What if your file of bonus recipients contains the bonus amounts, for example, like this?

```
10000   Meg Young
8000    Shelly Horwitz
7000    Tyler Rioff
5000    Eliot Mooiweer
9000    Elana Kleiman
11000   Kate Henoch
8000    Timothy Kenny
7000    Emily Miller
5000    Alexander Milona
6000    Becky Pittore
7000    Gabrielle Zandi
```

When you alphabetize things as letters, not as numbers, a 1 comes before an 8, no matter what, even if it's the first letter of 10. When you alphabetize things as numbers, 10 comes after 8, not before it. If you sort this file as letters, with this command:

```
sort bonus.recipients
```

you get this result:

```
10000   Meg Young
11000   Kate Henoch
5000    Alexander Milona
5000    Eliot Mooiweer
6000    Becky Pittore
7000    Emily Miller
7000    Gabrielle Zandi
7000    Tyler Rioff
8000    Shelly Horwitz
8000    Timothy Kenny
9000    Elana Kleiman
```

This result does not show the bonus amounts in any useful order. If you sort the file as numbers, with this command:

```
sort -n bonus.recipients
```

you get this more useful listing:

```
5000     Alexander Milona
5000     Eliot Mooiweer
6000     Becky Pittore
7000     Emily Miller
7000     Gabrielle Zandi
7000     Tyler Rioff
8000     Shelly Horwitz
8000     Timothy Kenny
9000     Elana Kleiman
10000    Meg Young
11000    Kate Henoch
```

If the file contains letters, not numbers, the -n option doesn't do anything useful. (We could explain what happens, but — trust us — you don't want to know.)

## That's a take — print it

Being able to print the output of a command is terrifically useful when you want to send to a printer something that normally appears on-screen. To print a listing of your files, for example, type this line:

```
ls | lp
```

Depending on your version of UNIX, you might have to use the lpr command rather than lp. Experiment; while you're doing that, feel free to rant and rave about people who can't even figure out how to misspell *print* consistently. (Chapter 9 explains how to determine which command to use and other information about printing. But here's a hint: BSD systems use lpr, and System V systems usually use lp.)

You can use more than one pipe if you want to be really advanced. To print a listing of your files in reverse order, for example, you can use this convoluted command:

```
ls | sort -r | lp
```

# Wild and Crazy Wildcards

When you type a command, you may want to include the names of a bunch of files on the command line. UNIX makes the typing of multiple filenames somewhat easier (as though we should be grateful) by providing wildcards.

*Wildcards* are special characters (still more of them to remember!) that have a special meaning in filenames. There are two wildcards:

?    means "any single letter."

*    means "anything at all."

## Pick a letter, any letter

You can use one or more ? wildcards in a filename. Each ? stands for exactly one character — no more, no less. To list all your files that have two-letter names, for example, you can type this line:

```
ls ??
```

The filename `budget??` matches all filenames that start with *budget* and have two — and only two — characters after *budget,* like `budget93` and `budget94`; the combination doesn't match `budget1` or `budget.draft`.

## Stars (***) in your eyes

The * wildcard stands for any number of characters. To list all your files that have names starting with a *c,* for example, type the following:

```
ls c*
```

This specification matches files named `customer.letter`, `c3`, and just plain c. The specification `budget.*` matches `budget.1994` and `budget.draft`, but not `draft.budget`. The name `*.draft` matches `budget.draft` and `window.draft`, but not `draft.horse` or plain `draft`. By itself, the filename `*` matches everything (watch out when you let the asterisk go solo!).

## Are kings or deuces wild?

Unlike some other kinds of operating systems (we won't name any, but one system's initials are *DOS*), UNIX handles the ? and * wildcards in the same way for every command. You don't have to memorize which commands can handle wildcards and which ones cannot. In UNIX, they all can handle wildcards.

Wildcards commonly are used with the `ls`, `cp`, `rm`, and `mv` commands.

## *Wildcards for DOS users*

Although UNIX wildcards look just like DOS wildcards and they work in almost the same way, they have a few differences:

- ✔ Because UNIX filenames don't have the three-letter extensions that DOS filenames use, don't use *.* to match all files in a directory. A simple * does the job.

- ✔ In DOS, you cannot put letters after the * wildcard — DOS ignores the letters following the asterisk. In DOS, D*MB is the same as D*, for example. It's dumb, we know. The good news is that UNIX is not so dumb. In UNIX, D*MB works just the way you want it to.

## Look before you delete!

The combination of wildcards and the rm command can be deadly. Use wildcards with care when you delete files. You should look first at the list of files you are deleting to make sure that it is what you had in mind. Before you type the following command, for example, to delete a bunch of files:

```
rm * 92
```

type the following line first and look at the resulting list of files:

```
ls * 92
```

There might be something worth keeping that you forgot about in that list of .92 files.

The most deadly typo of all is this one (*do not type this line!*):

```
rm * 92
```

There's a space between the * wildcard and the 92. Although you may have thought that you were deleting all files ending with 92, UNIX thinks that you have typed two filenames to delete:

  \*      This "filename" deletes all the files in the directory.

  92    This filename deletes a file named .92. By the time UNIX tries to delete this (nonexistent) file, of course, it has already deleted all the files in the directory!

You end up with an empty directory and lots of missing files. Watch out when you use rm and * together!

# Part III
# A Quick Tour In and Near Your Computer

# In this part...

**A**ll sorts of stuff is inside your computer, ranging from tiny and uninteresting microchips to large and uninteresting power supplies and disk drives. But on the off chance that you might want to know what makes the computer tick, either from plain curiosity (Naaah) or because you want to understand better why your computer never does quite what you want it to, here are a few words about what's inside the box.

# Chapter 7

# The Guts of the Computer

*T*his chapter is by necessity a little vague (as though the rest of the book isn't) because UNIX runs on a huge variety of computers, from enormous multimillion-dollar IBM mainframes and Cray supercomputers to itty-bitty notebook-style portables about the same size as this book (without the snazzy yellow-and-black cover). Fortunately, because all these computers have much more in common than you might expect, we forge ahead with a description of a generic UNIX computer.

## Meet Mr. Computer

In all but the smallest computers, you can distinguish easily between the computer and the various pieces of attached equipment, known as *peripherals*. All the parts of the system that might be of some use to a human being, such as the keyboard, monitor, mouse, and printer, are peripherals. The computer itself these days is just a boring box with maybe one light on it to show when it's turned on and a lot of wires coming out the back. People have different fancy names for the computer, like the *system unit*. A simple rule of thumb is that the part of the system that costs the most is probably the computer itself.

Storage devices, like disks and tapes, also are considered peripherals even though in smaller computers they're usually mounted inside the computer box.

Back in the good old days, the front of the computer had an attractive array of blinking lights. These lights told technicians what was going on and impressed people with what a bunch of extremely important stuff the computer was doing.

For an example of this, watch the old movie *Desk Set,* with Katharine Hepburn and Spencer Tracy. Kate believes that she's going to be replaced by a new computer, installed by Spencer, but she's not, of course, and gets to keep both her job and Spencer. The computer turns out to be a friendly ol' hunk of metal that would never put anyone out of a job, no way. The part of the computer is played by a 1950s IBM computer (IBM was never shy about getting publicity) that figures prominently in many scenes; the computer has a large panel several feet across, chock-full of impressive blinking lights. It didn't run UNIX, though, because UNIX wouldn't be written for another 15 years, so never mind.

Since the 1970s, the price of computer components has dropped so much that a humorless bean-counting bookkeeper discovered that the lights had become the single most expensive part of the computer, so out they went. What a shame.

# One Chip, Two Chips, Red Chip, Blue Chip

The heart of any computer is the central processing unit, or *CPU.* These days, in all but the largest computers, the CPU is a single microchip (a little, plastic package that looks sort of like a robot built by centipedes). The kind of chip it has determines the computer's personality, such as it is.

## Von Neumann machines? Do you mean Alfred E. von Neumann?

There turns out to be a surprisingly straightforward reason that all computers are pretty much the same these days. Way back before the dawn of time (1945, to be exact), a bunch of guys in Philadelphia built the first working, large, electronic computer, called the ENIAC. They didn't give much thought to how you would program it, so it turned out to be fiendishly difficult to program. In the entire project, in fact, only one person could program it, and there was far more programming necessary than she could do by herself.

Up in Princeton, New Jersey, meanwhile, was this place called the Institute for Advanced Study, a school so erudite that, although it had professors, it had no students to disturb the professors' deep thoughts. One of the professors, John Von Neumann, was a brilliant Hungarian mathematician, the sort of guy who solved two or three deep mathematical problems between lunchtime and the cocktail hour. (We hear that he also threw amazing parties on weekends.) He went down to Philadelphia one day, looked at the ENIAC, and said, "Build the next one in such-and-such a way, and it'll be a lot easier to program." They did, and it worked so well that every computer built since then has been built the way Von Neumann suggested. He was that kind of guy.

One practical effect this advice has had is to make it possible to write *portable* software, or programs moved easily from one kind of computer to another. UNIX is the best-known example of portable software because it runs on dozens, if not hundreds, of different kinds of computers.

CPU chips are named by using numbers, like 80486 and 68000. Technical people get into many arguments about the relative merits of different processor chips, but we'll let you in on a secret: They're all the same. That's right, the differences among the different chips are so nerdy that you don't care. The very largest machines, like mainframes and supercomputers, haven't yet been squeezed into single chips; from the point of view of a user or programmer, however, that turns out not to make much difference, either, except that single chip CPUs tend to be much cheaper to buy. (This discussion generally applies to large computers, even though they don't have single CPU chips.)

| Table 7-1: | Some CPU Chips You Might Be Stuck With | | | |
|---|---|---|---|---|
| **Name** | **Maker** | **Bits** | **Speed** | **Theology** |
| 80286 | Intel | 16 | Mediocre | CISC |
| 80386 | Intel | 32 | Mediocre | CISC |
| 80486 | Intel | 32 | Fast | CISC |
| Pentium | Intel | 32/64 | Really fast | CISC |
| 860 | Intel | 32 | Fast | RISC |
| 68020 | Motorola | 32 | Mediocre | CISC |

*(continued)*

# Well, OK — there are a few important differences

Maybe a few differences in CPU chips are worth mentioning. One is how much data a chip handles at a time. Nearly every CPU chip made these days handles 32 bits, a respectable handful. A few older CPU chips, notably the Intel 8086, 80186, and 80286 (also called the 86, 186, and 286 — those lazy typists are everywhere) handle 16 bits. A few of the newest ones can handle 64 bits at a time. The practical differences are as follows:

- The size of the program a CPU chip can handle is proportional to how many bits it handles. A 32-bit CPU chip can handle much larger programs than a 16-bit CPU chip can. This issue turns out to be a practical one because many new programs either don't fit on 16-bit ma-

chines or have to be perverted around internally in ways that make them slow or buggy.

-  CPU chips that handle more bits at a time are somewhat faster, although not as much as you might think.

- CPU chips that handle more bits can handle more RAM (see the section "I Hope That My Memory Doesn't Fail Me"), which in practice makes them faster.

Most CPU chips in UNIX machines are relatively fast 32-bit chips (see Table 7-1, if you care), which means that they're more or less equally capable.

| Table 7-1: | | Some CPU Chips You Might Be Stuck With *(continued)* | | |
|---|---|---|---|---|
| **Name** | **Maker** | **Bits** | **Speed** | **Theology** |
| 68030 | Motorola | 32 | Fast | CISC |
| 68040 | Motorola | 32 | Faster | CISC |
| 88000 | Motorola | 32 | Faster | RISC |
| 88100 | Motorola | 32 | Even faster | RISC |
| R2000 | MIPS | 32 | Fast | RISC |
| R3000 | MIPS | 32 | Faster | RISC |
| R4000 | MIPS | 32 | Really fast | RISC |
| Microvax | DEC | 32 | Varies with different models | CISC |
| Alpha | DEC | 64 | Blindingly fast | RISC |
| Precision | HP | 32/64 | Blindingly fast | RISC |
| RT PC | IBM | 32 | Mediocre | RISC |
| RS/6000 | IBM | 32 | Fast | RISC |
| SPARC | Sun/others | 32 | Mediocre to fast | RISC |

## RISC, CISC, and other four-letter words

You may hear UNIX wizards talk about "risk chips" and say to yourself, "That's odd; they don't look like poker players." They're not — RISC is the name of the latest fad in chip design. For a long time, CPU-chip designers spent all their time trying to cram into a chip as many complex features as they possibly could, on the theory that the more swell stuff they put in the chip, the faster programs would run.

Then some researchers tried checking exactly how much most programs used the complex features; it turned out that they didn't use them nearly as much as people expected. So the researchers and developers made a new round of CPU chips that had a lot less stuff in them, but the stuff they did have was really fast. The new chips ran programs much faster than the older,

more complex chips. The new chips are known as RISC, for *Reduced Instruction Set Computer;* the old ones are known pejoratively as CISC, for *Complex Instruction Set Computer* (pronounced "kisk").

The only little problem with the new RISC chips is that, because they aren't compatible with the older chips, none of the old programs runs with the new chips. One of the attractions (to technical types) of UNIX is that, because getting UNIX going on a new kind of computer is very easy, practically all the RISC computers have wound up running UNIX. But, as noted, from our point of view, the only interesting difference between CISC and RISC computers is that, all other things being equal (which they never are), RISC computers are faster.

# Memory Lane

The other key component your computer needs, in addition to a CPU, is main memory, or RAM. Lots of main memory. The more, the better. Main memory is where the computer puts the programs and data it is working on now. Less urgent data goes on the disk (discussed later in this chapter). The contents of main memory evaporate when the power goes off, which is one of many reasons to be sure that everything is saved properly before you shut off your computer.

## How much memory is enough?

Memory is measured in things called *bytes* (pronounced "bites"), as in "This here memory really bytes." Each byte is enough to store one letter, so the word *ketchup* takes seven bytes. A typed page of text is about 2,000 characters, so storing it takes about 2,000 bytes of memory. Memory sizes are measured in K, which stands for *kilobytes,* or about 1,000 bytes; M or MB, which stands for *megabytes,* is about a million bytes; and G, which stands for *gigabytes* (sounds sort of like "giggle"), is about a billion bytes, which is a lot. (Now we can say that the typed page takes 2K of memory.)

Actually, 1K is a little more than 1,000 bytes: it's 1,024 bytes, which happens to be an easy number to handle in a computer's internal binary code. A megabyte is 1K times 1K, which works out to 1,048,576 bytes; a gigabyte is 1K times 1K times 1K, which (as though you care) is exactly 1,073,741,824 bytes. Marketing people, as exuberant types, tend to call 1K a thousand bytes if it can make something they're selling look bigger. For example, 64K is actually 65,536 bytes (64 times 1024), which in sales literature somehow always ends up being called 65K. Don't be fooled, it's really 64K.

## Why RAM?

RAM stands for *random-access memory* because the CPU can fetch any particular piece of data stored there equally fast. Now you know. A long time ago, RAM was built from teensy, little, metal doughnuts called *cores,* so some hardcore nerds may still refer to something stored in RAM as being "in core."

The earliest versions of UNIX used moderate amounts of RAM; one version needed only about 50K. As people have stuffed features into UNIX, its memory appetite has grown so that these days you can't even begin to run UNIX with less than 2 megabytes; many workstations have 100 megabytes of RAM or more. Table 7-2 gives a quick summary of some commonly available chunks of memory and how they are labeled.

## More memory than I really have

UNIX also uses something called *virtual memory*, which enables you to run very large programs in very small amounts of memory (although perhaps not as fast as you want). You may be familiar with some other kinds of computers in which, for example, a 640K program won't run in a 512K computer. By using virtual memory, UNIX avoids that problem: although having extra RAM makes your computer faster, having less RAM doesn't prevent you from running large programs.

In reality, a program that has insufficient memory can slow down so much that it would have been a kindness if it hadn't bothered to run. We used to have a program that normally took about five seconds to start up, but, when we tried to run it on a computer with a lot less RAM, it took 15 minutes to start. If your computer doesn't have enough RAM, you will know — it feels like someone poured a jar of molasses into it.

Every kind of computer has a maximum amount of RAM that can be installed. For PCs, the maximum may be as low as 8M; for mainframes (big computers), it may be 1,000M or more. For microcomputers and minicomputers — as long as you haven't reached the memory limit — it's technically straightforward for your system administrator to add more RAM, by plugging in more RAM chips or

| Table 7-2: | How to Measure Memory | |
|---|---|---|
| *Amount* | *Techie name* | *Marketing name* |
| 1,024 | 1K | 1K |
| 65,636 | 64K | 65K |
| 262,144 | 256K | 262K |
| 1,048,576 | 1M | 1M, sometimes 1,048K |
| 268,435,456 | 256M | 268M |
| 1,073,741,824 | 1G | 1G |

## You can disregard this hopelessly technoid discussion of virtual memory

The way virtual memory works is, in principle, very simple. (Paying off the national debt is, in principle, very simple, too.) Every running program is divided into 4K chunks called *pages*. At any given moment, the program really uses only a small fraction of the pages it has been assigned. UNIX copies to the disk all the pages of memory that haven't been used lately and removes them from RAM. If the program later needs one of the pages out on the disk, the program freezes for a moment, UNIX quickly scurries around and finds some other unused page in RAM, copies the page to the disk, drags the newly needed page back into RAM, and lets the program continue. Amazingly, this entire shell game takes only about 1/10 second. As long as this process doesn't happen often, the program runs *virtually* (that word) as though all its pages were really in RAM. The more pages that really *are* in RAM, of course, the less often the shell game is required and the faster the program runs.

sometimes cards with the RAM chips mounted on them. (The hardest part is getting someone to pay for it.) If your computer is chronically too slow, a RAM boost is usually the best way to fix it.

# A Disk-usting Disk-ussion

The other kind of memory in UNIX computers is *secondary memory*. IBM calls the things that provide secondary memory *direct-access storage devices*, with the unpronounceable acronym DASD. (Maybe "dazz-dee"? Sounds like a diaper service.) The rest of us call the things *disks* because that's what they are. There are two general kinds of disks: removable disks and permanently mounted disks.

## Gimme some disks to go

Removable disks come in many varieties. They are called removable because (drumroll, please) you can take the disk out of the drive. They sometimes are also called *floppy disks* or *diskettes*, especially by PC and Macintosh users. Table 7-3 lists the most common kinds of removable disks.

| Table 7-3: | A Boring Table of Kinds of Removable Disks | | |
|---|---|---|---|
| **Kind** | **Changeable Contents?** | **Size (across)** | **Amount of data (bytes)** |
| Minifloppy | Yes | 5¼-inch | 300K to 1.2M |
| Microfloppy | Yes | 3½-inch | 400K to 2M |
| CD-ROM | No | 5¼-inch | 600M |
| Magneto-optical | Yes | 5¼-inch | 600M (sometimes more) |

## Minifloppies and microfloppies

PCs and Macs use these kinds of floppy disks (also called *diskettes*). Some kinds of workstations also can use them. Sometimes, workstations can even read and write disks that PCs or Macs have written, and vice versa. (Don't take this for granted — PCs and Macs can't read each others' disks, even though the disks are physically identical. Typical.) Every minifloppy comes in a little paper envelope that, if you're lucky, hasn't gotten lost yet. Microfloppies have a sturdy plastic case and a spiffy little metal shutter over the opening so that they don't need an envelope. Each kind of floppy comes in several varieties that look physically the same but that are incompatible from the computer's point of view. (Why do they do this?) Ask a local expert which kind of floppies work in your particular computer.

### Putting a floppy in a computer

The disk drive has a slot into which you insert the floppy disk. Because every floppy disk has a top, a bottom, and four sides, there are eight ways to put the disk in the computer, seven of which are wrong. The right way is with the label side on top and the business end of the disk — the part of the disk with the little opening (if it's a minifloppy) or the shutter (if it's a microfloppy) — going into the computer first. If the disk goes in vertically, the label goes to the left.

If you have to force the disk into the drive, you probably have it in the wrong way. Be sure that there isn't a disk in the slot already: There's room for only one at a time.

Sometimes the computer has a little lever you push to lock the disk into the computer. Particularly with microfloppies, you may have to try two or three times until the disk properly seats itself in the computer with a satisfying click.

### Taking a floppy out of the computer

To get the disk out, first wait for the computer to finish with the disk: Wait until the light on the disk unit is off and the disk unit stops humming and swishing. For most kinds of UNIX, before you can take the disk out, you must give an "unmount" command to tell the system to finish writing all its updated information to the disk.

After you're sure that you're ready to take the disk out, flip back the disk drive lever (if there is one); you should be able to pull the disk out. For microfloppies, you usually push a little button to pop the disk out like toast from a toaster; then pull the disk out the rest of the way.

### Off the record, er, CD

A CD-ROM is a computer disk that looks exactly like a regular compact disc full of music. Indeed, it is exactly like a compact disc: They record music on a CD by converting music to a whole lot of computer data. A CD player is really a specialized little computer that turns the data back into Elvis's Greatest Hits. Computer types saw no reason that they should be cut out of the fun, so they invented a sort of rewired CD player that skips the Elvis part and feeds the data directly into a computer.

The good thing about CD-ROMs is the same as the good thing about music CDs: They don't take up much space on the shelf, and they're sturdy. Like music CDs, CD-ROMs can be recorded only at the factory. The ROM in CD-ROM stands

# Helpful floppy disk hints to avoid digital amnesia

✔ Keep minifloppies in their paper envelopes when not in use. Don't confuse the *paper* envelope with the stiff *plastic* envelope in which the disk is permanently mounted. When someone tells you to take the disk out of the envelope, take it out of the *paper* envelope. Don't ever try to take it out of the permanent one: You will break the disk and everyone will make fun of you. This is the number 1 "stupid user" story passed around at help desks. Don't let it happen to you!

✔ When a minifloppy is out of its paper envelope, don't let your fingers touch the inner disk (the brown, shiny part).

✔ Do not store any kind of disk on a radiator, in direct sunlight, or near a strong magnet. (*Hint:* The back of every computer screen contains a strong magnet.) Keep disks away from tele-

phones, air de-ionizer gizmos, and refrigerator magnets.

✔ Don't use a disk as a coffee-cup coaster unless you're sure that you never want to use that disk in a computer again. Don't do it even if you are sure, because sooner or later you will confuse your coaster disk with a good disk, and then won't you feel foolish.

✔ While you're at it, don't put floppies near your coffee cup, and vice versa: A floppy with coffee spilled on it is a former floppy.

✔ Never remove a floppy from the computer until the computer is finished with it: Check that the disk light is out, the disk is not spinning, and the disk is "unmounted" (if your version of UNIX requires this step).

## Why they're called compact discs with a *c* but computer disks with a *k*

We have no idea. Sorry.

for *read-only memory* because your computer can read it but can't change it. Even though a CD-ROM is about the same size as a floppy disk, it holds much more data: about 600M as opposed to 1M or so for a floppy. (On a music CD, "Blue Suede Shoes" takes up about 35M of data on the disk — or 35 floppies' worth of space. But hey, it's worth it.)

Different models of computer CD players differ in how you insert the disk. For some, you just stick the disk in the way you do with your stereo. Others use a *caddy,* a little carrier in which you place the CD-ROM; then you insert the caddy in the CD player.

Some versions of computer CD players can also play music CDs, which is usually the real reason people want these kinds of players on their workstations. Music can make you much more productive when you are using a computer. At the least, music makes you somewhat less destructive because you're unlikely to throw things out the window in annoyance at the same time you're

## That disk doesn't look so scuzzy to me

You may hear people talking about *scuzzy disks.* This doesn't mean that the disks need to go in the dishwasher: they're actually talking about the Small Computer Systems Interface, abbreviated SCSI and pronounced *scuzzy* except in certain parts of California where they pronounce it *sexy.* Hmmmm.

SCSI defines some rules for the way disks and tapes and computers plug together so that if you take any SCSI-compatible disk or tape and plug it into a computer with a SCSI connector on the back (most workstations, many PC clones, and most Macs have these connectors), it will in all likelihood work. This is an astonishing degree of compatibility for the computer industry, so you'll be relieved to hear that committees are hard at work on mutant versions of SCSI with names like *SCSI-2* and *Fast and Wide SCSI*; there will soon be plenty of opportunity for things not to work.

In the meantime, the fact that all SCSI disks are pretty much interchangeable has made the disk market very competitive: Disk prices get significantly cheaper from one month to the next.

singing along to "Hound Dog." Your co-workers will understand, unless you get into the habit of humming along with the music.

The much less common *magneto-optical disk* is sort of a hybrid of a CD-ROM and a floppy. It physically resembles a CD-ROM, but your computer can change what's on it. Because you can change what's on it, you can use it more like a floppy disk. Magneto-optical players usually cannot play CD-ROMs; and they can never play music CDs, so they're nowhere nearly as much fun.

## I-never-get-to-go-anywhere disk storage

Most of the data in your computer is stored on *permanently mounted,* or *fixed, disks.* Fixed disks range in size from Maytags down to some nearly as small as matchboxes. The most common models are about the same size as a telephone. They don't look like disks: they look like metal boxes. The disks are permanently mounted inside the metal boxes, but we still call them disks.

The amount of data you can store on a fixed disk ranges from 20M up to about 20G for the largest models attached to mainframes. Sometimes the disk is mounted physically inside the computer. If there isn't enough space inside the computer box, the disk goes in a separate shoebox-sized case. (Computer wonks call these cases *shoeboxes.* Are they creative or what?)

Because fixed disks are permanently sealed at the factory, there isn't much you can do to break one other than to drop it off a table. Most people put shoebox cases on the floor to forestall this problem.

# Don't Scotch That Tape

One problem with permanently mounted disks is that, if one of them breaks, the information on the disk is permanently wrong. This is why people make backup copies of data on the fixed disk: as insurance against a possible disaster of unthinkable proportions. Although you could, in principle, make backup copies of the fixed disk onto floppy disks, a typical 300M fixed disk would take 300 backup floppies; it's hard to find people willing to sit around and feed 300 disks into a computer.

Tapes largely solve this problem. Computer tapes come in various sizes. The most common tape comes in a plastic cartridge about the same size as an old eight-track tape (remember them?). There are also smaller tapes a little bigger than a cassette. The big, old reels of tape you may remember from old movies are almost completely obsolete because cartridge tapes hold more stuff and cost a lot less.

Tape capacities range from 20M for the oldest varieties to 2G for the newest kind of cassette-style variety. The tape units are quite small; if you have a shoebox containing a fixed disk, it probably contains a tape unit also.

If you're lucky, you'll have a diligent system administrator who arranges to copy all the system's data to backup tapes every night. If this is true, in a disaster you'll never lose more than one day's work. Most of us are not so lucky, however, and you may have to do some of your own backing up.

Backup procedures are, sadly, wildly inconsistent from one system to another. Find a local wizard and ask him or her to write you a little two-line program that copies all your personal files to a backup tape, something the wizard can probably do in about a minute and a half. Then have your expert walk you through putting the tape in the tape unit, running the program, taking the tape out, and putting it on the shelf. Back up your data *every single day* before you go home. You'll be glad you did. It's not a bad idea to ask the wizard for help in getting a file or two back from the backup tape, just to be sure that you have all the stuff on the tape you think you do.

Many people think that backing up all that data is a pain. It's true, it is. Of course, you have to compare that to how much pain you're going to feel when your disk breaks and all your data disappears. We can tell you from experience that there are few smug grins quite as smug as the one you'll grin when your disk breaks and you know that all your precious stuff is safe on tape on the shelf.

For a stern lecture about backups and more information about how to make them, see Chapter 22.

---

## The care and feeding of tapes

Most of the advice about floppy disks also applies to tapes:

- Don't put your fingers on the tape.

- Don't store tapes in the sun, on the radiator, or next to your screen.

- As with disks, keep tapes away from magnets.

- Wait for the light on the tape unit to go out and for the unit to stop whirring before taking the tape out.

- Tapes and coffee don't mix any more than disks and coffee do. Tapes don't even make very good coasters.

# Just a Node on a Network

Most UNIX systems are attached to networks. *Networks* are highly sophisticated electronic communication facilities through which you can exchange gossip, innuendo, rumors, lies, slander, and other important information with your co-workers. Even if you have no personal interest in the network, you'll probably have to learn something about it because, in many cases, the disks that contain your files are in fact on some computer somewhere else on the network. Without the network, your computer will get a severe case of amnesia. You may also want to use the network's electronic mail program. We talk more about networks and files in Chapter 19, but here are a few helpful network tips.

The most common kind of network is something called *Ethernet*. Ethernet lets you connect an almost unlimited number of computers, including both UNIX and non-UNIX computers. Computers on the Ethernet can share files on each other's disks and print things on each other's printers. You can have computers with super-big disks (*file servers*) so that everyone can store files there. You can have computers with fancy, expensive printers so that everyone can print their résumés in the evenings with the highest possible print quality (these computers are called *print servers*). And you can have plain old computers like the one on your desk that are used to get work done. All the computers on the network are called *nodes*. (Don't you love all this fancy tech talk?)

## Getting wired

There are three (you knew this wouldn't be simple) kinds of wiring for Ethernet. Usually, you see a wire coming out of the wall that looks a lot like a cable-TV hookup. Some setups have a thicker cable, about the size of your thumb. If the network fails (you can tell when this happens because your computer largely freezes up and starts mumbling incomprehensible complaints about network servers not responding), the most likely problem is that the network wire has come unhooked from the computer. This is particularly likely with the thicker cables because the cable is quite heavy and the connector has an extremely clever little slide latch whose only shortcoming is that it doesn't hold very well.

The third kind uses telephone wire, and uses connectors similar to telephone plugs that actually work.

Look at the back of your computer. If the network cable has come unhooked, you can plug it back in. (Unlike practically every other part of the computer, networks are designed so that computers can be plugged into the network, and unplugged from them, while they are running. Wow!)

If replugging or wiggling the network connector doesn't help, you're out of luck and will have to call for help.

The great thing about networks is that you can share expensive disks and printers, share files, and send and receive electronic mail (see Chapter 18). The bad thing about networks is that, if someone kicks a network connector out of a socket in a cubicle on the other side of the building, you can't get any work done until it's fixed. Centralization, as always, has its drawbacks.

We talk about how to determine who is on your network in Chapter 17, use e-mail in Chapter 18, and share files over the network in Chapter 19.

# Chapter 8

# Baseball Bats and Other Attention-Getting Devices

*In This Chapter*

▶ Fun facts about your screen

▶ The care and feeding of keyboards

▶ How to determine the gender of your mouse and other important facts about pointing devices

*I*n Chapter 7, we went on at length about the parts of the computer that aren't very useful to you because A) you can't use them to tell the computer what you want to do and B) the computer can't use them to tell you what it did. In this chapter, we attempt to remedy the situation by talking about the devices you and the computer use to chat with each other.

## Smoke Screens and Other Visual Devices

Probably the largest single part of your computer is the screen. Some people call screens *monitors* (historically, early computer screens were adapted from the screens that TV stations used to monitor their broadcasts). Screens are sometimes called *displays* because they display stuff; sometimes they're called *CRTs* (cathode ray tubes) — because that's what electronic engineers call them — or *VDUs* (video display units) by people whose lives require a TLA (*t*hree-*l*etter *a*bbreviation) for everything they do. We call them *screens* because that's what they are.

The screen is easy enough to identify: It's the part of your computer that looks like a TV set.

Screens come in a variety of shapes, sizes, and styles. The smallest screens you usually find on a computer are about 12 inches diagonally (measured the same way you measure a TV); the largest screens are about 20 inches. Generally, bigger is better, but the price goes up radically as the screen gets bigger, so there's a compromise between what you want and what you can afford. (Isn't that always the case?)

Screens come in both black-and-white versions, often called *monochrome* (or *mono,* for short), and color. Depending on what you're doing, you may want a color screen or you may want black and white.

✔ At a particular size or price, a monochrome screen is sharper and clearer than a color screen. A color screen internally has three separate "guns" that separately display the red, green, and blue parts of the picture. Getting the three colors to appear at exactly the same place is difficult.

✔ A monochrome screen has only one gun and avoids the problem of mixing colors. If you are using a graphics system such as Motif or OPEN LOOK, the computer can update the picture on a monochrome screen considerably faster than it can update a color screen, again because there is only one color to draw rather than three.

✔ A monochrome screen is usually about half the price of a color screen of the same size and quality.

✔ Although color screens are usually more fun, monochrome screens often are better for getting work done.

On both color and monochrome screens, another issue relates more to the *display adapter* that connects the screen to the rest of the computer. The issue is the number of different colors the screen can display. Some monochrome screens just show black and white; others show various numbers of shades of gray that range from 4 shades to as many as 256 shades or more. Color screens range from 8 colors to millions of different colors. Most color screens use a *palette* from which the colors in any particular picture are drawn; although a screen may be capable of displaying 16 million colors, only 256 can appear in a single picture. This turns out not to be too much of a problem in most cases: Even 256 colors are enough to draw color pictures better than what you can get on a TV set.

The possible combinations of display adapters and screens vary widely from one type of computer to another. Terminals, both regular and X terminals, have a particular screen built in, take it or leave it. For low-end computers such as PC clones and Macs, there are dozens of screens for each one. For workstations, there is usually a smaller range of screens mated to particular models.

# Caring for your screen

Taking care of your screen is not difficult. By and large, leave the screen alone. You do have to turn it on by flipping a power switch, the location of which has probably been determined by a screen-design engineer with a sense of humor. The obvious place is on the front of the screen, but some screens have switches on the side, the back, and occasionally even on the bottom. You just have to hunt until you find it.

Screens typically have contrast and brightness adjustments on the front or side, and many other controls either on the back or inside a little door on the front. Fiddle with the brightness and contrast knobs until you like what you see. We usually turn the contrast all the way up and the brightness about two-thirds of the way up.

You usually should leave the other controls alone unless the picture looks really awful. There are controls that set the horizontal and vertical size of the picture, the horizontal and vertical position of the picture, and some other adjustments such as a "pincushion" (which deals with the fact that the picture-drawing gun inside the screen prefers to draw a picture that is circular, and you would rather it drew one that is square). Adjust these controls a little at a time — if you crank them all over the place, you may make your picture so deranged that it will take an hour to fiddle it back into place.

Here are some other things to do to keep your screen happy:

✔ On larger screens, you may have a button labeled Degauss. If the picture starts looking a little smudgy around the edges, or has missing dots in the middle, push the Degauss button for a second or two and see whether that helps. Don't go overboard: If you use the Degauss button as much as once a week, that's a lot.

✔ Every few days, wipe the front of the screen with a handkerchief or paper towel to remove the dirt. Unless you have a heavy smoker in the office, that's all you have to do to keep the screen clean. If you haven't wiped off your screen for a few weeks, you will be amazed at how much dirt sticks to it and how much brighter and clearer it seems afterward.

✔ One of our editors gave us this handy tip: Use a used dryer sheet (like Bounce or Snuggle) to clean the screen; the sheet reduces the static on the screen and seems to keep the dust off it longer.

✔ Most screens, particularly larger ones, generate a lot of heat, so they have vents in the case to let the heat out. Don't pile stuff on top of the screen because it blocks the vents and the screen can overheat.

✔ Never, never put your coffee cup on top of the screen. Better coffee warmers are available.

✔ Never, never open your screen's case. Screens use extremely high electrical voltages; if you touch the wrong thing inside the screen case, you can receive a nasty and dangerous shock — even if the screen is turned off and unplugged. There's nothing in there you can adjust or fix anyway.

## Should I turn off my screen?

People get into long and heated arguments about whether to turn off a screen — or the entire computer, for that matter — when it's not being used. This question is particularly important if you leave your screen turned on with the same picture on it for a long time. After a while, the picture gets "burned in" to the front of the screen and stays there like a faint, angry ghost regardless of what else is showing on the screen.

One way to avoid this problem is to turn off your screen, or at least turn down the brightness, when you're not using it, particularly if you're leaving it for a long time, like overnight. If you're going home for the weekend, it's a good idea to turn off the screen. Your terminal may have a screen saver program, which makes your screen go blank or displays a constantly moving pattern when you don't use the computer for a few minutes.

## Avoiding the hacker's crouch

The most important thing you can do to make your computer working environment physically comfortable is to put your screen in the right place. The screen should be directly in front of your face when you're sitting comfortably in your chair. If the screen is sitting directly on your desk or on top of a flat "pizza box" workstation, it's probably too low. If you find yourself hunching low in your chair or bending your head down so that your neck is curved like a flamingo's, your screen is probably too low. This position can make your neck hurt and make you feel terribly guilty because you're not sitting up straight, like your mom told you to.

Raising the screen isn't difficult. Some screens have a swivel base that lets you raise the screen by just twisting it. If you don't have that option, put something underneath the screen, like a few old phone books or a couple of those dusty computer manuals you never read. (At least then they're good for something.) Even if you think that your screen is already high enough, try boosting it up four inches or so. You might be surprised at how much more comfortable it is.

You may also want to lower your keyboard, as described later in this chapter.

## Why don't they use regular TV sets rather than expensive computer screens?

People often wonder why a 17-inch computer screen costs a thousand bucks and a 17-inch TV costs about a quarter of that amount. The answer is that the picture on the TV screen is, by computer standards, laughably vague and blurry. A 17-inch computer screen has at least 1,000 separately changeable picture elements (known in the computer biz as pixels) from top to bottom; a TV has less than 500. Look at your TV up close, if you can stand it, and you can see that the image is pretty fuzzy. Also, TV pictures move; computer pictures more often stand still. Blurriness is much more apparent in still pictures. TVs do fine at showing pictures because they can display a much larger range of colors than all but the best computer screens. For displaying readable text, however, color is less important than resolution (the number of pixels).

Use your TV as nature intended, to watch reruns of "I Love Lucy," and use your computer screen for your computer. (You can buy gizmos to play TV through your computer screen, but, because they cost more than a TV and still produce only a TV-quality picture, there's not much point to getting one.)

Your computer may run a graphical user interface, such as X Windows, Motif, or OPEN LOOK. These interfaces are explained in Chapters 10 and 11, but we mention them here because they usually include screen savers.

If your screen displays exploding fireworks or meandering roaches (pictures of roaches, that is) or has gone blank, don't panic. It probably means that your screen is being saved. To get the normal contents of your screen back, either move the mouse (if you have one) or push any key on the keyboard. It doesn't have to be a key that does anything: One of the Shift keys works well.

# *Nonmusical Keyboards*

The part of your computer with which you engage in the most hand-to-hand combat is the keyboard. It looks like a typewriter with a lot of extra keys that are in groups at the top, on the right side, and sometimes on the left side.

The typewriter part in the middle of the keyboard is easy enough to understand, but all those extra keys can be hard to fathom. Some of the extra keys are easy to figure out: They have other special symbols not found on regular type-writers — the reverse slash (\) and curly braces ({ }), for example. Here are some other keys you might encounter:

- ✔ Shift makes small letters into CAPITAL LETTERS.

- ✔ Ctrl or Control is a special kind of "control" shift used primarily to make the special combinations Ctrl-C and Ctrl-Z that are used to stop runaway programs.

- ✔ The Caps Lock key works much like it does on a typewriter. Usually, a little light on the keyboard comes on to tell you when Caps Lock is turned on. Sometimes, if you turn on Caps Lock, you can use the regular Shift key to get lowercase letters, which makes it easy to mAKE tYPING mISTAKES lIKE tHIS.

One of the most mysterious and most heavily used keys on the computer keyboard is called Esc, short for "escape." Escape? Escape from what? Nobody remembers. (On some early keyboards, the key was called AltMode, and nobody knew what that stood for either.) Make sure that you can find your Esc key; you will need it in order to use any text-editing programs. If you press Esc in other places, it may make something strange happen on the screen, but, otherwise, it doesn't do anything much.

Other keys usually have arrows that point up, down, left, and right and have useful-sounding labels like Insert, Delete, Home, and End. In most cases, the keys don't do anything useful. The reason is that most UNIX programs were written at places where there were dozens of different kinds of terminals, all with different keyboards. Rather than try to adapt every program to every kind of keyboard, people wrote programs to use only the keys they knew would always be present. These keys include the printing keys, the Enter key, maybe the Backspace key, and the mysterious Esc key just mentioned. (It may be mysterious, but it's standard.)

Then there are the function keys. For a while, workstation makers seemed to battle to see who could make the "manliest" keyboard with the most function keys. Early keyboards had a modest 3 or 4 function keys. Then the IBM PC had 10 function keys on the left side of the keyboard; soon, 12 appeared across the top. Function keys soon bristled everywhere — one steroid-crazed keyboard had 10 keys on the left, a dozen across the top, and 10 more on the right. What's really amazing is that no programs ever used all these function keys. For one thing, different keyboards had different sets of keys, so you couldn't count on the keys to be there. For another, most programs don't have 30 different things you can tell them to do, so all those keys were, for the most part, just decoration.

If your keyboard has a key marked F1, it most likely is the Help key in some programs. It doesn't hurt to try it if you're stuck.

## Life with your keyboard

The two best ways to ruin your keyboard are to drop it on the floor and stomp on it and to pour coffee or soda pop on it. Other than that, the keyboard is pretty sturdy. If you type on it eight hours a day, every day, eventually some keys will stop working. At that point, it's probably easier to buy a new keyboard than to try to fix it. They're not all that expensive.

If you do pour something on your keyboard, follow these steps:

1. Save your work if the keyboard still works.

2. Turn off your computer or terminal if you can (don't just hit the switch — follow the instructions in Chapter 1).

3. Turn the keyboard upside down and shake out the liquid, preferably not on your desk or in your lap.

4. Wipe it off as much as possible with paper towels or tissues. (In the process of doing this, you will type many strange characters and the UNIX shell will get upset if the computer is still on. That's its problem, not yours.)

5. Let the keyboard dry out.

At this point, the keyboard may still work, and you should resolve to be more careful in the future. If one or two keys don't work, your local computer-hardware-oriented wizard may have a bottle of spray electronic cleaner that can probably dissolve enough glop to get the keys working. If not, you must have a repairperson clean the keyboard or replace a broken key, which may be more expensive than buying a new one.

## Comfort at the keyboard

Most computer users put their keyboards on their desks, which is usually not at a comfortable height for typing. Your wrists may start to hurt; in the worst case, you may get something called carpal tunnel syndrome, or repetitive wrist strain (expensive medical terms for "very sore wrists").

The simplest thing you can do to relieve wrist strain is to put a palm rest in front of the keyboard to raise your wrists. A better option is to lower the keyboard; one way to do that is to get a typing table about six inches lower than a desk and put the keyboard and computer on it. (You definitely will want to raise the screen if you do this: See the discussion about screens earlier in this chapter.) Another way to lower the keyboard is to mount a keyboard drawer under the desk and slide it out when you want to use it. Both these methods cure wrist pain; the second method has the great advantage that it frees up valuable desk space otherwise occupied by the keyboard. We wouldn't type without a keyboard drawer.

# Pointing Devices: Mice, Trackballs, and More

If you use a window system like Motif or OPEN LOOK, you have a pointing device, most likely a mouse. A mouse is a little box you slide around on the desk. As you slide the mouse around, a little arrow or other shape moves around on-screen; by moving the mouse, you move the arrow to point at things on-screen.

The mouse has on it some buttons you push to tell the computer you're pointing at an item on the screen with which you want to do something. Different mice come with different numbers of buttons: as few as one or as many as three. With a UNIX system, you always want a three-button mouse because most X Windows programs (which include many of the programs you run under Motif and OPEN LOOK) were written with a three-button mouse in mind. In principle, all the programs can be reconfigured to work with a two-button or one-button mouse (probably by using the Ctrl or Shift key rather than the missing buttons), but life is too short to spend time fooling around with that. Demand three buttons.

Mice come in two general varieties: the mechanical kind with balls and the optical kind without, known tastelessly as male and female mice, respectively. Mechanical mice can roll on any surface, usually on your desk, and occasionally on your leg (very occasionally on someone else's leg, but this chapter has had enough tastelessness already). Even so, most people get rubber pads for their mechanical mice because the mouse rolls more smoothly on the pad. Optical mice come with a special reflective pad and work only on that pad.

People express strong opinions about which kind of mouse is better, but we find that we can get along well with either one. In recent years, manufacturers have switched to ergonomically shaped mice that are supposed to be more comfortable in your hand and that certainly look zoomier. Unless you spend all your time in a CAD or drawing program that requires constant mouse use, you won't use the mouse enough for an ergonomic mouse to make any difference.

## Caring for your mouse

If you have a mechanical mouse, you should turn it over every few months, twist the little cover over the ball, and dump the ball into your other hand. Wipe off the mouse with a tissue and put the mouse back together. That's all the care it needs. For optical mice, wipe off the pad now and then.

## What's the plural of mouse?

Once upon a time, goes a very old joke, a man plagued by snakes heard that the mongoose was an excellent snake hunter. He wanted two of them to de-snake his house. "Please send me two mongooses," he wrote. No, that looked wrong. "Please send me two mongeese." Not much of an improvement. "Please send me a mongoose. And, while you're at it, send me another one."

You might not expect the mouse to suffer the same pluralistic fate as the mongoose, but, sadly, you would be mistaken. One large computer com-

pany, which we won't name but will refer to by its initials (IBM), seems to think that, if you put one mouse next to another, you have two mouses. No doubt it has an excellent reason for doing so, but we can't figure out what it is.

We think that the plural of mouse is mice, and that saying "mouses" makes you sound as though you learned English from one of those schools that advertises on the back of a matchbook. So, unless you hear your boss saying "mouses," be normal and say "mice."

## *Finger-pointing alternatives*

Some people prefer to use trackballs rather than mice to point to things on-screen. Trackballs are just mechanical mice flipped over so that you roll the ball directly with your fingers. The trackball has the advantage that it stays at a fixed place on your desk (sometimes it's even built into the keyboard) so that it doesn't need the cleared desk area a mouse needs. We find a trackball a little more difficult to get used to, but not much different in practice from a mouse. Again, be sure to get a three-button model.

Occasionally you may see more exotic pointing devices, such as touch screens; you use them by pointing with your finger directly at the part of the screen you want (you can tell that it's a touch screen because it's covered with finger-prints). Other pointing devices include light pens that you also touch to the screen, cordless mice, and more. These devices either work just like mice do (and then the discussion in the preceding section applies) or they're entirely different (and then you have to ask a local expert).

# Chapter 9
# Printing (the Gutenberg Thing)

• • • • • • • • • • • • • • • • • • • • • • • • • • • • • • • • • • • • • • • • • • •

• • • • • • • • • • • • • • • • • • • • • • • • • • • • • • • • • • • • • • • • • • •

## Printing Stuff

Unless you happen to work in the paperless office of the future (reputed to be down the hall from the paperless bathroom of the future), from time to time you will want to print stuff. The good news is that it's usually easy to do so. The bad news is that nothing is as easy as it should be.

The major extra complication is that the way to print things is different on UNIX BSD and System V systems. (Remember which one you have? Refer to Chapter 2 if you don't. You may have written it on the Cheat Sheet in the front of the book.) We start by explaining how you print something already in a file; then we go on to the fancy stuff.

### There's a daemon in System V

If you use UNIX System V, the way you print stuff is, in theory, simplicity itself: You use the `lp` command. If you have a file called `myletter`, for example, you print it by typing this line:

```
lp myletter
```

UNIX responds with this important information:

```
request id is dj-2613 (1 file)
```

Usually, this is all you need to do. UNIX responds to your request to print by telling you the request ID of the print job, which you probably don't care about. Sometimes you will want to pretty up the way the printout looks by leaving wider margins; we talk about that later in this chapter.

The lp command doesn't print the file. That would be much too simple. What it does is leave a note for another program buried deep inside UNIX, and this buried program prints your file. The theory behind this arrangement is that a bunch of people may want to use the printer, and it would be a pain if you had to wait for the printer to be free. So lp puts your file on a list; the other program (called a *daemon*, and pronounced "dee-mon," not "day-mon") runs down the list and does the printing so that you don't have to wait. The *request ID* is the name lp gives to the note it leaves for the daemon. You can ignore it unless you change your mind and decide that you don't want to print that file after all.

## More daemons in BSD

If you use BSD UNIX, printing is just as easy as printing with System V, except that you use the command lpr rather than lp. If you have a file called myletter, for example, you print it by typing this line:

```
lpr myletter
```

Some systems, notably SVR4 and Solaris, have both the lp and lpr commands. If you have these versions of UNIX, either command should work equally well. Notice that the lpr command doesn't report a request ID.

## Finding Your Printout

As far as UNIX is concerned, its only job is to send your file to the printer. Now the real work begins: finding your printout.

If your UNIX system is attached to a network, chances are that your printer is attached to some other computer rather than to yours. This means that you may have to go looking for it to find your printouts.

You may have to ask people in nearby cubicles or stand very still in the center of the office and listen for the sound of printing (a gentle whir and click from most laser printers). If all else fails, ask your system administrator. There may be more than one printer your UNIX system can use, so your system administrator may be the only person who can tell you which printer your printout is on.

Aha! There's the printer! If you're lucky, no one else has printed anything recently, so the paper on top of the printer is all yours. It is more likely that lots of people have printed stuff and a pile of paper is on top of the printer, only some of which is yours.

Every printout should have in front of it a sheet that identifies the file printed, with the user name, time, and other odds and ends that seemed relevant to whomever configured the printer. It's considered tacky to root through the stack, pick out your own pages, and leave the rest in a heap. Instead, separate the printouts and leave them on the table or in printout racks (if there are any) with the user names visible. With luck, others will do the same for you. If you can't find your printout on the printer, maybe someone else has already separated and stacked the printouts. Other users may have decided that your printout looked more interesting than theirs and took it off the printer to read it.

## Printers, printers, everywhere

A reasonably large installation probably has several printers, either because there's too much work for one printer or because there are different kinds of printers. When you use the lp or lpr command, UNIX picks one printer as the default. If you use lp, you use the -d option (that's a lowercase *d* — remember that UNIX cares about these things) to identify the printer. To print your file on a printer called draft, for example, you type this line:

```
lp -ddraft myletter
```

If you use lpr, the analogous option is -P (that's a capital *P*); so the command you type is as follows:

```
lpr -Pdraft myletter
```

In either case, don't type a space between the -d or -P and the printer name.

## Calling all printers

The list of available printers depends entirely on the whims of the system administrator. Typically, one day she gets tired of putting up with the slow, illegible, or chronically broken previous printer, storms into the boss's office, gets the necessary signature, and buys the first printer available. Sometimes the old printer is thrown away, sometimes not.

It's generally not too difficult to get a list of printers known to the system. If you use the `lp` command to print, type this line to get a list of available printers:

```
lpstat -a all
```

This line means roughly, "Show me the status of all printers that are active." The `lpstat` program lists the status of all available printers, one per line, like this:

```
dj accepting requests since Thu Apr 25 13:43:50 1991
```

In this case, there is only one printer; its name is `dj`. The listing also shows you the vital fact that it was installed on a Thursday afternoon in April 1991. Whoopee. If you use the `lpr` command to print, try typing this line to get the same information:

```
lpq -a
```

---

## Woodsman, spare that file!

When you tell UNIX to print a file, the file doesn't print immediately. UNIX makes a note to print the file and remembers its filename.

What if you delete the file before UNIX has a chance to print it? If you print with `lp`, you get a nasty message because UNIX can't find the file. If you print with `lpr`, the file is printed normally because UNIX makes a copy of the material to print.

To force `lp` to copy the file, use the `<` command-line operator. To send a copy of the file `myfile` to the printer, for example, type this line:

```
lp < myfile
```

You can then delete or change `myfile` and not affect the printout.

If you are printing a large file, `lpr` can take a long time to make the copy of the file (which it doesn't really need to do because it's already in a file in the first place, isn't it?). You can use `lpr -s` to tell UNIX to print from the original file to save time and disk space. If you use the `-s` option, be sure not to delete or change the file until it's printed.

You can tell `lpr` to delete the file when it has finished printing it. This capability is sometimes useful when you made the file in the first place only so that you could print it. Use the `-r` option to remove the file after printing:

```
lpr -r myfile
```

For large files, you can use `-r` and `-s` together:

```
lpr -s -r myfile
```

The lpq program responds with a similar list, like this:

```
lp:
Rank      Owner    Job    Files         Total Size
1st       friday   7      longletter    4615 bytes
ps:
no entries
```

The lpq command stands for something like *line printer query*, and -a means *all* printers. In this case, there are two printers named lp and ps, and something is printing on the first one.

Keep in mind that not every printer the lpstat and lpq commands report is usable. Frequently, system administrators put in the table of printers some test entries that don't really represent printers you can use.

# Help! I've Printed, and It Won't Shut Up

The first time you print something large, you suddenly will realize that you don't really want to print the file because you have found a horrible mistake on the first page. Fortunately, you can easily tell UNIX that you have changed your mind.

If you tell UNIX to print a file that does not contain text, such as a file that contains a program or a database, in most cases UNIX prints it anyway. In a classic example of Murphy's Law (anything that can go wrong, will go wrong), files like that tend to print about 12 random letters on each of 400 pages. Every page has just enough junk on it so that you can't use it again. As you might expect, people who print a lot of files like that tend to become unpopular, particularly with co-workers whose 2-page memos are in line behind the 400 pages of junk.

## Cancel the order, System V

If you used lp to print the file in the first place, you use cancel (we don't know how that name slipped past the lazy typists) to cancel the print job. You have to give the cancel command the request ID that lp assigned to the job. If you're lucky, the lp command is still on your screen and you can see the request ID. If that information has vanished from your screen, remain calm. The lpstat command lists all the requests that are waiting for the printer:

```
lpstat
```

This command displays a list like this:

```
dj-2620              ness              34895   Dec 23 21:12 on dj
```

This list tells you these things:

- ✔ Your request was named dj-2620.
- ✔ It was done on behalf of a user named ness.
- ✔ The size of the file to be printed is 34,895 characters.
- ✔ The print command was given on December 23.
- ✔ The job is "on dj" (it's printing on the printer called dj).

You can cancel the request with the following command:

```
cancel dj-2620
```

UNIX responds with the following line:

```
request "dj-2620" cancelled
```

UNIX has a surprisingly convenient shortcut (surprising for UNIX, anyway) you can use. If you give the name of a printer, UNIX cancels whatever is printing on that printer. If you remember that the local printer is called dj, you can type this line to cancel whatever dj is printing:

```
cancel dj
```

## Cancel the order, BSD

If you made your printing mistake with the lpr command, you use lpq to find out the request ID, which — to add confusion — is called a *job number* here:

```
lpq
```

UNIX responds with a list of print jobs:

```
Rank    Owner    Job  Files                      Total Size
1st     jedgar   12   blurfle                    34895 bytes
```

You need to note the job number (12, in this case). Use that number with the
lprm command, which, despite its name, removes the request to print something and not the printer itself:

```
lprm 12
```

The lprm command usually reports back something about "dequeued" lines; this
information is meant to be reassuring, although it's not clear to whom. In response to the lprm 12 command, for example, UNIX displays this message:

```
dfB012iecc dequeued
cfA012iecc dequeued
```

## Some final words about stopping the printer

Most printers have something called an *internal buffer* in which data to be
printed resides before the printer prints it. An internal buffer is good and bad:
It's good because it keeps the printer from stopping and starting if the computer
is a little slow in passing your file to it; it's bad because, after data is in the buffer,
there's no way the computer can get it back. So, even after you cancel something
you want to print, some of it may still be in the buffer: as much as 2 pages of
normal text or about 20 pages of the junk that results from printing a nontext file.

There's no easy way to keep from printing the stuff in the printer buffer. One
really bad idea is to turn the printer off in the middle of a page: This method
tends to get the paper stuck and, on laser printers, lets loose a bunch of black,
smeary stuff that gets all over your hands and on the next 1,000 pages the printer
prints. If you insist, push the printer's Stop or Off-line button and wait for the
paper to stop moving; then you can turn the printer off relatively safely.

After your print request is canceled, the printer probably still has half a page of
your failed file waiting to print. You can eject that page by pushing a button on
the printer labeled something like Form Feed or Print/Check or even Reset.

# Caring for and Feeding Laser Printers

Laser printers are a different breed than traditional impact printers. You — or
your network — may have both kinds of printers. In many cases, you probably
can send your file to the impact printer for draft copies and save the laser printer

# Why you don't want to know about PostScript

You may have what's known as a PostScript printer. There are two general camps of laser-printer design: the Hewlett-Packard camp and the PostScript camp. Printers in the Hewlett-Packard camp are based on the design of HP's LaserJet line of printers; printers in the PostScript camp use the PostScript programming language designed by Adobe Systems. LaserJet printers are said to speak Printer Control Language (PCL), but PCL is not nearly as complicated or flexible (depending on how you look at it) as PostScript. To add to the confusion, many laser printers produced in the past year or two speak both PostScript and PCL.

You may reasonably ask, "What does a programming language have to do with a printer?" If you send a file that contains the text *Your mother wears army boots* to the simpler LaserJet, the printer prints Your mother wears army boots. If you send the same file to a PostScript printer, the printer doesn't print anything. The reason is that a PostScript printer is a powerful computer with a built-in programming language (that's PostScript) that can print stuff sort of as a sideline. To make a PostScript printer print anything, you have to send it a program to do the printing. Fortunately, such programs are widely available.

This arrangement isn't quite as deranged as it sounds. To print simple files of text, it's a pain, but for fancy typeset documents with lots of type-faces and figures and line drawings and such things, PostScript is considerably more flexible than PCL, enough so that people use PostScript to typeset entire books (like this one).

PostScript has two problems that may bite you. The first is sending a regular file to a PostScript printer. Usually, UNIX printer software is smart enough to figure out automatically that it must PostScript-ize the file in order to print it. If the printer software is not that smart, another program can do the PostScriptization. Adobe, the originator of PostScript, sells a widely used package called TranScript; TranScript includes a program called enscript that prints plain files. If the plain lp or lpr command doesn't work, try using the enscript command before you run for help.

The other problem you may encounter is that a file contains PostScript but prints like a regular file. PostScript files look like incomprehensible programs written in an obscure programming language, because that's what they are. The tip-off is that the first two letters on the first line are %!. To see what the file is supposed to look like, you must send it to a PostScript printer that can run the program in the file and print whatever the file contains. If it prints the PostScript program instead, most likely you're sending the file to a printer that doesn't speak PostScript. You may be out of luck unless you have access to another printer that does speak PostScript.

for the final versions of the file. The typical inexpensive laser printer isn't designed to be run continuously for 10 hours per day; if you do, it will wear out. Line printers are sturdier, or much cheaper to replace if they break, so you can save money overall if you use the line printer for drafts. (Your system administrator tries to keep operating costs down so that she can budget for another printer.) On the other hand, if you're lucky, you have a high-speed, heavy-duty laser printer on which you can print everything.

When you use the laser printer, keep in mind these pointers to keep your printer going:

✔ Laser printers usually take their paper from a tray that holds only 200 sheets; the printer can go through this amount in about 45 minutes. When the tray is empty, pull it out from the printer, find some blank paper and riffle it to make sure that the pages don't stick together, put it in the tray (make sure to get it underneath the little corner holders), slide the tray back into the printer, and push the Start button on the printer to tell it to go ahead. We realize that you're not a computer repairperson, but printers run out of paper so often that, if you can't refill the paper yourself, you will never get any work done. Get someone to show you how to refill the paper (it takes about half a minute) so that you too can be an expert.

✔ The printer uses *toner*, or dry powder that acts like ink. Toner comes in a plastic cartridge that lasts about 3,000 pages, or about 10 hours of continuous printing. When the toner is running out, printed pages get faint and streaky. You can often rejuvenate the toner for a few minutes if you stop the printer, open the top, remove the toner cartridge, do a little dance with it to shake up the powder inside, put the cartridge back in, and close the printer. If you want to know how to replace the toner cartridge, get someone to show you because the technique varies among models.

Dance carefully with your toner cartridge, and don't try to pry it open. Otherwise, you may get toner powder on your new washable silk shirt, and it will never come out!

✔ Make sure that you learn how to clean the *corona wire*, a delicate, hair-thin wire inside the printer that people always forget to clean. When the corona wire is dirty, it makes printed pages look crummy. On most models, you should replace the long, thin cleaner pad when you replace the toner cartridge — and most people don't. Print quality suffers if you don't replace the cleaner pad.

✔ Don't open the printer when paper is moving: It tends to make the paper jam and the toner smear. Press the Stop button and wait for the paper to stop feeding.

# Prettying Up Your Printouts

If you send a file full of plain text to the printer, the result can look ugly: no margins, titles, or anything else. You can use the `pr` command to make your file look nicer. Use it only with plain text files, not with files full of PostScript or document files from your favorite word processor or desktop publishing program.

## You probably don't care that there are three kinds of printers

Although we have been talking mostly about laser printers, you're likely to find one of three general kinds of printers attached to your computer: impact, inkjet, and laser. The oldest kind of printer is an *impact printer*, which works by hitting an ink ribbon with a little hammer against the paper, more or less like a typewriter. Most recent impact printers are *dot-matrix printers*, which means that, rather than have a hammer for every possible letter, a row of little pins hit the ribbon in various combinations to make the letters. The advantages of dot-matrix printers are that they are very cheap and they can make carbon copies and use continuous perforated paper. The disadvantages are that they are slow and noisy (they sound like something between a very small chainsaw and a very large mosquito), they can't use regular typewriter paper unless you feed every sheet by hand or buy an add-on sheet feeder that jams all the time, and the printed copy looks lousy.

The modern successor to a dot-matrix printer is an *inkjet printer*, which squirts itty-bitty drops of ink at the paper. Because you can make ink drops a lot smaller than you can make printer pins and because squirting ink makes very little noise, inkjet printers are much quieter than dot-matrix printers and produce much better-looking results. At the same time, they are still relatively inexpensive. Most inkjet printers use regular typewriter paper. The disadvantages are that they're still relatively slow and the ink can smear, particularly in large, black areas. You can get color inkjet printers also.

Most UNIX systems use *laser printers*, which work like photocopiers except that, rather than copy a paper original, they use a laser to draw a picture on the copier drum. Laser printers are somewhat more expensive than the other two kinds of printers, but they usually are faster than either kind and produce better-looking results.

Then there are two major kinds of laser printers: Hewlett-Packard and PostScript, but you already know about that (see the preceding sidebar).

## *Titles and page numbers make your printouts look much more official*

The simplest thing you can do with the pr command is to add titles and page numbers to your printout. By default, the title is the name of the file and the date and time it was last changed. You can use a pipe (defined in Chapter 6 as the vertical bar, |) to format with pr and print in a single line:

```
pr myfile | lp
```

(Remember to use the `lpr` command rather than `lp`, if appropriate.) This command tells the `pr` program to pretty up the file and to pass the results to the `lp` program.

You can set your own heading by using the `-h` option with the `pr` command:

```
pr -h "My Deepest Thoughts" myfile | lp
```

The result looks like this:

```
Feb 26 15:03 1993  My Deepest Thoughts Page 1
Call me Ishmael. ...
```

The `pr` command assumes that printer pages are 66 lines long. If that's not true for you, instead of the title appearing at the top of every page, it sort of oozes down from page to page. You can override the length of the standard page with the `-l` option. Suppose that the page length is 60 lines; you type this line:

```
pr -l 60 myfile | lp
```

If you want to use `pr` and not have any heading at the top of the page, use the `-t` option:

```
pr -t myfile | lp
```

(This example doesn't do anything interesting to `myfile`; later, though, you will see that it really is useful when you combine it with margins and stuff.)

## Marginally yours

You may frequently put printouts in three-ring binders. Normally, because printing starts very close to the left side of the page, the hole punch may put holes in your text and make the page difficult to read — not to mention look stupid. The `-o` option (that's a lowercase letter *o,* not a zero, for *offset*) pushes the stuff you print to the right, leaving a left margin. To leave five spaces for a left margin, for example, type the following command:

```
pr -o5 myfile | lp
```

Sometimes it's nice to leave a wider margin at the bottom of the page. You can do that by combining the `-l` option (described in the preceding section to set a page length) with the `-f` option that tells `pr` to use a special *form-feed character* to make the printer start a new page *now!* (Normally, the -1 option uses blank lines to space to the next page, like a typewriter.)

```
pr -o5 -l50 -f myfile | lp
```

This command tells UNIX to print just 50 lines per page, indented 5 spaces. That should be enough space in the margin for anyone.

## Seeing double

The -d option tells pr to double-space the printout:

```
pr -d myfile | lp
```

This command also puts a title on every page by default; use -d -t to avoid that:

```
pr -d -t myfile | lp
```

## One column can't contain me

If the lines in your file are short, you can save paper by printing the file in multiple columns. To print your file in two columns, for example, type the following:

```
pr -2 myfile | lp
```

Astute readers probably can guess what the options -3, -4, and up to -9 do. (If you're not that astute, these options specify the number of columns you want.) Columns normally run down the page, as they do in newspapers. If your file contains a list of items, one per line, and you want to print them in columns, you may want to change the order in which the lines print. If you want to print items across the page, move down to the next line, and so on (which is nowhere near as cool), use the -a option in addition to the -2 or -3 option.

For a truly baffling effect, you can arrange to print several files side by side with the -m option:

```
pr -m firstfile secondfile | lp
```

This command prints the first line of every file on the first line of the printout, the second line of every file on the second line, and so on. You can specify as many as nine filenames and have them print side by side in skinny, little columns. We never have been able to figure out much of a use for this option, but it is definitely a way to produce really odd printouts.

# Part IV

## Of Mice
## and Computers

The 5th Wave    By Rich Tennant

"Here at MIC, leaders in OEM, it's SOP to wish a happy retirement to a great MIS like Douglas U. Hodges, or, DUH as we came to know him."

# In this part...

*I*t's a new world here in UNIX-land! You may have to deal with a GUI (graphical user interface), a mouse, and cute little icons, which can be almost as cryptic as the commands they are designed to replace.

This part explains the newfangled concepts used by GUIs and tells you how to use the most popular UNIX GUIs: Motif and OPEN LOOK.

# Chapter 10

# I'd Rather Be GUI
# than a WIMP

● ● ● ● ● ● ● ● ● ● ● ● ● ● ● ● ● ● ● ● ● ● ● ● ● ● ● ● ● ● ● ● ● ● ● ● ● ● ● ● ● ● ● ● ● ● ● ●

## In This Chapter

▶ What's a GUI — should you care?

▶ How to determine which kind of GUI you're using

▶ Basic mouse skills for GUI survival

▶ How to work with windows

● ● ● ● ● ● ● ● ● ● ● ● ● ● ● ● ● ● ● ● ● ● ● ● ● ● ● ● ● ● ● ● ● ● ● ● ● ● ● ● ● ● ● ● ● ● ● ●

*T*o answer your first question, GUI stands for *graphical user interface* and really *is* pronounced "gooey." We prefer the term WIMP, which stands for *windows, icons,* and *mouse pointing,* but for some reason the term never caught on. Fast-track executives would rather be gooey than wimps, we suppose.

A GUI is a combination of a graphics screen (one that can show pictures in addition to text), a mouse or something like it, and a system that divides the screen into several windows that can show different things at the same time. All GUIs work in more or less the same way because they're all based on the same original work done at Xerox about 20 years ago; the details differ enough, though, to make you want to tear your hair out.

## The Big GUIs (The Big Gooey Whats?)

Most UNIX systems that have any sort of GUI use one based on the X Windows system. Older Sun workstations use systems called SunView or NeWS; NeXT machines use NeXTstep (are tHoSE wOrDS cAPiTaLIzed corREctlY?); other than those exceptions, however, you almost certainly will get X Windows. NeWS systems also support X (*X* is lazy author-ese for X Windows); there are frequently used X-under-NeXTStep packages too.

X has many advantages as a windowing system:

- ✔ It runs on all sorts of computers, not just those that run UNIX.

- ✔ It is *policy independent:* A program can make the screen look any way it wants; the screen is not constrained to a single style, as it is on the Macintosh. (As you might imagine, this capability is not an unmitigated blessing. More about this subject later.)

- ✔ It uses a *networked client-server architecture* (love those buzzwords). You can run X on one computer, but the programs that display stuff on-screen can be on entirely different computers connected by a network.

- ✔ MIT gives it away for free.

You can imagine which of these important advantages is the one that really made all the computer makers choose X. Even though MIT gives away the base version of X, unless you happen to be using one of the exact same kinds of computer the guys at MIT use, and unless you're willing to be enough of a programmer to compile tens of thousands of line of X program code, you don't get it for free. You must buy a version tailored for the particular kind of screen and adapter on your computer.

How your screen looks depends on which GUI you use. This chapter talks about things that are the same for all GUIs. Chapter 11 tells you how to tell which GUI you are using and how to do things that work differently for each GUI.

# *Basic Mouse Skills*

You have to know how to use a mouse to get anything done with X. Fortunately, mouse wrangling is pretty easy. Make friends with your mouse. One of us built a little mouse hole in the wall next to the computer desk, with a basket where the mouse can rest when it's not working, but that's probably excessive.

Mice (or mouselike things, such as trackballs) have a way to tell when you have moved them and some buttons you can push to tell the computer you want to do something. Different mice have different numbers of buttons. If your mouse has fewer than three buttons, it is a pain in the neck to use because many programs assign functions to the third button. The first button, by the way, is the one on the left (unless someone has configured your mouse to be left-handed, and then the first button is the one on the right).

 When you move the mouse on the pad or on your desk, a cursor (a little doohickey on-screen) moves along with it. You can pick up the mouse and put it back down somewhere else on the pad or desk without moving the cursor. This capability comes in handy when you find that you have moved the mouse to the edge of the pad and that the cursor is still in the middle of the screen: Just pick up the mouse and move it to a more convenient part of your desk. If you have an optical (female) mouse, it works only when you move it on the pad.

When you move the mouse, try to keep it square to the desk, with the cord (or the tail, depending on whether you're willing to put up with another cute term) pointing away from you. Particularly when the mouse is off to the side of your desk, it's easy to turn the mouse at an angle. Because the computer can't tell that you have done that, you find that you move the mouse down and to the right but that the cursor moves up because the mouse is twisted around. Fortunately, you get used to mousing pretty quickly and all this becomes second nature.

## With a click-click here

The two key mouse skills are clicking and dragging. Clicking is easy: You move the mouse until the cursor is on a screen item you want to activate and then you quickly press and release one of the mouse buttons, generally the first (the left) button. In window-ese, this process is called *selecting* the screen item; it means that you want to do something with the item you just clicked on.

Sometimes you need to *double-click* (click the same button twice quickly) to tell the screen item to do something particularly important. It can take some practice to train your finger to click the button quickly enough for the computer to recognize it as a double-click rather than one click and a second click, made when the nerve impulses finally get back to your finger. If you had practiced the piano when you were a kid, like your mother told you to, you would have the finger dexterity to do this the first time. (Really.) To keep your children from being at a disadvantage in the highly computerized land of the future, be sure that they take piano lessons and practice. Or maybe saxophone lessons would do as well and offer more upward political mobility. But we digress. Back to mouse skills.

## And a drag-drag there

Dragging the mouse is a slightly more complicated procedure. You move to a point of interest, press a mouse button, *hold it down,* move the mouse as you hold the button, and then let go of the button.

You use dragging in two main ways. The first is for *pop-up menus.* When you press one of the mouse buttons, a menu appears, with a list of possible things to do. While you are holding down the button, drag the cursor to the item on the menu you want and then let the button go. If you change your mind and don't want to do any of the things on the menu, drag the cursor entirely off the menu before letting go of the button.

The second way to use the drag technique is to outline some part of a window. You move to one corner of an area you want to select, press a mouse button, drag to the opposite corner of the area, and let go; at this point, a box on-screen shows the area you outlined.

## A few cool X programs

Because MIT gives away X Windows for free, X quickly became the standard window system at hundreds of colleges and universities around the world. Students, having as always a sincere dedication to doing something other than what they are supposed to be doing (not like the rest of us, no siree), quickly wrote all sorts of silly programs — nominally to test either X or their understanding of it, and generally to have fun. Assuming that these programs are installed on your computer, you have to type only their names in a window containing a UNIX shell to run them (more about this subject in the next chapter). A few of the better-known fun X programs are shown in this list:

✔ **xeyes.** Pops up a large pair of eyeballs that watch the mouse cursor as you move it around the screen. According to the manual, it checks up on you and reports back to the boss. Hmmm.

✔ **xsol.** Plays a game of Klondike solitaire against you. You click on the deck to turn over the next card and click and drag cards to move them around. It's as good a way as any to learn how to handle the mouse, or at least that's the excuse you can use when the boss comes by. Because the computer controls the card deck, you can't cheat, which means that it's practically impossible to win in one trip through the deck. We've won honestly once in about two years of play. The program allows

you to turn over the deck and try again, which lets you win nearly half the time, albeit without honor.

✔ **xphoon.** Displays in the background of your screen a detailed full-screen picture of the moon as it appears today. In a classic display of dedicated nerd programming, it correctly computes the relative angular positions of the earth, moon, and sun based on the current time and date, and shows the moon's current phase (full, quarter, half, or whatever). Useful for people who work in windowless offices in cities and have forgotten what the sky looks like.

✔ **xmille.** Plays the Parker Brothers game Mille Bornes against you. It keeps a running score and plays a mean game. Click on the deck with the first mouse button to draw a card, click on a card in your hand to play it, and click on a card with the second button to discard it. During the past year or so, we have won 34 games and lost 42, with each game consisting of about five hands.

✔ **xroach.** Lots of yucky roaches scurry around the screen and hide under the windows, just like in real life. If you run it with the `-squish` option, you can squish the roaches by clicking on them, leaving an authentic smudge of roach guts on your screen. (Nerds consider this to be humor at its finest.)

# Window Treatments

Now that you're a mouse expert, we discuss a few of the basic things you can do with X Windows. Suppose that you have two or three windows on your screen. How do you tell UNIX which window you want to use? The answer is (wait, no — how did you know this was coming?) *it depends*.

Most commonly, to select a window, you just move the mouse cursor into the window you want to use. You can tell when a window is *active* because the border around it changes color. Some systems are configured to use the "click to type" window-selection technique, in which you have to move the mouse to the window you want and then click one of the buttons to activate the window.

If you have to "click to type" and really hate it — or don't and really want to — a guru skilled in the ways of X (naturally called an X-pert) can change some parameters and turn "click to type" on or off. We recommend that you live with whatever you have; there are so many changeable parameters that, after you begin fiddling with them, it can become X-asperating to figure out X-actly how your X-pert left them, and you will utter an X-cess of X-pletives.

# Chapter 11

# OPEN LOOK, Motif, and Other Schools of Windowing Theology

**In This Chapter**

▶ How to tell which theology you subscribe to

▶ Window-wrangling skills

▶ How to log out

*M*ost windowing systems on most kinds of computers make programs use a consistent style. All Macintosh programs, for example, look pretty much the same: They all use the same menu, the same little window when you want to select a file, similar windows to turn options on and off, and so forth. One Microsoft Windows program looks a lot like all the others: They all use similar sets of windows. But do all X Windows programs have a consistent look? Of course not — that would be too easy. (This is what the X crowd means by *policy independence:* X Windows doesn't enforce any window-appearance policy.)

## Let's Go Window Shopping

A bunch of competing window "looks" are on the UNIX market (the best known are Motif and OPEN LOOK). To tell which one you're stuck with, er, have the pleasure to use, look at the border around the windows on your screen. If they have 3-D-style borders with sharp corners, as shown in Figure 11-1, you're using Motif. If they have rounded corners, as shown in Figure 11-2, you're using OPEN LOOK. If they have a thin border around the sides and bottom, and top borders like those shown in Figure 11-3, you're using a program called TWM, which comes with the base version of X and is widely used because it is simple and small.

```
                              xpcterm
          program, use the commands

               xgrabsc -Z >outfile.pzl
               puzzle -picture outfile.pzl


          To have xgrabsc sleep for three seconds before rubber-
          banding, display processing information, and have the result
          displayed with xwud,

               xgrabsc -Wvs3 | xwud
iecc:ttyp1:johnl>xgrabsc -W > mwmwd
iecc:ttyp1:johnl>xwud mwmwd
usage: /usr/bin/X11/xwud [-in <file>] [-noclick] [-geometry <geom>] [-display <d
isplay>]
          [-new] [-std <maptype>] [-raw] [-vis <vis-type-or-id>]
          [-help] [-rv] [-plane <number>] [-fg <color>] [-bg <color>]
iecc:ttyp1:johnl>xwud -in mwmwd
iecc:ttyp1:johnl>!xgrab
xgrabsc -W > mwmwd
iecc:ttyp1:johnl>!xw
xwud -in mwmwd
iecc:ttyp1:johnl>!xg
xgrabsc -W > mwmwd
```

**Figure 11-1:** A typical Motif window.

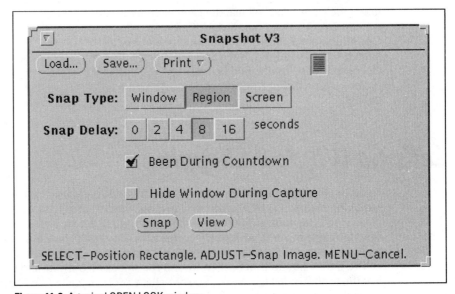

**Figure 11-2:** A typical OPEN LOOK window.

```
 X  xpcterm                                                                    
iecc:ttyp1:john1>who -a
              system boot  Dec 12 12:32
    .         run-level 2  Dec 12 12:32     2      0     S
bcheckrc         .         Dec 12 12:33   0:20       5   id=bchk term=0    exit=77
brc              .         Dec 12 12:33   0:20      15   id= brc term=0    exit=0
brc              .         Dec 12 12:33   0:20      19   id=  mt term=0    exit=0
rc2              .         Dec 12 12:49   0:20      23   id=  r2 term=0    exit=0
root          console      Dec 29 20:16   0:01   17956
sleep            .         Dec 12 12:49   0:20     130   id=  wt term=0    exit=0
john1         vt01         Dec 21 15:19   0:01    5938
LOGIN         vt02         Dec 29 20:16  20:48   17955
LOGIN         ttyd1        Dec 30 16:24   0:52    2827   492-3869
faxserve         .         Dec 26 11:45   0:20   24871   id=  F2
john1         ttyp2        Dec 30 17:16     .     3053   id=  p2 term=112 exit=2
john1         ttyp1        Dec 30 16:55     .     3054
john1         ttyp0        Dec 30 16:55   0:15    3055
john1         ttyp3        Dec 30 16:56   0:20    3086   id=  p3 term=112 exit=2
john1         ttyp4        Dec 30 16:12   1:04   19342   id=  p4 term=112 exit=2
john1         ttyp5        Dec 23 18:41   old    11186   id=  p5 term=112 exit=2
LOGIN            .         Dec 15 15:28   0:20   25517
LOGIN            .         Dec 15 15:30   0:20   25532
LOGIN         ttyd2        Dec 17 18:55   old     5561   id=  02 term=15   exit=0
iecc:ttyp1:john
iecc:ttyp1:john1>xgrabsc -W > twmwd
```

**Figure 11-3:** A typical TWM window.

You can and do mix different window styles on the same screen. If one of the programs you run is written with Motif and another is written with OPEN LOOK, each one displays its own windows by using its own style. The border around the windows, on the other hand, is controlled by a separate program called a window manager; if you have an OPEN LOOK window manager, you can have an OPEN LOOK border around a Motif window, or vice versa. This arrangement can look pretty strange, but fortunately it usually works smoothly.

# Opening a New Window

When you run a new X program, generally speaking, it opens a new window. In some cases, you want to tell a program that's already running to open another window (another file for a word processor, for example), but the way that you do that is specific to each program; you have to read the manual (gasp!) for the program.

You usually have at least one *terminal window* running. A terminal window isn't as sinister as it sounds; it's a window that acts like a terminal. The usual program is called `xterm`; it acts much like a DEC VT100 terminal. Most systems also have a modified terminal program that acts like the computer maker's favorite terminal. Hewlett-Packard systems have `hpterm`, for example, which acts like an

HP terminal, and PC UNIX systems have `xpcterm`, which acts like a PC console. For most purposes, all these terminal programs act the same. They start up running a UNIX shell, and you type commands just as we describe in this book.

There are two ways to start a new program that opens a new window: the GUI-oriented user-friendly way and the easy way.

Follow these steps for the GUI-oriented user-friendly way:

1. Move the cursor so that it's not in any of your current windows.

2. Click the Menu mouse button. This button is the last one (the rightmost button unless you have a left-handed mouse) in OPEN LOOK and the first button otherwise.

3. Drag the mouse up and down the menu that pops up until you find the program you want.

4. Let go of the button. Sometimes you have nested menus: When you pick an item from the first menu, a second menu pops up, and you must pick an item there too.

## Considerably more than you want to know about window managers, toolkits, and X

The X Windows system divides the work of controlling what's on-screen among three separate kinds of programs:

✔ The **X server**: the program that draws the pictures on-screen and reads user input from the keyboard and mouse

✔ The **window manager**: the program that controls where windows appear on-screen, draws borders around windows, and handles basic window operations, such as moving windows, shrinking windows to an icon (a little box representing that window), and expanding icons to windows

✔ **Clients**: programs that do some real work

For any particular screen, there is one X server, usually (but not always) one window manager, and a bunch of clients. Every client communicates with the server to tell it what to draw and to find out what you did; the server communicates

with the window manager when the user asks for a window-management operation such as changing the size of a window. Although the server, the window manager, and clients usually run on the same computer, X Windows allows them to exist on separate machines connected by a network. It is not unusual to have a setup in which the server runs in an X terminal, the window manager runs in a nearby workstation, and the clients are on machines scattered around the network.

The window manager is usually (except on a few X terminals) a regular UNIX program; you can stop one window manager and start another if you decide that you don't like the way your windows look. Client programs can ask the X server to ask the window manager to do some specialized operations. A terminal program, for example, can ask the window manager to enable the user to change the size of the window only to a size that

*(continued next page)*

The easy way to start a program has only one step:

1. Go to a terminal window and type the name of the program you want to run.

This approach is the same one you use to run any other program or to give a command. To display another terminal window, type xterm or the name of the terminal program you use.

Then there's the issue of where on-screen the new window appears. Some programs have strong opinions of their own, and the new window appears wherever the program thinks that it should. With other, less-opinionated programs, you make the call: A ghostly window that appears floats near the middle of the screen. You move the ghost around with the mouse and click when the window is where you want it. At that point, the ghost materializes into the regular window. This latter scheme is usually more convenient because the locations the opinionated programs choose for window placement are rarely where you want them. Beware of one thing, though: While the ghost is on-screen, all other windows are frozen. If you leave the ghost on-screen for a long time (while you're at lunch or overnight), all the others can get rather constipated waiting for the screen to unfreeze so that they can update their windows.

---

*(continued from previous page)*

is a whole number of lines of text. (This kind of communication starts to resemble that in the ancient Roman Empire, in which proconsuls could officially speak only to procurators who could speak to senators, and so forth. But computers are like that.) If there isn't a window manager, there aren't any window-management operations available.

Writing an X program is a lot of work. To make life easier for programmers, a programmer can build on *toolkits* of program code that are already written. MIT sends out X Toolkit (immediately called Xt by the usual lazy typists); this toolkit provides a set of basic window functions that most programs use. Starting with Xt, different people have produced libraries of *widgets,* or screen elements a program can use. A menu or a file-selection panel is a widget, for example. There is a Motif widget set for programs that want to look like Motif, an OPEN LOOK widget set (known as OLIT) for programs that want to look like OPEN LOOK, and a set of Athena widgets from MIT's Project Athena that

aren't particularly attractive but that many programs use because (where have we heard this before?) they're available for free. As a final extra level of bafflement, another widget set called xview contains OPEN LOOK widgets that look just like the ones in OLIT but are internally based on an earlier window system called SunView.

What all this means is that any particular X client uses one of the widget sets to control what that client's window looks like. A program that uses OLIT, for example, is an OPEN LOOK program. But because clients are separate from window managers, the Motif window manager (named mwm — the lazy typists strike again) can be running and draw a Motif border around the OPEN LOOK-based clients' windows, which produces ugly results indeed.

There is a school of thought that says we all would be better off if X Windows had picked a window style and stuck with it so that we would have a single window manager and a single set of widgets — as every other window system does — but it's far too late now for that.

Some systems have desktop manager programs (unrelated to window manager programs) that attempt to make it easier to handle programs and files. Desktop managers have sets of icons you click on to start common programs; they let you click on file names to edit the file, and so forth — sort of like the Macintosh Desktop. Opinions vary on how useful these desktop managers are. We haven't been crazy about them, but it's worth trying them for a few minutes because some people find them much easier to use than menus and shell commands.

# Icon Do It with a Picture

GUIs are crazy about pictures (they're graphical, after all), especially cute, little ones. The cutest, littlest ones you run into are icons. An icon is a little picture in a little box on-screen that represents a window. When you tell X Windows to *iconify* a window, the window disappears and an icon remains. When you click (or double-click in Motif) on the icon, the window comes back just as it was before. Being able to reduce windows to icons lets you shove programs out of the way and not lose what you were doing — one of the best things about window systems. Figure 11-4 shows a pair of icons, one for an electronic-mail program and one for a terminal program. If new mail arrives, the little flag on the mail icon flips up, which is almost useful enough to make up for its X-treme cuteness.

**Figure 11-4:** Icons are windows in a miniature disguise.

# Rearranging Windows

You frequently will find that you don't like the way the windows on your screen are arranged. You can do lots of things to alleviate this problem and simultaneously waste lots of time. In fact, we have found that, by giving your dedicated attention to window management, you can spend the entire day at the computer apparently working but not accomplishing anything. A little rearrangement is inevitable, so the following sections are thumbnail sketches of what you can do and how to do it in each of the three major windowing systems:

- **Change the layering.** Change which windows are in front of other windows, much like shuffling the papers in the pile on your desk. Unless you're a masochist, you want the active window (the window you're using) to be the one in front.

- **Move windows around the screen.** This is even more similar to shuffling the papers on your desk.

- **Turn windows into icons and vice versa.**

- **Change the size of windows.** Create larger areas for long files you're editing, for example.

## The chic window dresses in layers

To bring a window to the front of a stack of windows, move the cursor to the bar at the top of the window (known as the *title bar* because it shows a title for the window) and click the first mouse button. Astonishingly, you do this the same way in Motif, OPEN LOOK, and TWM. Motif also lets you do this: Move the cursor into the window, hold the Alt or Meta key, and press the F1 key.

You can also banish a window to the back of the pile:

- In Motif, you do this by holding the Meta or Alt key and clicking the first mouse button in the title bar; alternatively, hold Meta or Alt and press F3.

- OPEN LOOK makes it considerably more difficult: You click on the little triangle at the left end of the title bar to make a window-operations menu pop up; then you select Back from that menu.

- In TWM, you place the cursor in the title bar and click the third mouse button to move that window to the back.

## Where, oh where, has my window gone?

You can move a window to the exact location on-screen that you want it to be.

- In Motif or OPEN LOOK, put the cursor in the title bar, press the first mouse button, and drag the window to where you want it (move the window as you hold the mouse button). This action also brings the window to the front because you use the same button to do that.

- TWM works the same way, except that you use the *second* mouse button to move the window.

You can move windows so that they are partially off the edge of the screen, sort of like pushing papers to the side of your desk so that they hang over the edge (except that windows are less likely to fall on the floor). This ability is sometimes useful if the interesting stuff in the window is all at the top or all on one side.

## Stashing your extra windows

The title bar of the window has on it little things you can click, depending on which window system you use. One of them changes the window to an icon:

- ✔ Motif puts a bunch of strange-looking blobs in a window's title bar. On the left is a box that contains a little bar; if you click on it, a menu of window operations pops up. (You can do all the window-management tricks by using that menu, but there are easier ways to do them all.) Near the right of the title bar is a little box that contains a small dot; when you click on it, the window turns into an icon. To the right of that box is a third little box we discuss later in this chapter (don't be impatient, we're writing as fast as we can).

- ✔ In OPEN LOOK, the window-operations menu pops up when you click on the little triangle at the left end of the title bar; select Close to change the window into an icon.

- ✔ In TWM, you click on the X at the left end of the title bar to iconify the window. (You're probably starting to see why people like TWM.)

When the window disappears, an icon appears and replaces it. (Remember that the window isn't really gone — it's hidden away in a safe place, sort of like storing storm windows in the basement during the summer.) The icon is located either where the window used to be or off in one corner of the screen that has been made into an icon ghetto. You move icons the same way you move windows: Drag them with the first mouse button in Motif or OPEN LOOK and with the second mouse button in TWM.

To get the window back, double-click on the icon with the first mouse button in Motif or OPEN LOOK; single-click on the icon in TWM. The icon disappears and the window reappears, as though it had never been gone (and it's nowhere near as dusty as the storm windows in the basement).

## Changing window sizes

The last little bit of window magic involves changing window sizes. Motif and OPEN LOOK have gone to a lot of trouble to let you change the size of your windows, which tells us that they gave up trying to make them the right size in the first place. Oh, well. In both cases, little "grab bars" are in each corner of most windows. (The few windows you can't resize don't have the grab bars.)

You move the cursor to one of the grab bars, click the first mouse button, drag the corner to where you want it (which makes the window larger or smaller), and release the button. Then do it again two or three times because you never get it right on the first try. Motif also has grab bars on the top, bottom, and sides of every window that let you change the height of a window without changing the width or vice versa.

Motif and OPEN LOOK also have shortcuts to let you expand a window to fill the entire screen. In Motif, click on the little box-in-a-box at the right end of the title bar. In OPEN LOOK, double-click anywhere in the title bar. In both cases, the window swells to take over the entire screen. If you do the same thing again, the window shrinks back to normal size.

TWM takes a different approach to window resizing: You click on the little blob at the right side of the title bar and, while you hold the mouse button, drag the cursor around. Whenever the cursor crosses one of the edges of the window, the cursor drags that edge along with it. Release the button to set the window size. Although this process sounds kind of strange, it is very easy to use. TWM has no special way to make a window fill the entire screen because it turns out that, in practice, you rarely want to do that. (The full-screen option was a lot more important when screens were smaller.)

# Getting Rid of Windows

Your screen often becomes cluttered with windows you no longer need. You already know how to turn them into icons to get most of the screen space back, but sometimes you just want to make the program go away.

If you have 57 different programs running, even if most of them are snoozing behind their icons, it can put enough of a load on your computer to slow down the ones you want to use.

Most programs have a natural way to exit. In terminal windows, you log out from the shell by typing exit or logout in the terminal window. Real windows-oriented programs usually have menus of their own with a Quit or Exit entry that cleans up and makes the program stop. But because some programs just won't die, you have to take drastic measures.

Motif and OPEN LOOK both take the same approach to drastic measures. In Motif, click on the little bar in the box at the left end of the title bar; a menu of window operations pops up. (The program can tell Motif not to show that little box, and then you display the window-operations menu by holding Meta or Alt and pressing the spacebar.) From that menu, select Close either with the mouse or by typing c. The window and its associated program go away.

OPEN LOOK takes a similar approach: You pop up the window-operations menu by clicking on the triangle in the title bar and then selecting Quit.

Motif and OPEN LOOK use confusing and inconsistent names in the window-operations menu. In Motif, Close means to destroy the window and the program, and Minimize turns the window into an icon. In OPEN LOOK, Close turns the window to an icon, and Quit destroys the window.

TWM doesn't have an easy way to murder a program. Move the cursor outside any window and press the first or second mouse button (it varies depending on the version of TWM) until you see a menu called Window Ops; from that menu, select Destroy Window. The cursor then turns to a menacing skull and cross-bones. Move it to the window you want to get rid of and click the first mouse button to do the window in.

# Ta-Ta for Now

The last little detail is how to tell X Windows you're finished with it. The way you do that (we're getting tired of saying this) varies from one system to another. You have to stop the startup program, which is usually a terminal window named `login` or the window manager itself. If there is a window named `login`, go to the login window and type `exit` or `logout` to exit that shell, or kill it as explained in the preceding section.

If your startup program is the window manager, you must persuade the window manager to exit. You can't kill it the way you kill other programs because the window manager doesn't have a particular window. In OPEN LOOK or Motif, you move the cursor outside any window, press the first mouse button, and select the item labeled Exit from the menu that pops up. In TWM, the general plan is the same, but you may have to use the second or third button to find the menu and then select the Exit item.

# Part V
# Getting Things Done

## In this part...

*W*ell, so far, we have talked about the computer, UNIX, the shell, files — you name it. What about getting some real work done?

To get useful work done, you need software. This part talks about some useful programs that come with UNIX, including text editors. It also discusses buying and installing other programs.

# Chapter 12
# Writing Deathless Prose

* * *

* * *

*I*n the land of UNIX, many programs handle text. Where you come from, you may be accustomed to the idea of using a word processor when you want to type something and print it. Not in UNIX. There are four kinds of programs to do this, just to keep things interesting.

## Just the Text, Ma'am

A text editor handles files that contain text. No fancy formatting, no fonts, no embedded graphics, or junk like that — just text. It lets you do the following things:

✔ Create a file full of text

✔ Edit the text

You can print the file by using the lp or lpr programs, described in Chapter 9, but text editors can't do boldface, running headers or footers, italics, or all that other fancy stuff you need in order to produce really modern, overformatted, professional-quality memos.

You may want to use a text editor to write letters and reports. You certainly will use one to send electronic mail (see Chapter 18).

The most commonly used text editors in the land of UNIX are ed, vi, and emacs. We have strong opinions about these editors, which will be abundantly clear in the later sections of this chapter, where we tell you how to use each of them.

# Text Formatters Aren't Really Editors

*Text formatters* are programs that read text files and create nice-looking formatted output. You use a text editor to make a text file that contains special little commands only the formatter understands; the .I command, for example, makes something italic. When you run the text formatter, it reads the text file, reads the special little commands, and creates a formatted file that you then can print. You use pr or lpr to print the output of the text formatter.

The most common UNIX text formatter is troff, pronounced "tee-roff" (described later in this chapter). Some people use nroff, or "en-roff" (an older version of troff) or TeX, pronounced "tecccch" (like yecccch). With luck, you will never have to use any of them.

# Cuisinarts for Text: Word Processors

Word processors combine the capabilities of text editors and text formatters. Most word processors are supposed to be WYSIWYG (an acronym for *what you see is what you get,* and pronounced "wizzy-wig") so that you can see on-screen how the documents (that's what they call their files) will look when you print them.

Word processors for UNIX include WordPerfect (available also for PCs and Macintoshes) and Microsoft Word (available for at least XENIX and SVR4 as well as for Macs and PCs). Most UNIX users think that word processors are for wimps (*what you see is all you've got*) because they like the unintelligible and unmemorable commands used by text formatters and prefer to imagine what their text will look like when it is printed rather than be able to see it on-screen. To be fair, text formatters can do more complex things than word processors can, like format complicated mathematical expressions, lay out multipage tables, and fetch reference citations from a database. But that's probably not your problem. (We are using troff to write drafts of this book, so it just goes to show ya....)

# Desktop Publishing Does It All

A desktop publishing program (DTP) resembles a very fancy word processor. It can do everything a word processor can, plus things you need only if you are printing a book, newsletter, or something else that looks fancy. DTPs include facilities for creating tables of contents and indexes, maintaining cross-references — you name it. For writing an occasional memo, a desktop publishing program is definitely overkill.

The two most common desktop publishing programs for UNIX are Interleaf (available for PCs also) and FrameMaker (available for PCs and Macintoshes also).

TeX and some versions of troff are available for free, which explains why they remain so popular (big surprise, eh?). All word processors and desktop publishers are commercial products that cost extra. Lots extra.

# Ed *and* Vi *and* Emacs *Are Your Friends*

The rest of this chapter explains how to use each of the Big Three text editors (ed, vi, and emacs). Even if you use a word processor or desktop publishing program, you may need to use a text editor to do things like these:

- ✔ Write electronic mail (see Chapter 18)
- ✔ Create or edit text files called *shell scripts* to allow you to create your own UNIX commands (see Chapter 14)
- ✔ Create or edit special text files that control the way your UNIX setup works (see Chapter 28)
- ✔ Write C programs (just kidding!)

## Talk to Mr. ed

The ed program is the original editor that has been a part of UNIX since the beginning of time. When you use it, you begin to appreciate how far software design has progressed since 1975. The ed program is a *line editor,* which means that ed assigns line numbers to the lines in the file; every time you do something, you must tell ed which line or lines to do it to. If you have used the EDLIN program in DOS, ed should look familiar.

If there is *any way* — repeat — *any way* you can get another text editor to use, do it. If you don't think that ed can really be that bad, just peruse the next few pages and you will run screaming to your system administrator for vi or emacs (preferably emacs).

To run ed, type this line:

```
ed important.letter
```

(Type the name of your file rather than important.letter.) If no file has the name you specify, ed makes one. UNIX responds to this command with a number, which is the number of characters (letters, numbers, punctuation, and spaces) in the file, just in case you are getting paid to write by the letter.

If you receive an error message when you try to run ed, talk to your system administrator. Congratulate her on getting rid of that Neanderthal text editor and find out which text editor you *can* use.

### Hey Wilbur, which command was that?

All ed commands are one letter long (like h).

Remember *not* to capitalize ed commands unless we specifically say to; ed commands are almost all small letters.

## Emergency exit from ed

To get the heck out of ed — in case someone used your computer and left it running — follow these steps:

1. Type a period on a line by itself and press Enter (or Return). This action gets you into command mode in case you are in input mode. If you were already in command mode, a line of the file prints on-screen. Ignore it.

2. Type q and press Enter.

   If changes to the file have been saved or if there were no changes, this action quits ed and you see a UNIX shell prompt. If changes to

the file haven't been saved, ed displays a question mark, meaning, "Yo, you're about to throw away your changes. Are you cool with this?" Type q again and press Enter again. This time, ed exits. If someone has used your computer and run ed, and didn't save the work, to heck with it. And if *you* ran ed by mistake and are fighting to get out, you probably don't want to save any changes anyway.

In most versions of ed, you can also use the capital Q command, which means, "*Q*uit — and don't ask any questions!"

The ed program is always waiting for one of two things: commands or text (a.k.a. input). When ed is waiting for a command, it is in *command mode.* When it is waiting for text, it is in *input mode.* Normally, it is up to you to figure out which mode ed is in at any particular moment (it doesn't give you a clue). Whether ed is waiting for a command or for text input, it just displays a blank line — truly among the most unhelpful, not to say hostile, programs ever designed.

At the time the lazy typists who created UNIX wrote ed, they were using old, slow, noisy Teletype terminals and wanted to save themselves from having to type any character they could. But why should that be your problem?

Relatively recent versions of ed (since, oh, about 1983) have a P command (that's a capital *P,* one of the few uppercase commands) that turns on a prompt. If you type P and press Enter, ed prompts you with an asterisk when it's in command mode and waiting for a command. Is that incredibly user-friendly or what? It actually allows you to determine when you are in command mode! Must have snuck that one in when the lazy typists weren't looking.

If you are in input mode and want to give a command, type this character:

```
.
```

That's just a single period on a line by itself. Typing this character switches ed to command mode.

In the remainder of this discussion about using ed, whenever we tell you to type a command, it works only if you are in command mode. If you are not sure, type a period and press Enter first.

If you are in command mode and want to type some text, you switch to text input mode. But first you must decide whether you are going to *append* (by using the a command) after the current line the lines of text you will type or *insert* (by using the i command) the lines of text before the current line. More about the current line and the a and i commands in a minute.

### Help, Wilbur!

The ed program has a fascinating and totally self-explanatory error message that you see if you type anything wrong:

```
?
```

That's it — that's the whole thing. Luckily, you can humbly ask ed for more information about what went wrong. Just type this command and press Enter:

```
h
```

The ed program displays a short message that gives you a hint about the problem. In most versions of ed, if you type a capital H, ed not only explains the current complaint but also any others that occur later on. Be warned: The explanations are not as helpful as they might be, but what did you expect?

### What's my line?

The ed program thinks of your file (if we may anthropomorphize a bit) as a series of lines of text. It numbers the lines and works with them one at a time. And so must you, to get anything done using ed.

For most commands, you tell ed which line or lines to work with. When you insert lines, for example, you tell ed which line to insert the new lines in front of.

If you don't specify the line or lines you want to work on, ed assumes that you want the *current line*. The current line is the line you last worked with. If you last worked with a bunch of lines, it's the last one. When you start using ed, the current line is the last line in the file.

### Mr. ed *gets lunch*

Let's create a file and feed some text to it. Start the process by typing this line:

```
ed eating.peas
```

You can name your file something other than eating.peas, if you want. UNIX responds with a question mark, just to keep you on your toes. (This time, the question mark tells you that ed just created a new file for you.)

To add (append) new lines of text to the end of the file — in this case, the end of the file is the same as the beginning because the file is empty — type the following:

```
a
```

UNIX responds by saying absolutely nothing, which is your indication that ed is now in input mode and waiting for you to type some text. Type some pearls of wisdom, like this:

```
I eat my peas with honey,
I've done it all my life.
It makes the peas taste funny,
but it keeps them on the knife.
.
```

When you finish typing text, type a period on a line by itself to switch ed from input mode back to command mode. Not that ed gives you a hint that this is going on, unless you have used the P command to tell it to prompt you.

The lines of text are now in your file. This would be a good time to save the file, just in case you kick the plug of your computer out of the wall in your frustration at having to use such a brainless program.

### Saving a file

The following command saves your text in a file. If you are in input mode, remember to type a period on a line by itself to switch to command mode before giving this command:

```
w
```

That's w for *w*rite. UNIX responds with the number of characters now in the file. Be sure to give this command before leaving ed so that your deathless prose is saved in the file, eating.peas, in this case (or whatever filename you used when you ran ed).

### Show me the file, please

Now that you have text in the file, how can you see it or change it? By using the p (print) command. This command doesn't print anything on the printer, it just displays it on-screen — another example of superb software engineering. (Well, it printed on those old Teletypes.) If you type the p command by itself, like this, ed displays the current line:

```
p
```

In the case of the sample eating.peas file, the current line is the last line in the file. You can also tell ed which lines to display by typing their line numbers. To display lines 1 through 4, for example, type this line:

```
1,4p
```

## What if ed commands end up in my text?

If you are in input mode and type an ed command, ed doesn't do the command. Instead, it thinks that you are typing text and stores the letter or letters of the command as just some more text in your file.

If this happens, delete the lines you don't want (we explain how to delete lines later in this chapter). The next time you want to enter a command, be sure to type a period on a line by itself first.

You can also use the symbol $ to stand for the line number of the last line in the file (in case you don't know how many lines are in the file); the following command always displays the entire file:

```
1,$p
```

### Take a number, please

We know — you shouldn't have to see line numbers when you just want to write a simple memo or whatever, but, because ed uses line numbers with its commands, displaying line numbers can be useful. To display lines with line numbers, use n rather than p. Type the following line, for example, to see a complete listing of your file with line numbers:

```
1,$n
```

The result is something like this:

```
1    I eat my peas with honey,
2    I've done it all my life.
3    It makes the peas taste funny,
4    but it keeps them on the knife.
```

### Now you see it, now you don't

To delete the current line of text, type the following:

```
d
```

Watch out when you type lines that start with the letter *d* whenever you are using ed! If ed decides that you are in command mode when you type a *d,* ed deletes the current line (or whatever lines you specify) with no warning or confirmation. We suggest that you use the p and n commands a lot as you go along, to see what your file looks like.

## Accidental input

Most other lowercase letters are ed commands too. (We just didn't think that you would want to know about them.) When you are in command mode, typing almost any letter (or even some other symbols) tells ed that you want to do a command. So, watch what you type when you're in command mode.

After you add or delete lines, ed renumbers the lines in the rest of the file. Use the n command often to confirm your line numbers.

You can specify which lines you want ed to delete by typing the line number or numbers, like this:

```
4d
```

Or like this, to delete lines 1 through 2:

```
1,2d
```

The comma tells ed to delete lines starting with 1 and ending with 2, inclusive.

### A miserable way to edit

You can change the contents of a line of text with ed, but it involves giving commands that look like this:

```
12,13s/wrong/right/
```

This command substitutes right for wrong in lines 12 through 13, inclusive. Totally primitive and painful, isn't it? For the amount of editing you probably do in ed, it is almost easier to delete the line with the typo and insert a new line. We recommend that you immediately ask your system administrator for a better text editor.

### Make me better again, doctor

But, wait — there is one useful, humane command in ed after all! The u command lets you "undo" the last (and only the very last) change you made to the file. If you delete a line by mistake with the d command, for example, you can type this line to undo the deletion:

```
u
```

# Yikes — it keeps displaying lines!

If you are in command mode and press Enter without having typed any command, ed assumes that you want to see the next line of the file. It moves down one line in the file and displays that line — rather convenient, really, if you are expecting it.

Also, if you are *already* in command mode and you type a period on a line by itself (are you following this?), ed displays the next line in the file.

Be sure that you don't make any other changes before using the u command; it undoes only the very last thing you did.

### Give my regards to Broadway, ed

When you finish making changes and you want to leave ed (or even if you're not finished making changes and you want to leave ed anyway), type the following:

```
q
```

If you are in input mode, first type a period on a line by itself to get into command mode. Then type q to quit.

If you haven't saved your work by using the w command, ed just doesn't quit. Instead, it displays a question mark to tell you that it was expecting a w command first. To save your changes, type these two commands:

```
w
q
```

If you don't want to save the changes to the file, type q again at the question mark. This time, ed believes that you really want to leave and exits. Not a moment too soon!

As a review, Table 12-1 lists the commands you use most commonly with ed.

| Table 12-1: | Commands in ed |
| --- | --- |
| *Command* | *Description* |
| a | Add lines after the current line and enter input mode |
| d | Delete line or lines |
| h | Display extremely terse help message right now |
| H | Display terse help messages whenever anything goes wrong |
| i | Insert lines before the current line and enter input mode |
| n | Display line or lines with line numbers |
| p | Display line or lines |
| P | Display an asterisk whenever ed is in command mode |
| q | Quit the whole thing |
| Q | Quit regardless of whether changes have been saved |
| u | Undo last change |
| w | Write (save) the file |

### *Oh, no! It's my* ex*!*

An improved version of ed, called ex, understands all the same commands, so everything we have said about ed applies to ex. It is a little better about letting you know what's going on. In particular, ex prompts you with a colon at the beginning of the line when it's in command mode (is that user friendly, or what?) It also has considerably more informative error messages.

But the most important thing about ex is that it's the same program as vi! If you find yourself in ex (which sometimes happens when you send electronic mail), just type vi as a command to ex, and — Poof! — the ugly toad of ex turns into, well, the somewhat less ugly toad of vi, which we describe next.

# *Shy* Vi*, the princess of text editors*

The vi text editor is head and shoulders above ed in every way. It is a *screen editor* rather than a line editor; it shows you as much of the file as it can fit on-screen. You don't have to beg it to display bits and pieces of your file — definitely a step forward.

The bad news is that command-wise and mode-wise, vi works just like ed because deep down it's just a souped-up version of ed. Two modes with no clue about which one you are using, cryptic one-letter commands — the works. You're still better off learning emacs, but vi really is better than ed.

The vi program is available on almost all UNIX systems, which is the major reason it is so widely used.

To run vi, type this line:

```
vi eating.peas
```

Remember to substitute the name of the file you want to create or change for eating.peas. If the file you name doesn't exist, vi creates it.

### *Screens full of text*

The vi program shows you a full-screen view of your file. If the file isn't long enough to fill the screen, vi shows tildes (~) on the blank lines beyond the end of the file. Figure 12-1, for example, shows the file eating.peas (created in the preceding discussion about ed) as it would appear in vi.

The cursor (the point at which you are working) appears at the beginning of the first line of the file.

- ✔ If you get an error message when you try to run vi, talk to your system administrator.

- ✔ If the screen looks weird, your terminal type may not be set right — another reason to talk to your system administrator.

```
I eat my peas with honey,
I've done it all my life.
It makes the peas taste funny,
but it keeps them on the knife.
~
~
~
~
" eating.peas" 4 lines 115 characters
```

**Figure 12-1:** Tildes fill up the blank lines in a vi file.

### Royal commands and edicts

All vi commands are one letter long (like ed commands). Some are lowercase letters and others are capital letters. When you type vi commands, be sure to use the correct capitalization.

The vi program has two modes, just like ed: command mode (waiting for a command) and input mode (waiting to accept text input). You have to keep track of which mode you are using because vi doesn't tell you.

If you are in input mode and want to give a command, press the Esc key.

Whenever we tell you to type a command, it works only if you are in command mode. If you are not sure which mode you're in, press Esc first. If you are already in command mode, pressing Esc just makes vi beep.

To switch from command mode to text-input mode, you tell vi to add the text after the character the cursor is on (by using the a command) or to insert the text before the current cursor position (by using the i command). You can see where the cursor is in your file, which is a big improvement over ed.

## An emergency exit from vi

To escape from vi, do the following:

1. Press Esc at least three times. The computer should beep.

2. Type this line and press and Enter:

   :q!

   This line tells vi to quit and not save any changes.

Because vi deep down is still a souped-up version of ed, you can use the same old commands we talked about earlier in our discussion of ed. To do so, first be sure that you're in command mode by pressing Esc, if necessary. Then type a colon (:), followed by the ed command, and end with Enter (as always, with ed commands). With rare exceptions, this procedure isn't worth the effort.

### Help! I need somebody!

The guy who wrote vi didn't believe in help, so there wasn't any. (Do you remember Bill, the grouchy guy who's 6'4" and in excellent physical condition? Same guy.)

Fortunately, vi has been used in so many introductory computing courses that Bill eventually relented and added a "novice" mode. Rather than type vi to run the editor, type vedit to get the same editor with some allegedly helpful messages. In particular, whenever you're in input mode rather than command mode, vi displays a message like INPUT MODE, APPEND MODE, CHANGE MODE, or OPEN MODE at the bottom of your screen. All these messages mean the same thing (except to Bill, evidently): Text you type when these messages can be seen is added to the file rather than interpreted as commands.

### Easy text-entry techniques

Let's make a new file with some more deathless prose so that you can practice entering text in vi. Run vi with a new filename:

```
vi madeline
```

To add text after the current position of the cursor, type the following:

```
a
```

We tell you how to move the cursor in a minute, when there's some text to move around in. Because vi is a full-screen editor, you do *not* press Enter after a command. You can type a, for example, to add this text to the newly created madeline file:

```
In an old house in Paris
All covered with vines
Lived twelve little girls
In two straight lines.
```

To get back to command mode, press Esc. Press Esc whenever you finish typing text so that you are ready to give the next command.

Other commands you can use to enter text include i to insert text *before* the current cursor position, A to add the text at the end of the line the cursor is on, and O to add the text on a new line before the current line.

### All around the mulberry bush: moving the cursor

You can use dozens of commands to move the cursor around in your file, but you can get to where you want with just a few of them:

✔ The arrow keys ($\leftarrow$, $\rightarrow$, $\uparrow$, and $\downarrow$) usually do what you would expect: They move the cursor in the indicated direction.

Sadly, there are terminals on which vi does not understand the arrow keys. If this is true for you, use h to move left, j to move down, k to move up, and l to move right. Bill chose these keys on the theory that, because those keys are a touch typist's home position for the fingers on the right hand, you can save valuable milliseconds by not having to move your fingers. Really. In some versions of vi, arrow keys work only in command mode; in others they work also in input mode.

✔ Enter or + moves to the beginning of the next line.

✔ The hyphen ( - ) moves to the beginning of the preceding line.

✔ G (the capital letter) moves to the end of the file.

✔ 1G moves to the beginning of the file. (That's the number 1, not the letter *l*. Why ask why?)

### A makeover for vi

To modify the text you have typed, follow these steps:

1. Move the cursor to the beginning of the text you want to change.

2. To type over (on top of) the existing text, type the letter R (just a capital *R*).

3. Type the new text. What you type replaces what is already there. Press Esc when you finish replacing text.

4. To insert text in front of the current cursor position, type the letter i (a lowercase *i*.)

5. Type the new text. What you type is inserted without replacing any existing text. Press Esc when you finish inserting text.

### Take a little off the top

To delete text, follow these steps:

1. Move the cursor to the beginning of the text you want to delete.

2. To delete one character, type the letter x. To get rid of five characters, type xxxxx. You get the idea.

3. To delete text from the current cursor position to the end of the line, type a capital D.

4. To delete the entire line the cursor is on, type dd (the letter *d* twice).

### I liked it better the way it was

Like ed, vi has a way to "undo" the most recent change or deletion you made. Type the following to undo the change:

```
u
```

If you type the following (a capital *U*), vi undoes all changes to the current line since you moved the cursor to that line:

```
U
```

### Write me or save me, just don't lose me

To save the updated file, type the following:

```
:w
```

That's a colon and a *w*; then press Enter. This command is the same one you used in ed to save (or write) a file. You should give this command every few minutes, in case the confusing nature of vi commands makes you delete something important by mistake.

### Good-bye, vi

To leave vi, type the following:

```
ZZ
```

Be sure to press Esc a few times so that you are in command mode before giving this command. To quit and not save the changes you have made, type the following line:

```
:q!
```

Then press Enter. This means, "Leave vi and throw away my changes. I know what I'm doing."

Most other letters, numbers, and symbols are vi commands too, so watch what you type when you are in command mode. Table 12-2 lists the most common commands you use with vi.

## A novel concept in editing: emacs makes sense

We don't want to get your hopes up, but emacs is much easier to use than ed or vi. The reason is that it doesn't have the mysterious modes that require you to remember at every moment whether the program is expecting a command or text.

| Table 12-2: | Commands in vi |
|---|---|
| *Command* | *Description* |
| Esc | Return to command mode |
| Enter (or Return) | Move to beginning of next line |
| + | Move to beginning of next line |
| - | Move to beginning of preceding line |
| a | Add text after cursor |
| A | Add text at end of current line |
| dd | Delete entire current line |
| D | Delete from cursor to end of line |
| G | Move (go) to end of file |
| 1G | Move to beginning of file |
| h | Move one space left |
| i | Add text before cursor |
| j | Move down one line |
| k | Move up one line |
| l | Move right one space |
| 0 | Add text on new line before current line |
| :q! (followed by Enter): | Quit vi, even if changes aren't saved |
| R | Replace text |
| u | Undo last change |
| U | Undo changes to current line |
| x | Delete one character |
| :w (followed by Enter) | Save (write) file |
| ZZ | Quit vi |

On the other hand, commands in emacs aren't exactly intuitive. But we like them better. In case you are wondering, the name *emacs* comes from *editor macros* because the original version of emacs was written as an extension to an early text editor called teco, an editor that makes ed look like the winner of the Nobel prize for user-friendliness. (Scary thought, isn't it?)

Although emacs doesn't come with UNIX, a popular version called GNU Emacs is distributed for free, so most systems have it or can get it. Also available are commercial versions of emacs, including Epsilon and Unipress Emacs.

To run emacs, type the following line:

```
emacs eating.peas
```

You replace eating.peas with the name of the file you want, of course. If the file you name doesn't exist, emacs creates it. Like vi, emacs displays a full-screen view of your file. On the bottom line of the screen is the *status line*; it tells you the name of the file you are editing and other less interesting information.

✔ If you get an error message when you try to run emacs, ask your system administrator what's up. On some systems, GNU Emacs is called gmacs, so you would type gmacs rather than emacs. The emacs program may have another name on your system. If your system administrator says that you don't have emacs, plead with him to get it.

✔ If emacs looks or acts weird (weirder than usual, that is), your terminal type may not be set correctly. Again, ask your system administrator to straighten this out.

### *How to Meta-morphose* emacs

Rather than have two modes, as do ed and vi, emacs treats normal letters, numbers, and punctuation as text and sticks them in your file when you type them. (Pretty advanced concept, huh?) Commands are usually given by pressing combinations of the Ctrl (or Control) key and a letter. You also give some commands by pressing the Meta key and a letter.

## An emergency exit from emacs

To stop using emacs, follow these steps:

1. Hold the Ctrl (or Control) key and press X.

2. Hold Ctrl and press C.

This procedure doesn't save any changes you made to the file in emacs. It just gets you out. Some versions of emacs may ask whether you want to save the file the editor was looking at, or say something like "Buffers not saved. Exit?" (Translation: "Do you really want to quit without saving your changes?") Press y for yes or n for no, as appropriate. If you just want to get out, say n to the "Do you want to save" question or y to the "Buffers not saved" question.

On most computers, the Meta key is the Esc key. If your keyboard has an Alt key, it may be the Meta key. In the following section, we tell you to press Esc.

### Another novel concept: type to enter text

To enter text, just start typing! The text is inserted wherever your cursor is.

### Tripping hither, tripping thither

To move the cursor around in your text, use the following keys:

- ✔ Arrow keys usually move the cursor up, down, left, and right.

  In a few situations, emacs doesn't understand the arrow keys. If this is true for you, use Ctrl-B to move *b*ackward a character, Ctrl-F to move *f*orward a character, Ctrl-P to move to the *p*receding line, and Ctrl-N to move to the *n*ext line. At least they tried to make them mnemonic.

- ✔ Ctrl-A moves to the beginning of the line (you hold Ctrl and press A).

- ✔ Ctrl-E moves to the end of the line.

- ✔ Esc-< (press Escape and then hold Shift and press the comma key) moves to the beginning of the file.

- ✔ Esc-> (press Escape and then hold Shift and press the period key) moves to the end of the file.

### A small change

Even though emacs is a better text editor, you still might make typos, change your mind, and think of brilliant improvements to your text. To change text, follow these steps:

1. Move the cursor to the beginning of the text you want to change.

2. Type the new text. The text is inserted wherever the cursor is.

3. Delete any text you don't want.

It's that simple. No weird commands required.

### More than one way to delete a character

There are several commands for deleting stuff:

- ✔ To delete the character the cursor is on, press Ctrl-D (hold the Ctrl key and press D).

- ✔ To delete text from the cursor to the end of the word (up to a space or punctuation mark), press Esc and then D.

- ✔ To delete text from the cursor to the end of the line, press Ctrl-K (short for *k*ill).

### *Someone saved my file tonight (sorry, Elton)*

To save the text in the file, press Ctrl-X Ctrl-S (press and hold the Ctrl key, type XS, and then release the Ctrl key). You should save your work every few minutes. Even though emacs isn't as frustrating as ed or vi, lots can still go wrong.

### *Bidding* emacs *adieu*

When you finish editing and want to leave emacs, press Ctrl-X Ctrl-C (press and hold the Ctrl key, type XC, and then release the Ctrl key). You leave emacs and see the UNIX shell prompt.

If you didn't save your work, emacs politely points out that your "buffers" (the stuff you have been working on) aren't saved and asks whether you really want to exit. It suggests n as the safe default in case you want to return to emacs to save the file. To leave without saving, press y and Enter.

It takes many fewer emacs commands to make a file and type some stuff, make a few changes, and then save the file and leave than it does with ed or vi. The emacs program has tons of commands, most of which are utterly useless. Table 12-3 lists the commonly used emacs commands.

TIP

## Moving text in emacs

Although this discussion is beyond the scope of this quick introduction to emacs, here's how to move text from one place to another in the file. It turns out that, when you use Ctrl-K to kill the text from the cursor to the end of the line, it stores the killed information in a temporary place called the *kill buffer.* You can copy the information from the kill buffer back into your file by pressing Ctrl-Y (yank it back into the file). To move some text, kill it with Ctrl-K, move to the new location, and press Ctrl-Y to insert the text where your cursor is.

| Table 12-3: | Commands in emacs |
| --- | --- |
| **Command** | **Description** |
| Ctrl-A | Move to the beginning of the line |
| Ctrl-B | Move back one space |
| Ctrl-D | Delete one character |
| Ctrl-E | Move to the end of the line |
| Ctrl-F | Move forward one space |
| Ctrl-K | Delete to the end of the line |
| Ctrl-N | Move to the next line |
| Ctrl-P | Move to the preceding line |
| Ctrl-X Ctrl-C | Leave emacs |
| Ctrl-X Ctrl-S | Save the file |
| Esc-< | Move to the beginning of the file |
| Esc-> | Move to the end of the file |
| Esc-D | Delete to the end of the word |

# Chapter 13

# Umpteen Useful
# UNIX Underdogs

- - - - - - - - - - - - - - - - - - - - - - - - - - - - - - - - - - - - - - - - - - -

## In This Chapter

▶ A grab bag of useful programs

▶ Sorting and comparing files

▶ Stupid calendar tricks

▶ Squashing files to make them smaller

▶ Some other odds and ends

- - - - - - - - - - - - - - - - - - - - - - - - - - - - - - - - - - - - - - - - - - -

*W*ebster's defines an underdog as a victim of injustice or persecution; we certainly have been persecuting UNIX in this book. But UNIX actually has some fairly handy programs lying around. In this chapter, we look briefly at some of them. All these programs have a severe case of what is known as Feature Disease (closely related to the greasy fingerprints mentioned in Chapter 2): They all are bristling with features and options. Most of the features and options aren't worth mentioning, so we won't.

## Comparing Apples and Oranges

When you have used your UNIX machine for a while, you have piles of files (say that six times quickly) lying around. Often, many of the files are duplicates, or near duplicates, of each other. Two programs can help sort out this mess: cmp and diff.

The simplest comparison program is cmp; it just tells you whether two files are the same or different. To use cmp to compare two files, type the following line:

```
cmp onefile anotherfile
```

You replace onefile and anotherfile with the names of the files you want to compare, of course. If the contents of the two files are the same, cmp doesn't say anything (in the finest UNIX tradition). If they're different, cmp tells how far into the files it got before it found something different. You can compare any two files, regardless of whether they contain text, programs, databases, or whatever, because cmp cares only whether they're identical.

A considerably more sophisticated comparison program is diff; this program attempts to tell you not only whether two files are different but also how different they are. The files must be plain text, not word processor documents or anything else, or else diff gets horribly confused. Here's an example that uses two versions of a story one of us wrote. We compared files tse1 and tse2 by typing the following command:

```
diff tse1 tse2
```

Enter the name of the older file first and then the name of the new, improved file. The diff program responds with the following:

```
45c45
< steered back around, but the sheep screamed in panic and reared back.
---
> steered back around, but the goats screamed in panic and reared back.
46a47
> handlebars and landed safely in the snow.
```

The changes between tse1 and tse2 are that, in line 45, the sheep changed to goats, and a new line 47 was added after line 46.

In its first line of output, 45c45, diff reports that there are changes (that's what the c stands for) in lines 45 through 45 (that is, just line 45). Then it displays the line in the first file, starting with a <, and the line in the second file, starting with a >. We think of this as diff's way of saying that you took out the lines starting with < and inserted the lines starting with >. Then diff reports that a new line appears between lines 46 and 47 of the original file, and it shows the line that was added. This is a great way to see what changes have been made when you get a new revision of a document you have written.

BSD versions of diff can compare two directories to tell you which files are present in one and not in the other and to show you the differences between files with corresponding names in the two directories. Run diff and give it the names of the two directories.

# Assorted Files

Computers are really good at putting stuff in order. Indeed, there was a time when a third of all computer time was spent sorting. UNIX has a quite-capable sorting program, cleverly called `sort`, that you may remember meeting briefly in Chapter 6. Here, we talk about some other ways to use it.

The `sort` program sorts the lines in a file in alphabetical order. From `sort`'s point of view, a line is anything that ends with a new-line character (that is, you pressed Enter). If a file contains a list, with one item per line, `sort` alphabetizes the list.

The easiest way to use `sort` is to sort one file into another. That is, you take the original file and tell `sort` to place the sorted version in another file. This way, you don't risk screwing up the original file if the sort runs amok. To sort the original `myfile` into a second file called `sortedfile`, type the following:

```
sort myfile > sortedfile
```

Although you can sort a file back into itself, you can't do it in the obvious way. The following line, for example, doesn't work:

```
sort myfile > myfile
```

The problem with this command is that UNIX clears out `myfile` before the sort starts (with the result that, when `sort` tries to sort something, it finds that `myfile` is empty). You can use the `-o` (for output) option to tell `sort` where to put the results, like this:

```
sort myfile -o myfile
```

This command works because `sort` doesn't start to write to the output file until it has read all its input.

Normally, `sort` orders its results based on a strict comparison by the internal ASCII code the computer uses. The good news is that this command sorts letters and digits in the correct way, although there are some peculiarities: Normally, uppercase letters sort before lowercase letters, so *ZEBRA* precedes *aardvark*. You can use the `-f` (for *f*old cases together) option to sort regardless of uppercase and lowercase letters:

```
sort -f animals -o sortedanimals
```

Although we could have used the > redirection symbol here, with sort it's safer to use -o. You can use several other options also to tell it to sort:

- -b Ignore spaces at the beginning of the line.

- -d Use dictionary order and ignore any punctuation. You usually use this option with -f.

- -n Sort based on the number at the beginning of the line. With this option, 99 precedes 100 rather than follows it, as it does in usual alphabetical order. (Yes, the normal thing the computer does is pretty dumb. Are you surprised?)

- -r Sort in the reverse order of whatever would have been done otherwise. You can combine this option with any of the others.

We find sorting to be particularly useful in files in which every line starts with a date. For example:

```
0201      Margy's birthday
1204      Meg's birthday
0510      John's birthday
```

We can type sort -n to sort this file by date. Notice that we wrote February 1 as 0201 and May 10 as 0510 so that a numeric sort would work.

You can do much more complex sorting and treat every line as a sequence of "fields" that sort uses to decide the final sorted order. If you really need to do this, talk to someone who knows something about sorting.

# *Time Is Money — Steal Some Today!*

All UNIX systems have internal clocks. You can ask it what the date and time are with the date command:

```
date
```

UNIX responds with the following information:

```
Mon Jan 4 15:43:50 EST 1993
```

Many options let you tailor the date format any way you want. Don't waste your time. UNIX has an idea about the time zone too, and even does daylight savings time automatically.

You can schedule things to be done later with the at command. You say something like this:

```
at 5:15pm Jul 4
sort  -r myhugefile  -o myhugefile.sort
pr  -f  -2 myhugefile.sort | lp
```

And then you press Ctrl-D to indicate that you're finished giving commands.

You give the at command and specify a time and date. Then you enter the commands you want to run at that date and time; press Ctrl-D on a separate line to
tell UNIX that you're finished listing tasks. In this example, we sort a huge file
and then print it in two columns, all on the Fourth of July when presumably no
one will be around to complain that it's taking too long. If you omit the date,
UNIX assumes that you mean today if the time you give is later than the current
time; otherwise, UNIX assumes that you mean tomorrow.

Any output that normally would go to the terminal is sent back to you by electronic mail, so you should at least skim Chapter 18 to find out how to read your
mail.

# Calendar Games

Another handy program is calendar, which keeps a "tickler" file of important
dates. You keep a file, also called calendar, in which every line has a date and
an event. The date format is quite flexible:

```
Feb 1    Margy's birthday
1/15,March 15,6/15,Dec 15    Pay estimated taxes
```

When you run calendar, it looks in the current directory for a file called
calendar and prints any lines that have today or tomorrow's dates (today or
Monday's dates if a weekend intervenes). If you have a calendar file in your
home directory, the system automatically runs the calendar program every
day at midnight; if any lines are printed, UNIX sends them to you through electronic mail.

If you want to see a calendar for the current month, type this line:

```
cal
```

UNIX responds by displaying the following:

```
    January 1994
 S   M Tu  W Th  F  S
                    1
 2   3  4  5  6  7  8
 9  10 11 12 13 14 15
16  17 18 19 20 21 22
23  24 25 26 27 28 29
30  31
```

UNIX can do calendars for any month and year, back to the year 1. You can type `cal 1993` to display all 12 months of 1993 or `cal 7 1776` to display July 1776. (The fourth was a Thursday.) If you type `cal 93`, you get a calendar for the year 93 A.D., which is probably not what you want. In a typical bit of UNIX over-implementation, because `cal` knows that the calendar in use in the United States changed from the Julian to the Gregorian calendar in September 1752, `cal 9 1752` produces a most peculiar calendar missing the 11 days by which the calendar was adjusted at that point. We suggest that you not point that out to your friends unless they have pocket calculators hanging from their belts.

A final time-related command is `sleep`. You use it to delay something for a while. If you're going out to lunch, for example, and want to print `bigfile` ten minutes later, type the following command:

```
sleep 600 ; lp bigfile
```

The 600 is 600 seconds, or 10 minutes (the `sleep` command insists on taking the sleep time in seconds). The semicolon separates two commands on the same line; it works for any shell command. You can't use UNIX while it is sleeping (for GUI users, you can't use the window that is sleeping). For delays of more than an hour or so, or if you want to do something with your computer in the meantime, it's easier to use the `at` command. If you change your mind and decide that you didn't want to wait after all, you can interrupt `sleep` with the usual interrupt character, usually Del or Ctrl-C.

# Squashing Your Files

One problem that is common to all UNIX systems — indeed, to nearly all computer systems of any kind — is that there is never enough disk space. UNIX comes with a couple of programs that can alleviate this problem: `compress` and `pack`. They change the data in a file into a more compact form. Although you can't do anything with the file in this compact form except expand it back to the original format, for files you don't need to refer to very often, it can be a big space saver.

You use `compress` and `pack` in pretty much the same way. To compress a file called `sleuth1.doc`, for example, type the following line:

```
compress -v sleuth1.doc
```

The optional `-v` (for *verbose*) option merely tells UNIX to report how much space it saved. If you use it, UNIX responds with the following information:

```
sleuth1.doc: Compression: 49.79%—replaced with sleuth1.doc.Z
```

The `compress` program replaces the file with one that has the same name with `.Z` added to it. The degree of compression depends on what's in the file, but 50 percent compression for text files is typical. On a few files, the compression scheme doesn't save any space, in which case `compress` is polite enough not to make a `.Z` file.

To get the compressed file back to its original state, use `uncompress`:

```
uncompress sleuth1.doc.Z
```

This command gets rid of `sleuth1.doc.Z` and gets back `sleuth1.doc`. You can also use `zcat`, a compressed-file version of the `cat` program, which sends an uncompressed version of a compressed file to the terminal, without changing the compressed file or storing the uncompressed version in a file. It is rarely useful by itself but can be quite handy with programs such as `more` or `lp`:

```
zcat sleuth1.doc.Z | more
```

This command lets you see one page at a time what's in the file. Unlike `uncompress`, `zcat` does not get rid of the `.Z` file.

A similar but older program that uses a different compacting scheme is `pack`. To use it, type the following line:

```
pack sleuth1.doc
```

UNIX responds with the following information:

```
/usr/bin/pack: sleuth1.doc: 37.1% Compression
```

You get packed files back with `unpack`; you can look at packed files with `pcat`. Packed files end in `.z` (that's a lowercase *z*, to confuse the innocent). Like `compress`, `pack` leaves the file untouched if packing doesn't save any space. In most cases, `pack` doesn't save as much space as `compress` does, although it occasionally does better. Sometimes it's worth it to try both.

# How does file compression work, anyway?

This discussion is pretty technical. Don't say we didn't warn you.

Normally, every character in a file is stored by using 8 bits (binary digits, 1s and 0s, the smallest unit of data a computer can handle). Suppose that a file contains 800 As followed by 100 Bs and 100 Cs. That's 1,000 characters, at 8 bits apiece, or 8,000 bits. For this particular file, the pack program can use much shorter codes. It can use a 1-bit code for *A* and 2-bit codes for *B* and *C*. That makes the total size 800 bits for the As, and 200 bits apiece for the Bs and the Cs — a total of 1,200 bits rather than 8,000. The packed file is a little larger than that (1,408 bits) because pack has to put at the front of the packed file a table that indicates which codes correspond to which letters.

The issue of *optimal codes* (codes that use the least number of bits for a particular file) was a hot topic in the late 1940s, challenging the deepest thinkers in the field. In 1952, a student named David Huffman published a paper that any high-school student could understand showing how to use simple arithmetic techniques to construct optimal codes. Oops. Ever since then, this kind of code has been known as *Huffman coding*.

The compress program uses a dictionary-compression scheme, which is kind of backward from the way pack works. Rather than try to find the shortest code for every letter, compress runs through the file trying to find frequently occurring groups of letters it can encode as a single dictionary entry, or *token*. By using the same file that pack just worked through, compress reads letter by letter and notes that it has seen *AA* more than once; then it notices that it has seen *AAA*

more than once, and so forth. It enters longer and longer runs of As into its dictionary until it has runs of more than 300 As, each represented by a single dictionary entry and a single token in the compressed file. When it encounters the Bs and then the Cs, it does the same thing, and enters long runs of Bs and Cs in the dictionary also.

Using a clever technique (at least, it's clever to data-compression wonks), compress doesn't have to store the dictionary in the compressed file because uncompress can deduce the contents of the dictionary that compress was building from the sequence of tokens in the compressed file. As a result, compress does a fantastic job on this file, and squashes it to a mere 640 bits from the original 8,000.

Compression techniques are still a hot topic in the computer biz, and many techniques have been patented. The particular technique compress uses is known as LZW, after *L*empel, *Z*iv, and *W*elch, the three guys who thought of it. Welch, who works for Unisys and made some improvements to an earlier scheme designed by Lempel and Ziv, has a patent on it. It's such a cool technique, in fact, that two other guys named Miller and Wegman, who work for IBM, invented it at about the same time and they also have a patent on it. Because the patent office is not supposed to grant two patents on the same invention, some people use this situation to suggest that issuing patents on software isn't a very good idea. Fortunately, because neither Unisys nor IBM has ever objected to the compress program and because both companies ship it with their respective versions of UNIX, you can go ahead and use it.

# What's in That File?

Sometimes you have a bunch of files and no recollection of what they contain. The file command can give you a hint. It looks at the files you name on the command line and makes its best guess about what's in the files.

To have file try to figure out what's in the files in the working directory, type the following line:

```
file *
```

UNIX responds with the following bunch of seemingly incomprehensible information:

```
sleuth1.doc: data
sleuth1.ms: [nt]roff, tbl, or eqn input text
tse1: ascii text
tse2.Z: compressed file - with 16 bits
```

This mess says that file figured out that the sleuth1.ms file is a text file coded for input to the troff text formatter (those other programs are some of troff's helpers), that tse1 contains text, and that tse2.Z is compressed. (The "16 bits" stuff tells basically which version of compress was used; it doesn't really matter because current versions of compress can read any compressed file.) The file program guesses "data" whenever it has no idea what's in a file. The first file, sleuth1.doc, was a Microsoft Word document, something file doesn't know about, so it guesses that it's data.

# A Desk Calculator

UNIX comes with a severely overimplemented desk calculator program called bc. You run it and then type arithmetic expressions to which UNIX gives answers. To run it, type this line:

```
bc
```

It doesn't say anything, so it's ready for you to type a formula. If you type the following line:

```
2*3
```

It responds with the following:

```
6
```

You can use parentheses to tell bc the order in which to perform the calculations:

```
(2+9)*3
```

It says:

```
33
```

You can ask bc to do things with really big numbers, like this:

```
238735743473874874854854754874547*929726435540695684947958695859656
```

It responds this way:

```
2219589318161235893764880347174617659766790965431481781919832
```

Answers can get so long that they don't fit on one line. If you type the following line:

```
2^900
```

you get this response:

```
845271249817064394163743655866426570430155721657794435404737134442678\
244090759775159067609420251500631479031989211405886211756095204296859\6
008623655407033230534186943984081346699704282822823056848387726531379\0
144663684526840249878214143503802725836238326172943638079733376
```

That last example is 2 to the 900th power (2 multiplied by itself 900 times). The bc program doesn't believe in rounding off. By golly, if the answer to some calculation is a 14,000-digit number, it computes all 14,000 digits exactly, even if it takes a while. The people in your accounting department who are always after you to explain the missing 14 cents on your expense report will like this feature of bc.

To leave bc, type quit or press Ctrl-D.

# A Really Dumb Program

Lest we leave you with the impression that UNIX is full of useful programs, we end this chapter with banner. If you type this line, for example:

```
banner "Eat at" "Joe's"
```

UNIX responds with the following:

```
#######
#          ##      #####                    ##      #####
#         #  #       #                     #  #        #
#####    #    #      #                     #    #      #
#        ######      #                     ######      #
#        #    #      #                     #    #      #
#######  #    #      #                     #    #      #
         #                     ####
         #    ####   ######  ####    ####
         #   #    #  #       #  #   #
         #   #    #  #####    #      #####
  #      #   #    #  #                    #
  #      #   #    #  #              #    #
  #####   ####   ######            ####
```

All banner does is print words in large, ugly letters. If you want it to print two words separated by a space, put them in quotation marks, like we did. Perhaps this program was useful at one point for printing separator pages on the printer. Then again, perhaps not.

# Chapter 14

# I'm Not a System Administrator — I Can't Install Software!

· · · · · · · · · · · · · · · · · · · · · · · · · · · · · · · · · · · · · · · · ·

*In This Chapter*

▶ Where does software come from? (The software stork?)

▶ Where to put software

▶ Writing shell scripts, or files full of commands

▶ Writing aliases for your favorite commands

· · · · · · · · · · · · · · · · · · · · · · · · · · · · · · · · · · · · · · · · ·

*H*ey, calm down. No, we're not about to train you to be a system programmer. Every user has a few favorite programs, and you will wear out your welcome quickly if you go off to your local wizard every time you want to use a new program. In many cases, installing new programs is easy enough that you can do it yourself.

If you are a DOS or Macintosh user, you probably are thinking just the opposite: "Sure, I can install new programs. What's the big deal? I just stick in a floppy disk and type INSTALL, right?" No. In UNIX, it's not that simple, of course. There are issues of paths, permissions, and other technical-type stuff we have been protecting you from.

## *The Software Stork*

Interesting software comes from many places:

    ✔ Some other user on the same machine already has it for his or her own use and you want to use it too.

    ✔ Some other machine on the network has a program you want for yourself. See Chapters 19 and 20 for the gory details of copying it from other machines on the network.

✔ Someone sends you programs through electronic mail. (Yes, it's possible.)

✔ You create files that contain frequently used commands so that you don't have to type them repeatedly. In UNIX-speak, these files are called *shell scripts.* In essence, you make your own UNIX commands.

First, let's talk about where you should put your own software; then we can go into more detail about the mechanics of putting it there.

## *You've* bin *Had*

Every UNIX user should have a bin directory. It's just a directory called bin in your home directory. If it's not there, you can make it by going to your home directory and typing this line:

```
mkdir bin
```

The thing that's special about bin is that the shell looks for programs there. Most system administrators automatically set up a bin directory for users. If not, and you had to create it yourself, you may have to do some fiddling to tell the shell to look for programs there. See the sidebar entitled "Your search path" for the bad news.

TIP

### Why is it called bin?

Early on, bin was short for *bin*ary, because most programs that people put there were, in fact, compiled binary code. In the late 1970s, a famous professor of cognitive science at the University of California published a paper called "The Trouble with UNIX," in which he complained bitterly about how difficult it was to use UNIX. One of the items on his list was that bin was difficult to remember. One of the UNIX guys at Bell Labs published a witty rebuttal and pointed out that many of the allegedly "more natural" command names the professor suggested were merely the names the computer system at his university used. The UNIX guy reported that many Bell Labs users thought that a bin was the obvious place to stash their programs. So, it's still bin.

The famous professor has come around somewhat and is reputed to even use UNIX now and then, because he now works for Sun Microsystems, a large maker of UNIX workstations. But he probably shuts his door so that no one can see.

# *Stuffing the* bin

To put programs in your bin directory, you just copy them there by using the cp command. Alternatively, you can move them there by using the mv command, a text editor, or any other way to create or move a file.

### *A* bin *of shells*

You can also make your own commands (that is, shell scripts) and put them in your bin directory. Here's an example in which you make a one-line shell script:

```
cd bin
ed myscript
```

UNIX responds with the following line:

```
?myscript
```

Type the following line (remember that, because we're using ed, we're back to weird commands):

```
a
```

This line tells ed to start appending text to the end of the myscript file. Then type this line:

```
echo This is my script.
```

Then tell ed to write the file by pressing Esc to return to command mode. Type this line:

```
w
```

UNIX responds with the information that you have a file with 24 characters:

```
24
```

You quit ed by typing the following:

```
q
```

You see the shell prompt again. Now type these two command lines:

```
chmod +x myscript
myscript
```

UNIX responds by running the `myscript` program file. The program displays the following message on-screen:

```
This is my script.
```

### What did I just do?

Now let's go through that process again line by line: First, you go to the `bin` directory. Then you use the `ed` editor to create a one-line file called `myscript` that contains the text `echo This is my script`. (The `echo` command is used when you want to tell UNIX to print whatever follows on the line.) Feel free to use a better editor. The next line is magic: `chmod +x` marks the file as an executable program rather than as a mere file. Then you type the program name, `myscript`, and it runs. All this program does is print the text `This is my script`. The script-writing technique has more productive uses.

You're not quite finished, though. Observe what happens when you go to another directory. Type the following two commands to go to your home directory of `bin` and give the `myscript` command there:

```
cd
myscript
```

UNIX responds with this message:

```
myscript: Command not found.
```

Now type these commands to get UNIX to do what you want:

```
rehash
myscript
```

Finally, UNIX responds by running the program file:

```
This is my script.
```

What's going on? Well, it's Mr. too-smart-for-his-own-good Shell. Because programs don't appear and disappear very often, when the shell starts up, it makes a list of all the commands it can access and where they are. Because there are frequently five or six command directories, this process saves considerable time (the alternative is to check every directory for every command every time you type one). The `rehash` command tells UNIX to rebuild its list, known in geekspeak as a *hash table,* because you have added a new command (the `myscript` file is really a command, remember?). If the command still doesn't work, you will have to fiddle with your search path — not a pretty job. See the sidebar titled "Your search path."

## Your search path

You can ignore this section unless you have put a command in your `bin` directory and the shell can't find it. Still reading? Sorry to hear it. The shell has a list of directories that contain commands; this list is known as the *search path*. On any sensible UNIX system, your `bin` directory is already in your search path. If it's not, you have to put it there. There are two stages: putting it in once and putting it in permanently.

To see what your current search path is, type this line if you are using the C Shell:

```
echo $path
```

If you have the Bourne or Korn Shell, type this line:

```
echo $PATH
```

Yes, one's uppercase and one's lowercase. Arrgh. The C Shell responds with something like this:

```
/bin /usr/bin /usr/ucb/bin /usr/local/bin .
```

The Bourne or Korn Shell shows something like this:

```
/bin:/usr/bin:/usr/ucb/bin:/usr/local/bin:.
```

What you have to do is add your `bin` directory to the path.

If you use the C Shell, type this magical incantation:

```
set path=($path ~/bin)
```

That's a space and a tilde (~) in the middle. It tells the C Shell to set the path the same as the current path ($path), plus the `bin` subdirectory of your home directory (~).

If you use the Bourne or Korn Shell, type this even more magical incantation:

```
PATH=$PATH:$HOME/bin
```

```
export PATH
```

Notice that the second time you type PATH and HOME in the first command, you include a dollar sign ($) in front of them. It tells the Bourne or Korn Shell to set the path the same as the current path ($PATH), plus the `bin` subdirectory of your home directory ($HOME). Same song, different words.

Now you should be able to run the `myscript` script regardless of which directory you're using.

This new, improved path lasts only until you log out. To put your `bin` directory on the path every time you log in, you must add the incantation you used earlier to the end of the shell script that runs automatically whenever you log in. If you use the C Shell, add it to the `.login` file. If you use the Bourne or Korn Shell, add it to the `.profile` file.

Yes, these filenames begin with periods. File names that start with periods usually don't show up in file listings, which is why you haven't noticed these files in your home directory. Type the following line to list all your files, including these hidden ones:

```
ls -a
```

In principle, you only have to edit the file, go to the end, and add the necessary lines. In practice, it's easy to screw up, so — unless you're feeling particularly brave — you're probably better off asking for expert assistance.

## You, too, can be a scriptwriter!

The most common things to put in your `bin` directory are shell scripts. You already have created a little one called `myscript`, so let's look in more detail at exactly what you did.

To create a shell script, use any text editor (see Chapter 12). Enter the commands one per line. If you frequently search for files with names that begin with *budget,* for example, you probably are tired of typing this command over and over:

```
find . -name budget* -print
```

(Check out Chapter 26 to see how the `find` command works.) Instead, you can put this command in a shell script and perhaps call the script `findbud`. To do this, create a text file named `findbud` that contains just one line: the command.

## Don't give me any arguments!

Shell scripts can be complete programs. Every shell program has lots of swell programming features you don't want to know about. But one is so useful that we're going to tell you anyway: Your shell scripts can use information from the command line. That is, if you type `foogle dog pig`, your script called `foogle` can see that you ran it saying `dog` and `pig`. The things on the line after the name of the command are called *arguments.* The word *dog* is the first argument, and *pig* is the second one. In shell scripts, the first argument is called `$1`, the second `$2`, and so forth. In shorthand, `$*` means "all the arguments."

Suppose that you want to write a script called `2print` that prints files in a two-column format. (You do that by using the `pr` command, described in Chapter 9.) Create a file called `2print` that contains the following line:

`pr -f -2 $* | lp`

Then use the `chmod` and `rehash` commands to make `2print` an executable script. If you want to print several files, one right after the next, in two-column format, you can type this line:

`2print onefile anotherfile yetanotherfile`

In reality, you are saying this:

`pr -f -2 onefile anotherfile yetanotherfile | lp`

This line prints all three files, with each one in two-column format. (Note that you may need to use `lpr` rather than `lp` in this shell script. Refer to Chapter 9.)

### Making a screenplay from a text file

Now you must tell UNIX that the text file you have created is executable — that it's more than a mere text file. To do this, type the following line:

```
chmod +x findbud
```

This line marks the findbud file as *executable* (it's a script the shell can run).

### Take 1

To run the shell script, just type its name:

```
findbud
```

Voila! You have just created your own UNIX command!

Type rehash to tell the shell that you have added a new command and that you want it to rebuild its list of available commands to include this one. If you don't give the rehash command and you change directories, you can't use the newly created shell script during this login session.

We could write an entire book about shell scripts (others have). The finer points naturally vary depending on which shell you use, but this explanation gives you the general idea. Shell scripts aren't limited to one line: They can be as long as you want, which is handy when you have a long list of commands you want to run regularly.

# Borrowing Other People's Programs

Lots of times, someone else has a cool program you want to be able to use. There are several approaches to getting what you want, and both are pretty easy. Suppose that your friend Tracy's bin directory has a program called pornotopia. (No, we don't know what it does, either.) How can you run it?

## The long way

If you use the C Shell, you can run the program from Tracy's directory by typing this line:

```
~tracy/bin/pornotopia
```

If you use the Bourne or Korn Shell, you can type this line:

```
/usr/tracy/bin/pornotopia
```

If home directories aren't all in /usr, you will have to substitute the actual location of Tracy's directory.

## The easier way

It is a pain to type this long string of letters and symbols every time you want to run the program. A better way is to put in your bin directory a link to the cool program so that you can run it directly. (Links are described in Chapter 26.) You use the ln command to create a link, which makes the file appear to be in your own bin directory too.

Try the direct approach. Move to your home directory and create a link:

```
cd
ln ~tracy/bin/pornotopia bin/pornotopia
```

With any luck, this method will work, by creating a link from Tracy's file to your bin directory. After a quick rehash, you're all set.

The ln command doesn't work, however, if you and Tracy have files on different disks. (All this is explained in Chapter 26.) In this case, you may get this unhelpful message:

```
ln: different file system
```

If you get this message, it's time for Plan B. BSD and SVR4 systems have things called *symbolic links* that work across different disks (these are explained in Chapter 26, too). Try this line:

```
ln -s ~tracy/bin/pornotopia bin/pornotopia
```

If it works, it makes a symbolic link to the file you want. You're all set. The link to pornotopia refers to Tracy's version; after a rehash, you're ready to go.

## Using an alias

Well, if you were named pornotopia, you probably would want an alias too. Fortunately, the C and Korn Shells give you this ability to invent a short name for a long command. In the C Shell, type this line:

```
alias dobudget '/usr/tracy/bin/pornotopia'
```

This line tells the shell that, when you type `dobudget`, you really want to run Tracy's program. Heh, heh. To avoid inadvertent ease of use, the Korn Shell's `alias` command works in almost the same way, but it is punctuated slightly differently:

```
alias dobudget='/usr/tracy/bin/pornotopia'
```

(In both cases, the quotes are optional if the command doesn't contain any spaces or special characters, but it never hurts to use them.)

You can define aliases for any frequently used one-line command. The alias can contain spaces, pipes, and anything else you can type on a command line. In the C Shell, for example:

```
alias sortnprint 'sort -r bigfile | pr -2 | lp'
```

this line makes the new `sortnprint` command sort your `bigfile` in reverse alphabetical order, format it in two columns with `pr`, and send the result to the printer. Aliases also can be useful if you are subject (as we are) to chronic miswiring of the nerves in your fingers. We always type `mroe` when we mean `more`, so an alias fixes it:

```
alias mroe more
```

(That's the C Shell version; the Korn Shell would have an equal sign rather than a space between `mroe` and `more`.)

Aliases you type directly to the shell are lost when you log out. If you want them to be available permanently, you must put the `alias` commands in your `.login` or `.profile` file, in the same way we mentioned earlier, in the sidebar about changing your search path.

## The last resort

If you are using the Bourne Shell and cannot use aliases, try Plan D to use Tracy's program: a one-line shell script. Although we use the `ed` program because it's easier to show, you should use a real editor. Start by revving up `ed`:

```
ed bin/pornotopia
```

You get the following helpful response:

```
?bin/pornotopia
```

Now tell ed to add some text to the file:

```
a
```

You are now in append mode. Type the command line you want to include in the shell script:

```
/usr/tracy/bin/pornotopia
```

Press Esc to switch back to ed's command mode and type the following:

```
w
```

This line writes the new shell script file and prints the size of the new file, which should be 26. Then type the following to quit ed:

```
q
```

Type this command to make your new shell script runnable:

```
chmod +x pornotopia
```

Give this command to tell UNIX to redo its hash table:

```
rehash
```

Now your script named pornotopia will run Tracy's original program called pornotopia. At least one of these plans should work for any program lying around anywhere on your system.

We don't even discuss software copyrights, licenses, and ethics here, but, if you use a copyrighted program, you should pay for it unless you like to think of yourself as a thief.

# Stealing Software from the Network

If you are on a network, zillions of programs are on the network and are free for the taking. You can get copies of programs in the same way you get copies of anything else on the net. See Chapter 20 for the inside scoop.

# Sneaking Software Through the Mail

It is possible to disguise programs as mail messages so that you can mail them around. This method is often the only way to do samizdat software distribution when networks and system administrators are uncooperative. For short programs and shell scripts, the usual way to send stuff is as a *shar* message: a shell script that, when you run it, re-creates the files in question. (If you care, shar rhymes with cigar and is lazy-typist-ese for *shell ar*chive.) Shar files are also a convenient way to mail groups of text files as a unit.

Shar messages usually start with lines like this:

```
#!/bin/sh
# This is a shell archive (produced by shar 3.49)
# To extract the files from this archive, save it to a file, remove
# everything above the "!/bin/sh" line above, and type "sh file_name".
#
# made 01/05/1993 19:41 UTC by johnl@iecc
# Source directory /usr/johnl/bin
```

Recovering the files is a three-step process:

1. Save the message in a separate file, called something like `incoming-shar`. See Chapter 18 for instructions about how to do this.

2. Use any text editor to delete all the lines from the beginning of the file to the first line that starts with a #. If you delete a few of the # lines, don't worry: The shell ignores them anyway.

3. Feed the edited file to the shell by typing this line:

```
sh incoming-shar
```

This command runs the script in the file and creates the program files or whatever else is in the shar file. (Near the front of most shar messages is a manifest that lists the files contained in the file.) When you see the UNIX prompt, it is done. Delete the `incoming-shar` file and move the files it created to the appropriate place, probably to your `bin` directory.

Shar files don't work well for binary programs, so a widely adopted scheme called `uuencode` disguises them as text. If you receive a file coded in `uuencode`, the message looks something like this:

```
begin 775 pornotopia
M3'$$'!C?&RRRRRR4@"0',"!P"P$+'O"S"P"9"#:"0"""$"-"""<
M#4"+G1E>"0"""<T"""T",PP"P"0""""'-I1""""((""""YD
```

Recovering the binary file from the uuencode file is a two-step process:

1. Save the message in a file with a name something like uu-incoming.

2. Feed the file to the uudecode program by typing the following line:

```
uudecode < uu-incoming
```

You don't have to edit the encoded file to delete the first lines in the file because uudecode ignores them for you. When you see the UNIX prompt, it is finished. Then get rid of the uu-incoming file and move to the appropriate place the binary file that is created.

# *Real Software Installation*

In case you are wondering, there are official software-installation procedures for purchased software. To install these pieces of software, you must log in as *root* (the superuser — the one who can clobber anyone's files anywhere) and run a program called install. The install program directs you to load tapes, CD-ROMs, or floppies, as appropriate, reads in the programs, and then asks a bunch of configuration questions, like "Does this system support DES-protected NFS mounts across router boundaries?" We suggest that you leave this procedure to trained professionals.

# Chapter 15

# How to Run a Bunch of Programs at a Time

*I*f you have a plain, old terminal with no windowing system, you may be envious of users with fancy window systems who can pop up a bunch of windows and run umpteen programs at a time.

Well, don't. Any UNIX system lets you run as many programs simultaneously as you want; nearly all the systems let you stop and restart programs and switch around among different programs whenever you want.

If you're used to an old-fashioned, one-program-at-a-time system, such as DOS (without Windows) or the Mac (at least the pre-System 7 Mac), you might not see the point of doing several things at a time. Suppose, however, that you're doing something that takes a while and that the computer can manage with little or no supervision from you, like copying a large file over a network, which can take 10 or 15 minutes. There's no reason for you to sit and wait for that process to finish — you can do something useful while the copy runs in the background.

Or, suppose that you're in the middle of a program and you want to do something else: You're writing a memo in a text editor and need to check some e-mail you received to make sure that you spelled someone's name right. One way to do that is to save the file, leave the editor, run the mail program, leave the mail program, start the editor again, return to the same place in the file, and pick up where you left off. What a pain. UNIX lets you stop the editor, run the mail program, and resume the editor exactly where you left it. For that matter, you can run *both* the editor and the mail program and flip between them as necessary.

In the interest of fairness, we must point out that *job control*, the feature that lets you flip back and forth, was written by Bill, the same guy who wrote the C shell, vi, and NFS. In contrast to our opinion of some of his other efforts, we think that job control is pretty cool.

# Starting Background Processes _____

Starting a background command is simplicity itself. You can run any program you want in the background: When you type the command, stick a space and an ampersand (&) at the end of the line just before you press Enter.

Suppose that you want to use troff to print a file (even though we warned you not to use it). This process is bound to take a long time, for example, so typing the ampersand to run it in the background is wise:

```
troff a_really_large_file &
```

The shell starts the command and immediately comes back to ask you for another command. It prints a number, which is the *process ID* (or PID, as described in Chapter 23) assigned to the command you just started. (Some shells print a small number, which they call the *job number*, and a larger number, which is the PID.) If you know the PID, you can check up on your background program with the ps command. If you get tired of waiting for the background process, you can get rid of it with the kill command and the PID, as you will see in Chapter 23.

You can start as many programs simultaneously as you want in this way. In practice, you rarely want more than three or four because only one computer is switching back and forth among the various programs; the more simultaneous things you do, the slower each one runs. (It also slows down all the other users on the machine, which doesn't make you real popular.)

When your background program finishes, the C Shell, Korn Shell, and SVR4 Bourne Shell tell you that it's finished; older versions of the Bourne Shell say nothing.

If you know that a program is going to take a long time (a program that crunches for a long time to produce a report, for example), you can use the nice command with that program. The nice command tells the program to run in a nice way so that it gets a smaller share of the computer than it would otherwise. The niced program takes longer to run, but other programs run faster, which is usually a good trade-off if the niced program was going to take a long time anyway. To use it, you just type nice followed by the command to run:

```
nice genreport Tuesday.raw &
```

You almost always use nice to run programs in the background because it would take an inexplicably saintly user to want to slow down a program he was going to sit and wait for.

If you want to wait for background programs to finish, the wait command waits for you until they're all finished. If you get impatient, you can interrupt wait with Ctrl-C (or Del, depending on your system); these keystrokes interrupt only the wait and leave the background processes unmolested.

# The Magic of Job Control

Quite a while ago (in about 1979), people (actually, our pal Bill) noticed that, many times, you run a program, realize that it's going to take longer than you thought, and decide that you want to switch it to a background program. At the time, the only choices you had were to wait or to kill the program and start it over by using an & to run it in the background. Job control lets you change your mind after you start a program. To do so, press Ctrl-Z.

The job-control business requires some cooperation from your shell. In SVR4, all three shells handle job control. In some earlier versions of UNIX, only the C Shell, or sometimes the C Shell and Korn Shell, handled job control.

Suppose that you start a big, slow program by typing the following line:

```
bigslowprogram somefile anotherfile
```

The program runs in the foreground because you didn't use an ampersand (&). Then you realize that you have better things to do than wait, so you press Ctrl-Z. The shell should respond with the message Stopped. (If it doesn't, you don't have a job-control shell. Sorry. Skip the rest of this chapter.) At this point, your program is in limbo. You can do three things to it:

- ✔ You can continue it in the foreground as though nothing had happened, by typing fg (which stands for *foreground*).

- ✔ You can stick it in the background by typing bg (for *background*), which makes the program act as though you started it with an & in the first place.

- ✔ You can kill it if you decide that you shouldn't have run it at all. This method is slightly more complicated; details follow.

# Take this job and...

UNIX calls every background program you start a *job*. A job can consist of several processes (which, as you will see in Chapter 23, are running programs). To print a list with titles of all your files in all your directories, for example, you can type this line:

```
ls -lR | pr -h "My files" | lp &
```

This command lists the files with ls, adds titles with pr, and sends the mess to the printer with lp, all in the background. Although you use three different programs and three separate processes, UNIX considers it one job because each of the three programs needs the other two in order to get work done.

Every regular command (those you issue without an &) is also a job although, until you use Ctrl-Z to stop it, that's not a very interesting piece of information. You can use the jobs command to see which jobs are active. Here's a typical response to the jobs command:

```
[1] - Stopped (signal) elm
[2] + Stopped vi somefile
```

This listing shows two jobs, both of which have been stopped with Ctrl-Z. One is a copy of elm, a mail-reading program; the other job is the vi editor. (The difference between Stopped (signal) and plain Stopped is interesting only to programmers, so we don't discuss it.) One job is considered the *current job* — the one preceded by a plus sign (+); it's the one most recently started or stopped. All the rest are regular background jobs, and they can be stopped or running.

### ...Stick it in the background

You can tell any stopped job to continue in the background with the bg command. A plain bg continues the current job (the one marked by a plus sign) in the background. To tell UNIX to continue some other job, you must identify the job. You identify a job by typing a percent sign (%) followed either by the job number reported by jobs or by enough of the command to uniquely identify it. In this case, the elm job can be called %1, %elm, or %e because no other job used a command starting with an e. %% refers to the current job. Some other % combinations are available, but no one uses them. Typing bg %e, for example, continues the elm job in the background.

### ...Run it in the foreground

To put a process in the foreground, where it runs normally and can use the terminal, you use the fg command. Continuing a job in the foreground is such a common thing that you can use a shortcut: You just type the percent sign and the job identifier. Typing %1 or %e, for example, continues the elm job in the foreground; typing %v or %% continues the vi editor in the foreground.

### *...Shove it*

To get rid of a stopped or background job, use the `kill` command with the job identifier or (if it's easier, for some reason) the PID. You can get rid of the `vi` editor job by typing this line:

```
kill %v
```

Typically, you start a job, realize that it will take longer than you want to wait, press Ctrl-Z to stop it, and then type `bg` to continue that process in the background.

Alternatively, you interrupt a program by pressing Ctrl-Z, run a second program, and, when the second program is finished, type `fg` or `%%` to continue the original program.

You don't often bring in the gangster `kill` to turn out the lights on a program, but it's nice to know that you have friends in the underworld who can put a nasty program to sleep for good. Chapter 23 talks more about it.

## *What happens when two programs try to use the terminal?*

Suppose that a program running in the background tries to read some input from your terminal. Severe confusion can result (and did, in pre-job-control versions of UNIX) if both the background program and a foreground program — or even worse, two or three background programs — try to read at the same time. Which one gets the stuff you type? Early versions of UNIX did the worst possible thing: A gremlin inside the computer flipped a coin to decide who got each line of input. That was, to put it mildly, not very satisfactory.

With the advent of job control, UNIX enforced a new rule: Background jobs can't read from the terminal. If one tries, it stops much as though you had pressed Ctrl-Z. Suppose that you try to run the `ed` editor in the background:

```
ed some.file &
```

UNIX responds:

```
[1] + Stopped (tty input) ed
```

As soon as `ed` got started and wanted to see whether you were typing anything it should know about, the job stopped. You can continue `ed` as a foreground program by typing `fg` or `%%` if you want to type something for `ed`. Or you can kill it (which is all that `ed` deserves) by typing `kill %%`.

## Full-screen programs and job control

Programs that take over the entire screen, notably the vi and emacs editors and mail programs such as elm, treat the Ctrl-Z interrupt in a slightly different way. Just stopping the program and starting it again later isn't adequate; the screen would still show the results of what you did in the meantime. To solve this problem, full-screen programs make arrangements with UNIX to be notified when you press Ctrl-Z, and again when you continue them so that they can do something appropriate, like redraw the screen, when you continue. This process generally is all automatic and obvious, although people occasionally are confused when the screen is magically returned after they give the fg command.

### Taming background terminal output

Any program, foreground or background, usually can scribble on-screen anything it wants at any time it wants. More often than not, that's OK because most programs are well behaved about not blathering when they're in the background.

In some cases, however, particularly when you use a full-screen editor, the interspersed output gets on your nerves. Fortunately, job control lets you solve this problem. You can put your *terminal in terminal output stop* mode: When a background program wants to send something to the terminal, it stops, just as it does when it wants to read something; the next time you're talking to the shell (when your foreground program finishes or you type Ctrl-Z), you hear about the stopped job:

```
[1] + Stopped (tty output) ed
```

You then have the same alternatives to continue that program in the foreground if you want to see what it has to say or kill it if you don't. To turn on output stop mode, type this command:

```
stty tostop
```

To turn off output stop mode, type this line:

```
stty -tostop
```

The stty command is used to make all sorts of changes to the setup of your terminal. See Chapter 28 if you want to know what else it can do.

## Do windows and job control mix?

If you use a GUI system such as Motif or OPEN LOOK, you can run lots of programs in lots of windows; is there any need for this Ctrl-Z nonsense? By and large, the answer is no; it's much easier to pop up three windows to run three programs than it is to flip the programs around in one window. (Chapter 11 shows you how to pop up new windows.)

Even if you use a GUI, it doesn't hurt to learn about job control, though. It's not hard to use, and someday you may be stuck in a single window (when you use `telnet` to access another system) or be banished to a regular non-X terminal; then you will appreciate what job control has to offer.

# Chapter 16
# The DOS-to-UNIX Rosetta Stone

. . . . . . . . . . . . . . . . . . . . . . . . . . . . . . . . . . . . . . . .

## In This Chapter

▶ UNIX commands that do the same things as the DOS commands you wish you could use

▶ UNIX command options that make UNIX commands act more like DOS commands

. . . . . . . . . . . . . . . . . . . . . . . . . . . . . . . . . . . . . . . .

For those of you who know DOS, this chapter provides a translation of your favorite DOS commands into UNIX. For those of you who have stayed far away from DOS, skip this chapter.

DOS was based largely on UNIX, so some commands act the same in both systems, like `mkdir` to make a directory. Other commands are basically the same but have subtle differences that can trip you up. `cd` (or CD), for example, changes directories in both DOS and UNIX, but, if you don't specify the directory to change to, DOS and UNIX do two different things. Other commands are similar but have different names, like UNIX's `ls` and DOS's DIR. Some DOS commands have absolutely no counterparts in UNIX (thank heavens), like the notorious RECOVER command, found in earlier versions of DOS.

For each commonly used DOS command, we explain how to get UNIX to do the same thing, more or less. Unless we indicate otherwise, we're talking about DOS 5. To make clear which commands are DOS and which are UNIX, we capitalize the DOS commands and keep the UNIX commands in the `special font` you have become used to. (DOS doesn't care whether you type commands in capital or small letters. As you know, UNIX does care, and most of its commands are spelled with small letters.)

# The Most Important Differences

Slashes! You know how you finally learned to type backslashes (\) in all your DOS filenames? It's time to flip them all around because UNIX uses regular slashes (/) instead. This takes months of getting used to, but there's no way around it.

On the other hand, it surely is nice that filenames can be longer in UNIX than they can in DOS. You're not limited to eight little characters with a three-letter extension. Go nuts with your filenames; name your next file this way:

```
terrific.file.name.possible.only.in.UNIX
```

While we are talking about filenames, remember that, even though DOS doesn't care about capitalization, UNIX does. In UNIX, capital and small letters are considered to be different letters, so don't mix them up.

# APPEND, JOIN, and SUBST

These DOS commands do weird things to make files seem to be in places where they are not. APPEND makes files in other directories seem to be in the current directory. SUBST does the opposite of APPEND: It makes a directory seem to be a separate disk drive. JOIN does a combination of the two.

UNIX has no equivalents to JOIN and SUBST because UNIX users usually don't want to deal with disk drive letters (like A:, in the DOS world). These are weird, sick commands anyway.

If you miss the DOS APPEND command, use the UNIX ln command to create links so that files can appear in more than one directory at a time. (See Chapter 26 for an explanation of how to use ln).

# ASSIGN

The DOS ASSIGN command lets you change the names (A: and B:, for example) of DOS disk drives. There's no such thing in UNIX because disk drives don't have letter names. DOS 6 took the hint and doesn't have ASSIGN either.

# ATTRIB

The DOS ATTRIB command lets you change the *attributes* of files, such as whether they are hidden or read-only or need to be backed up (archived).

## ATTRIB +H

The DOS ATTRIB +H command makes a file *hidden* so that it doesn't show up on directory listings. To do this in UNIX, rename the file with a filename that begins with a period. A file named `.secret`, for example, does not appear on ls listings. To ask for a listing of all files, including hidden files, you can type this line:

```
ls -a
```

## ATTRIB -H

The DOS ATTRIB -H command "unhides" files; the thing you do in UNIX is rename files so that they don't begin with periods. Watch out, though: Some hidden files must stay hidden in order to work. The `.login` and `.profile` files, for example (your shell executes one of these every time you log in) don't work if you rename them to anything else.

## ATTRIB +A and ATTRIB -A

In DOS, the ATTRIB +A and ATTRIB -A commands flip the archive bit, the bit that indicates whether the file has been backed up. UNIX files record the last time they were changed; UNIX backups store all the files changed since the last backup time.

## ATTRIB +R and ATTRIB -R

The DOS ATTRIB +R and ATTRIB -R commands control whether a file is *read-only*. In UNIX, every file is owned by someone; the owner can control who can read it (r), change it (w), and, for a program, run it (x). Chapter 28 discusses this stuff in more detail.

To set permissions for a file you own so that no one (not even you) can change it (equivalent to DOS's read-only attribute), type this line:

```
chmod ugo-w filename
```

To set permissions so that only you can change the file, type these two commands:

```
chmod go-w filename
chmod u+w filename
```

We talk more about the inscrutable `chmod` command in Chapter 28.

# BACKUP, RESTORE, and MSBACKUP

In DOS, the BACKUP and RESTORE commands (now MSBACKUP in DOS 6) store stuff on floppy disks in a specialized backup format. In most cases, your UNIX system administrator handles backups. If this is not true in your case, programs called `tar` (for *tape archive*), `cpio` (for *copy in or out*), and `pax` (for *portable archive exchange*) save and restore UNIX files to and from tapes and floppies. If you need to do your own backups, get a local expert to write a little script that does the backup; the details of controlling disks and floppies vary wildly among versions of UNIX. Chapter 22 talks about making and using backups.

# CHDIR, or CD

The DOS CHDIR or CD command changes directories — that is, it makes another directory the working directory. It works in pretty much the same way as the UNIX `cd` command, except when you type the command by itself, like this:

```
cd
```

If you don't tell the DOS CD command where you want to move, it doesn't move anywhere. Instead, it tells you where you are now. The UNIX equivalent is the `pwd` command, which tells you where in your directory structure you are.

The UNIX `cd` command moves you back to your home directory if you don't type a directory name (see Chapter 5).

# CHKDSK

The DOS CHKDSK command checks the current disk for logical problems. Then it tells you how much space on the disk is used and how much is free.

On UNIX, unless you are the system administrator, you should try not to think about the possibility of your disk having logical problems. To find out how much space is free on your disk, type the following:

```
df
```

This command shows the free space on all disks (see Chapter 19), so you have to figure out which disk is yours by looking for the one that matches the beginning of your home directory name (the one that pwd displays).

You can also type the following line to find out how much space your files are using:

```
du
```

The du command (for *disk us*age) reports the amount of space used by the files in each directory and subdirectory. (If a directory has subdirectories, the space used in the subdirectories is included in the amount for the directory.)

# CLS

Ahh, a real complicated one. The DOS CLS command clears the screen. In UNIX, type the following to do the same thing:

```
clear
```

# COMP and FC

The DOS COMP and FC commands compare two files and tell you about their differences. The UNIX command cmp is like COMP: It indicates whether two files are identical. The diff command does a much better job than FC does of showing the differences between files (see Chapter 13). Type this line to compare two files in UNIX:

```
diff afilename anotherfilename
```

DOS 6 gets rid of COMP, and uses FC for both, but UNIX still has two commands: diff for text files and cmp for everything else.

# COPY and XCOPY

The DOS COPY and XCOPY commands copy files (no kidding). The UNIX cp command works in almost the same way (see Chapter 4). In DOS, you can omit the directory you are copying to if you want to copy to the current directory. In UNIX, you can't do this. Instead, you have to type a period (.) to indicate that you want to copy to the working directory.

In DOS you type the following line, for example, to copy the LETTER.WP file from the \DOCS directory to the current directory:

```
COPY \DOCS\LETTER.WP
```

In UNIX, you type this line to do the same thing:

```
cp /docs/letter.wp .
```

The period at the end of the line tells UNIX to copy the file to the working directory.

# COPY A + B C

You can use the DOS COPY command to combine two text files. To stick one file at the end of the other in DOS, for example, you type this line:

```
COPY FILE1 + FILE2 COMBO
```

This command creates a new file called COMBO that contains the contents of FILE1 followed by the contents of FILE2. You don't use the UNIX cp command to do this; you use cat to display the files and redirect the output to a new file, like this:

```
cat file1 file2 > combo
```

# COPY FILENAME+,,

This bizarre DOS usage changes the date and time associated with the file and doesn't change anything else. The UNIX `touch` command does the same thing in an almost sane way. Type this line:

```
touch filename
```

This line changes the date and time of the file to today, right now.

# XCOPY /S

The DOS XCOPY command, unlike COPY, can copy more than just the current directory. The /S option tells XCOPY to copy all subdirectories of the current directory too.

In most versions of UNIX, you can use the `-r` option with the `cp` command to do the same thing (see Chapter 4):

```
cp -r /usr/margy/* .
```

With this command, UNIX copies to the working directory not only all the files in /usr/margy but also all the subdirectories. If any subdirectories are in /usr/margy, UNIX creates corresponding subdirectories in the working directory and then copies the files that are in them. This is a great way to make a backup copy of all the files in your home directory, including any subdirectories.

# DATE and TIME

The DOS DATE and TIME commands display the date and time and let you change them. In UNIX, type this line:

```
date
```

The `date` command displays both the date and time. You shouldn't need to change them. If you do, talk to your system administrator.

# DEBUG

The DOS DEBUG command lets you edit files that contain programs. You can look at their contents as characters (ASCII) or numbers (hexadecimal, no less). You have to be kind of nuts to try this. The ed, vi, and emacs programs let you edit files, if you must (see Chapter 12). If you really want to look at the bits in a file, the od command (for *octal display*) lets you display a file in octal, hex, decimal, ASCII, and about 45 other formats.

# DEL and ERASE

The DOS DEL and ERASE commands delete files. The UNIX rm command works in the same way (see Chapter 4). In both systems, *be careful!* The rm command doesn't ask you for confirmation if you try to delete all the files in a directory, so be even more careful. The rm command does ask for confirmation if you try to delete a file that is protected so that you can't write to it. If you really want to delete a protected file, type y when UNIX asks for confirmation.

# DIR

Everyone's favorite DOS command is DIR: It lists the files in a directory. It is similar to the UNIX ls command, but the options are different (see Chapter 4). To get a UNIX listing that looks like the regular DOS DIR file list, type this line:

```
ls -l
```

This command shows the size, date, and owner of every file in the directory.

## DIR /W

The DOS DIR /W command displays just the filenames in several columns across the screen. UNIX can do this too; indeed, most versions of UNIX automatically display listings in columns. If your version of UNIX doesn't, try this approach:

```
ls -x
```

# DIR /P

DIR /P pauses after filling up the screen with a directory listing so that you have time to read the filenames. The UNIX equivalent redirects the output of ls to the more command, which does the pausing (see Chapters 4 and 6):

```
ls | more
```

# DIR /A

DIR usually doesn't list hidden files. The /A option tells DIR to list all files. The UNIX equivalent is this (see Chapter 4):

```
ls -a
```

# DIR /O

DIR usually lists the files in any old order (actually, it's the order in which they occur in DOS's internal recordkeeping system, which is more or less the order in which the files were made). The /O option sorts them in alphabetical order. The UNIX ls command sorts them this way automatically.

# DIR /S

The /S option tells the DOS DIR command to include all the files in any subdirectories of the current directory. The UNIX equivalent is this:

```
ls -R
```

# DISKCOPY and DISKCOMP

The DOS DISKCOPY and DISKCOMP commands copy and compare (respectively) a floppy disk. Because UNIX almost never uses floppy disks, it doesn't have equivalent commands.

# DOSKEY

DOSKEY is a cool little DOS command, new in DOS 5, that lets you give the same command without retyping it. In UNIX, doing this depends on which shell you use. See Chapter 2 for descriptions of the Big Three shells and which one you are using (you may even have written it down on your Cheat Sheet card in the front of the book).

If you are using the C Shell (csh), type this line to repeat the last command:

```
!!
```

If you use the Korn Shell (ksh), type the following:

```
r
```

If you use the Bourne Shell (sh), you are out of luck. (Sorry!)

# DOSSHELL

DOSSHELL runs the DOS shell, a graphical user interface for DOS. The UNIX equivalents are various user-friendly shells under Motif and OPEN LOOK (see Chapter 11).

# EDIT and EDLIN

EDLIN is the yucky old DOS line editor that nobody uses if there is any alternative (it's gone in DOS 6); EDIT is the DOS editor (new in DOS 5). To edit files in UNIX, use ed, vi, or emacs (see Chapter 12).

# FIND

If you think that the UNIX equivalent to the DOS FIND command is the find command, you are wrong. Far too easy. The DOS FIND command examines a file and looks for the characters you specify. It's like a weaker version of the UNIX grep command (see Chapter 26 for how to use grep). The UNIX find command looks in directories for a filename you specify! It's covered in Chapter 26, too.

# FORMAT

The DOS FORMAT command prepares a floppy disk for use, by erasing anything that was on it. Although many UNIX systems don't even use floppy disks, the ones that do usually have a `format` command that formats a floppy. Ask an expert for help.

# HELP

The DOS HELP command displays some help text about the command you specify. In UNIX, use the `man` command (see Chapter 27). To get help about the `ls` command, for example, type this line:

```
man ls
```

On most UNIX systems, it shows you the info a page at a time. On some systems, however, the manual page flies by too fast to read, in which case you run it through `more`:

```
man ls | more
```

Some UNIX systems even have a `help` program. Try typing this line to see whether yours does:

```
help
```

Most `help` programs show you a little menu that lets you choose what to get help for. One choice is usually `quit`, so you press q to leave.

# LABEL and VOL

The DOS LABEL command lets you give a disk a name. The VOL command tells you the name of a disk. UNIX disks have names, but it's more trouble than it's worth to try to change them. Besides, no programs care about disk names.

# MEM

MEM tells you how much of your computer's memory is free and how much is being used (that's RAM memory, not space-on-the-disk memory). All current UNIX systems have virtual memory, so the amount of memory in use isn't your problem.

# MKDIR, or MD

The DOS MKDIR or MD command makes a new directory, just like the UNIX `mkdir` command does (see Chapter 5).

# MORE

DOS has filters just like UNIX! The DOS MORE filter acts almost the same as the UNIX `more` filter (see Chapter 6). In DOS, however, you can't type this line to see a file one screen at a time, as you can in UNIX:

```
more filename
```

With DOS, you must stick a < after the `MORE`: `MORE < filename`.

# PATH

The DOS PATH command tells DOS which directories to look in when it has trouble finding the program you want to run. In UNIX, you use a shell variable to contain this information. We were hoping not to have to tell you that were such things as *shell variables,* but there's one anyway.

In UNIX, the shell variable called `PATH` or `path` contains a list of the directories UNIX searches whenever you ask it to run a program. Your system administrator probably set it up for you, and you probably don't need to change it.

To see the current value of the `PATH` variable in the Bourne or Korn Shell, type this line:

```
echo $PATH
```

To see it in the C Shell, type this line:

```
echo $path
```

This is the UNIX equivalent of typing just PATH in DOS.

Changing your path (that is, adding a directory to the path) is kind of a pain. If you really need to do so, see Chapter 14.

# PRINT

Hardly any DOS people use the PRINT command to print a text file. The UNIX equivalent is the `lp` or `lpr` command, described in gory detail in Chapter 9.

# PROMPT

The DOS PROMPT command changes the prompt from the ever-unpopular `C>` to something more helpful. You can do this in UNIX, too, but you should get a UNIX wizard or your system administrator to help you so that the prompt is changed permanently rather than just until you log out.

We like our prompts to contain the current working directory so that we have an idea where we are. If you are working on a network, it can be nice to see also the name of the computer you are using. Ask your local wizard for his or her opinion: People who use UNIX heavily always have strong opinions about what type of prompt is best.

It no longer is considered particularly funny to change your prompt to something like "Yes, master?" or "I wait to do your bidding, all-powerful one!" If you ask a UNIX expert to help you do this, he or she will feel that you are wasting time, so watch out.

# RENAME, or REN

The DOS RENAME command renames a file. In UNIX, you use the `mv` command (see Chapter 4). RENAME can't move a file to a different directory at the same time, but `mv` can.

# REPLACE

The REPLACE command copies a file from one directory to another and updates older copies. It has several options that control the way the copying proceeds. Consider this DOS command:

```
REPLACE A:NEWFILE.DOC C:\ /S
```

It searches all the directories on drive C for files named NEWFILE.DOC. If it finds any, it replaces them with the NEWFILE.DOC file on the floppy disk in drive A.

To do the same thing in UNIX, you have to use the find command (see Chapter 26). If you have a file called newfile.doc in the current directory and you want to update any file by that name in your home directory and all its subdirectories (/usr/you, for example, if your user name is you), type something like this:

```
find /usr/you -name newfile.doc -exec cp /newfile.doc {} \;
```

This wild and crazy command tells find to start its search in /usr/you and look for files with the name newfile.doc; if it finds any matches, find will execute the UNIX command cp /newfile.doc and replace the {} with the place where it found the file. This is a bit confusing, but you probably never have used the DOS REPLACE command either.

# RMDIR, or RD

The DOS RMDIR, or RD, command removes a directory. In DOS, before you can remove a directory, you first must delete all the files and subdirectories in it so that it is empty. The UNIX rmdir command works in the same way (see Chapter 5). If you don't want to delete everything in the directory beforehand, however, you can use the rm command to delete, in one devastating stroke, both the directory and everything it contains:

```
rm -r directoryname
```

The -r option (which stands for *recursive*) tells rm to delete all files and subdirectories (and subdirectories of subdirectories, and so on) of the directory you name.

You can delete lots of important files in a hurry with this command. Watch out! To make it safer, add the `-i` option, which interactively asks you before deleting each file:

```
rm -ir directoryname
```

In UNIX, you can't abbreviate the `rmdir` command as `rd`. Amazingly, the UNIX lazy typists didn't allow that abbreviation, so you have to type the full name. The `rmdir` command is dangerous enough, UNIX figures, that you should have to do a little typing if you want to use it.

# *SET*

The DOS SET command sets or displays the contents of DOS environment variables. UNIX has environment variables, also called shell variables, which we have tried not to talk about in this book.

To display the contents of a UNIX shell variable, type this line (use the actual name of the variable):

```
echo $VARIABLENAME
```

Most shell variable names are capitalized, for no particular reason. To set an environment variable in the Bourne Shell or the Korn Shell, type this line:

```
VARIABLENAME=whatever
```

In the C Shell, type this line:

```
setenv VARIABLENAME whatever
```

The `PATH` or `path` shell variable, for example, contains the list of directories UNIX searches whenever you want to run a program. To see it, type this line in the Bourne or Korn Shell:

```
echo $PATH
```

Or type this line in the C Shell:

```
echo $path
```

To change it (a bad idea, actually) in the Bourne or Korn Shell, type this line:

```
PATH=/bin:/etc:/usr/you:
export PATH
```

Or in the C Shell:

```
set path=(/bin/etc/usr/you)
```

You can see why you should not change this variable unless you know the list of directories that contain programs on your system.

# SORT

The DOS SORT command works in almost the same way as the UNIX sort command (see Chapter 6). In UNIX, however, don't use a < before the filename if you are sorting a file. In DOS, you type this line: SORT < FILENAME

In UNIX, you just type this line:

```
sort filename
```

# SYS

The DOS SYS command copies the DOS operating system files to a floppy disk or hard disk. There are just three DOS system files, and they are small.

The UNIX operating system files are so large and extensive that they don't fit on any known floppy disk and take up gobs of space on your (or someone's) hard disk. There is no command like SYS in UNIX.

# TREE

The DOS TREE command displays an ugly but readable picture of the directory structure of a disk. The closest UNIX equivalent is ls -R, although lots of free X Windows programs are floating around that show spiffy directory trees on-screen. If you are running X Windows, ask around to see whether a directory-structure program is available.

# UNDELETE and UNFORMAT

The DOS UNDELETE command (new in DOS 5) undeletes files you erased accidentally — under certain circumstances, anyway. UNFORMAT tries to reverse the process of formatting a disk. UNIX doesn't come with any commands like these unless you have the Norton Utilities for UNIX, in which case you undelete files with nue. See Chapter 22 for what to do if you accidentally delete a file.

# VER

The DOS VER command tells you which version of DOS you are using. To find out which UNIX version and shell you are using, see Chapter 2.

# Obscure DOS Commands

Some DOS commands are used mainly in batch files, so we do not get into them here. They are BREAK, CALL, ECHO, EXIT, FASTOPEN, FOR, GOTO, IF, LOADHIGH, MIRROR, MODE, PAUSE, REM, SHARE, SHIFT (yuck), and VERIFY.

Then there are the DOS commands we have *never* heard of anyone using, like CHCP, COMMAND, COUNTRY, CTTY, EMM386, EXE2BIN, GRAPHICS, GRAFTABL, KEYB, NLSFUNC, RECOVER, and SETVER. We won't tell you their UNIX equivalents because we can assure you that you couldn't care less.

# DOS batch files and UNIX shell scripts

If you have used batch files in DOS, you can use similar things, called shell scripts, in UNIX. In case you don't know, a DOS *batch file* is a text file that contains a series of DOS commands, one per line. Amazingly, a UNIX *shell script* is a text file that contains a series of UNIX commands, one per line. In DOS, batch files have names that end with the BAT extension. In UNIX, you can name a shell script anything you want and use `chmod +x` to mark it as a script. See Chapter 14 for some hints about writing shell scripts.

In DOS, if you have a batch file named AUTOEXEC.BAT in the root directory of the disk you load DOS from, DOS runs that batch file automatically whenever you start DOS (that is, whenever you start or restart the computer). UNIX has a similar shell script.

If you are using the Bourne Shell or the Korn Shell and have a file called `.profile` in your home directory, this file is executed automatically whenever you log in. The C Shell equivalent file is `.login`. You can edit these files with a text editor. Your system administrator probably already has given you a `.profile` or `.login` file full of stuff to set up your local environment. Don't take anything out without consulting your system administrator. If you want to add commands, add them at the end of the file.

The DOS CONFIG.SYS file contains information about your hardware and software configuration. When you turn on your computer, after it loads DOS but before it runs the AUTOEXEC.BAT file, the system looks in this file to configure DOS for your system.

UNIX configuration is entirely different and, in most cases, is not your problem. In most cases, UNIX systems automatically adapt themselves to whatever hardware is attached to the computer (pretty advanced concept, eh?).

# Part VI

## The World Outside the UNIX Biosphere

"C'MON BRICKMAN, YOU KNOW AS WELL AS I DO THAT 'NOSE-SCANNING' IS OUR BEST DEFENSE AGAINST UNAUTHORIZED ACCESS TO PERSONAL FILES."

## In this part...

Most computers that run UNIX are connected to other computers. Many are parts of networks, and many have telephone connections to UNIX computers in other places. This part talks about how to send messages and share files with other people on your computer, other people on your local network, and other computers out there in UNIX-land.

# Chapter 17

## Who's Out There?

● ● ● ● ● ● ● ● ● ● ● ● ● ● ● ● ● ● ● ● ● ● ● ● ● ● ● ● ● ● ● ● ● ● ● ● ● ● ● ● ●

### In This Chapter

▶ Find out who else is using your computer

▶ Communicate with them

● ● ● ● ● ● ● ● ● ● ● ● ● ● ● ● ● ● ● ● ● ● ● ● ● ● ● ● ● ● ● ● ● ● ● ● ● ● ● ● ●

*F*rom the beginning, UNIX was designed as a multiuser system. In the early years of computing, it was considered greedy to keep to yourself an entire PDP-11/45 (a 1972 vintage minicomputer about the speed of a PC AT but the size of a trash compactor). It was also kind of expensive. These days, the cost argument is much less compelling — unless your computer is a Cray or the like — but UNIX remains multiuser partly because it always was and partly because multiuser systems make it easier to share programs and data.

Even if you have your own workstation but are attached to a network, your machine is potentially multiuser because other people can log in to your machine over the net (as we technoids call a network). (On the other hand, you can log in to their machines too. See Chapters 19 and 20 for details.)

In this chapter, you see how you can nose around and find out who's on your system and on other systems on the network. Then you can look into getting in touch with them.

If you are the only person who uses your computer and you don't have a network (your UNIX computer is all alone in the world); skip this chapter and the next three.

## Finding Out Who's on Your Computer

There are two main commands you can use to find out who's using your machine: who and finger. The simple way to use either one is just to type the command:

```
who
```

The typical response is something like this:

```
root      console    Dec 29 20:16
john1     vt01       Dec 21 15:19
john1     ttyp2      Jan 6  16:36
john1     ttyp1      Jan 6  17:20
john1     ttyp0      Jan 6  16:36
```

You see the user, the terminal, and the login time. User `john1` is logged in five times because he has a bunch of X terminal windows, each of which counts as a login session. The exact output from `who` varies from one version of UNIX to another, but it always contains at least this much. You can also type `who am i` and UNIX prints just the line for the terminal (or terminal window) in which you typed the command.

A considerably more informative program is `finger`:

> `finger`

This command produces a more useful report than `who` does:

```
Login      Name           TTY   Idle  When        Office
root    0000-Admin(0000)   co   1:11  Tue  20:16
john1   John R. Levine     vt   1:11  Mon  15:19   x3712
john1   John R. Levine     vt   1:35  Tue  16:47   x3712
john1   John R. Levine     p2   1:11  Wed  16:36   x3712
john1   John R. Levine     p1         Wed  17:20   x3712
john1   John R. Levine     p0         Wed  16:36   x3712
```

Although `finger` reports the same stuff as `who` does, it also looks up the user's real name (if it's in the user password file) and tells you how long the terminal has been idle (how long it's been since the user last typed something). If the system administrator has entered the data, it also usually gives an office phone number, room number, or some other handy info about where the user works.

You can also use `finger` to ask about a specific user, and UNIX looks up some extra info about that user. Here, we used it to look up one of the authors:

> `finger john1`

UNIX returned this information:

```
Login name: johnl           In real life: John R. Levine
Directory: /usr/johnl       Shell: /bin/sh
On since Dec 21 15:19:45 on vt01      1 hour 27 minutes Idle Time
Project: Working on "UNIX for Dummies"
Plan:
Write many books, become famous.
```

The Project and Plan lines are merely the contents of files called .project and
.plan in your home directory. (Yes, the filenames start with periods.) It has
become customary to put a clever remark in your .plan file, but please don't
overdo it. If the user is logged in on more than one terminal or terminal window,
finger gives a full report for each terminal. The finger johnl command we
gave, in fact, reported five times — one for each login — but we edited it for
practicality.

# Finding Out Who's on Other Computers

If your machine is on a network, you can use rwho and finger to find about
other machines. You type the system name you want to check up on after an @
(at sign.) (See Chapter 18 for more information about system names.) We can
check a nearby system, for example:

```
finger @spdcc
```

The spdcc machine turns out not to be very busy:

```
[spdcc.com]
Login    Name            TTY Idle    When     Office
uucp     Uucp Daemon     02          Wed 20:13
johnl    John R. Levine  03          Wed 20:44   Shepard Str 555-2368
dyer     Steve Dyer      p0   1      Wed 08:13
```

You can also ask about an individual by putting that user's name in front of
the @:

```
finger johnl@spdcc
```

This command gives the same sort of report as a local `finger` does:

```
[spdcc.com]
Login name: johnl              In real life: John R. Levine
Directory: /var/users/johnl    Shell: /bin/csh
On since Jan 6 9:22:45 on tty02        2 minutes Idle Time
Plan:no plan
```

If you're on the Internet, you can — in principle — finger any machine on the net. Because there's no rule that says machines must answer when you call, in many cases you get a "connection refused" response or even no response.

Some systems, particularly main network machines at universities, have set up `finger` to return user-directory information. Suppose that you ask who's at MIT:

```
finger @mit.edu
```

You get an introduction to their on-line directory:

```
[mit.edu]

Student data loaded as of Dec 15, Staff data loaded as of
Dec 19. Notify the Registrar or Personnel as appropriate to
change your information. This service is maintained by
Distributed Computing and Network Services.

Send Comments regarding this service to mitdir@mit.edu.
Use finger help@mit.edu for some instructions.
```

You can try to finger a particular individual at MIT too:

```
finger chomsky@mit.edu
```

Now you can see the public data on that individual:

```
[mit.edu]
   .
   .
   .
There was 1 match to your request.
```

```
       name: Chomsky, Noam A
      email: CHOMSKY@ATHENA.MIT.EDU
      phone: (617) 555-7819
    address: 20D-219 ·
 department: Linguistics & Philos
      title: Institute Professor (on Leave, Year)
      alias: N-chomsky
```

You can engage in wholesale nosiness by using rwho; this command attempts to compile a list of all the people using all the machines in the local network.

# Chatting with Other People on Your Computer

After you have figured out who is on your computer, you may want to send them a message. There are two general schools of message sending. The first is the real-time school, in which the message appears on the other user's screen while you wait, presumably because it's an extremely urgent message. The write and talk commands let you do that. Excessive use of real-time messages is a good way to make enemies quickly because you interrupt people's work all over the place. Be sparing in your blather.

The second school is electronic mail, or e-mail, in which you send a message the other user looks at when it's convenient. E-mail is a large topic in its own right, so we're saving that for Chapter 18.

Real-time terminal communication has been likened to talking to someone on the moon because it's so slow: it's limited by the speed at which people type. Here on Earth, most of us have telephones, so the most sensible thing to do is to send a one-line message asking the other user to call you on the phone.

The simpler real-time communications command is write. If someone writes to you, you see something like the following on your screen:

```
Message from john1 on iecc (ttyp1) [ Wed Jan 6 20:28:42 ] ...
Please call me at extension 8649
<EOT>
```

Usually the message appears in the middle of an editor session and scrambles the file on your screen. You will be relieved to know that the scrambling is limited to the screen — the editor has no idea that someone is writing to you; the file is OK.

In either vi or emacs, you can tell the editor to redraw what's supposed to be on-screen by pressing Ctrl-L (if you're in input mode in vi, press Escape first).

To write to a user, use the write command and give the name of the user to whom you want to talk:

```
write margy
```

After you press Enter, write tells you absolutely nothing, which means that it is waiting for your message. Type the message, which can be as many lines long as you want. When you finish, press Ctrl-D (the general end-of-input character) or the interrupt character, usually Ctrl-C or Delete. write copies every line to the other user's screen as you press Enter, so reading a long message sent by way of write is sort of like reading a poem on old Burma-Shave signs as you drive by each one.

You want to send an important message, for example, to your friend Joe, so you type these lines:

```
write joe
Yo, Joe, turn on your radio. WBUR is rebroadcasting
Terry Gross's interview with Nancy Reagan!
```

You press Enter at the end of each line. After the last line, you press Ctrl-D.

## *I'm talking — where are you?*

Sometimes, write tells you that the user is logged in on several logical terminals:

```
john1 is logged on more than one place.
You are connected to "vt01".
Other locations are:
ttyp1
ttyp0
ttyp2
```

The write command is pretty dumb. If the user you are writing to is logged in on more than one terminal — or more typically, is using many windows in X — write picks one of them at random and writes there. You can be virtually certain that the window or terminal write chooses is not the one the user is looking at. To maximize the chances of the user seeing your message, use the finger command to figure out which terminal is the most active (the one with the lowest idle time)

and write to that window. Remember the results of the `finger` command, for example, from a few pages back:

```
Login       Name            TTY Idle  When       Office
root    0000-Admin(0000)    co  1:11  Tue 20:16
johnl   John R. Levine      vt  1:11  Mon 15:19
johnl   John R. Levine      vt  1:35  Tue 16:47
johnl   John R. Levine      p2  1:11  Wed 16:36
johnl   John R. Levine      p1        Wed 17:20
johnl   John R. Levine      p0        Wed 16:36
```

The best candidates to send a message to are `ttyp1` and `ttyp0`. (The `finger` command cuts out the `tty` from terminal names.)

To write to a specific terminal, give `write` the terminal name after the user name:

```
write johnl ttyp1
```

If you are writing back to a user who just wrote to you, you should use the terminal name that was sent in his `write` message (in this case, it was also `ttyp1`).

# Can we talk?

You can have a somewhat spiffier conversation with the `talk` command, which allows simultaneous two-way typing. You use it the same way you use `write`: by giving a user name and optionally a terminal name. The other user sees something like this:

```
Message from Talk_Daemon@iecc at 20:47 ...
talk: connection requested by johnl@IECC
talk: respond with: talk johnl@IECC
```

If someone tries to talk to you and you're interested in responding, type the `talk` command it suggests. If you're in the middle of a text editor or other program, you must exit (or press Ctrl-Z) first.

While `talk` is running, it splits your screen and arranges things so that what you type appears in the top half and what the other user types appears in the bottom half. Unlike `write`, `talk` immediately passes what you type — without waiting for an Enter — which means that you can see all the other user's typing mistakes and vice versa. When you get tired of `talk`, exit by pressing Ctrl-D.

# Chatting with Other People on Other Computers

The `talk` command is designed to talk to users on other computers. If the other computer is a long way away or the person you're chatting with has trouble hearing or speaking, typing rather than talking can make sense. As networking stretches around the world, you may find yourself "talking" with someone for whom English is not a native language. In that case, typing can be faster than trying to understand someone with a strong accent across a noisy phone connection.

Computers have names, too, which usually are called *machine names* (more about this submect in Chapters 19 and 20). To talk to someone on another computer, give `talk` the user name and machine name:

```
write johnl@iecc.mycorp.com
```

After you're connected, `write` works just like talking to a local user, except that sometimes it can take several seconds for characters to get from one machine to another on an intercontinental link.

# Reading the Writing on the Wall

For the truly megalomaniacal among you, a program called `wall` blats what you type to every single terminal and window on your entire computer. You use it much like `write`:

```
wall
Free pizza in the upstairs conference room in 5 minutes!
```

As with `write`, you tell `wall` that you're finished by pressing Ctrl-D. Be sparing in your use of `wall` unless you want a bunch of new enemies.

Note that `wall` affects only the people who use your computer, not everyone on your network.

# Chapter 18

# Automating Your Office Gossip

* * *

* * *

*E*lectronic mail (or *e-mail*) is the high-tech way to automate interoffice chatter, gossip, and innuendo. Using e-mail, you can quickly and efficiently circulate memos and other written information to your co-workers, including directions to the beer bash this Saturday and the latest Dave Barry column. You can even send and receive e-mail from people outside your organization, if you and they use networked computers.

If your organization uses e-mail, you probably already have some. In fact, there may be vitally important but unread mail waiting in your mailbox at this very moment. Probably not, but who knows? You can tell whether unread messages are in your mailbox because UNIX displays this message when you log in:

```
You have mail.
```

## What You Need in Order to Use E-Mail

Any UNIX system handles e-mail for users on that system. To exchange e-mail with the outside world, your computer must be on a network — or at least have a phone line and a modem. You definitely don't want to know how to set up a mail network or make connections to other computers — if your computer doesn't already have e-mail on it, it's time to talk to a UNIX wizard.

In the great tradition of UNIX standardization, there are about 14 different mail-sending and -receiving programs. (Fortunately, they can all exchange mail with each other.) To find out whether your computer can do e-mail, try using the simple mail program to see whether you have any mail waiting. Just type this line:

```
mail
```

UNIX says `No mail` if no mail is waiting, or it blats a copy of the first unread message on your screen. In the latter case, if you don't want to read your mail right away, type x (for exit) and press Enter to get out. We talk more about reading your mail later in this chapter.

# Addressing the Mail

E-mail, like regular mail (usually referred to by e-mail advocates as *snail-mail*), needs an address, usually called a *net address*. To send mail to a person, you send it to his user name (see Chapter 1 for information about logging in with a user name). If the other user uses a different computer than the one you use, the mail system has to know which computer the other person is on — and the address gets more complicated.

## Sending mail to people on your computer

For people who use the very same computer you do (you both use terminals connected to the same computer running UNIX), the mail address is just their user name. If you enter georgew for your user name, that's your mail address too. Make sure that you don't use capital letters in the mail address unless the user name also does.

## Sending mail to people on other computers

You can send mail to people who use other computers if your computer is connected to their computer on a network. For people who use other computers, you send mail by telling the mail system which computer they use.

Computers have names too, you know. They sometimes have boring names that indicate what they are used for, like marketing or corpacctg. Sometimes all the computers in an organization are named according to a more interesting scheme, like naming them all after fish, spices, or cartoon characters. One company we worked for had computers named haddock, cod, and flounder. The next company used `basil`, `chervil`, `dill`, `fennel`, and `ginger`. If your company has boring computer names, try talking your system administrator into lightening up and naming the next computer `bill_the_cat`.

When you are writing to someone on another computer on your network, include the computer name in the mail address by using an at sign (@) to indicate where they are "at." If your friend Nancy, for example, has the user name `nancyb` and uses a computer named `ginger`, her mail address is `nancyb@ginger`.

A few mail systems still use an older address scheme, based on the `uucp` communication program, that uses exclamation points, in which case the address would be `ginger!nancyb` (yes, the system name goes first). If you have to use a `uucp`-style address, remember that, because the C Shell treats exclamation points specially, you would have to type the address in a `mail` command as `ginger\!nancyb`.

A skillful system administrator can automatically note which computer each user in an organization uses. With luck, you can merely send mail by user name, and the system automagically figures out which computer to send it to.

If you have trouble with addresses, the easiest way to send a message to someone is to wait until they send a message to you and then reply to it. All mail programs have a command (usually `r`) that replies to the message you just read. Messages almost always have return addresses, and the `r` command lets you send a message without typing an address.

## Sending mail to people "out there"

If your computer network has phone connections to the outside world, you can probably also send mail to people out in the wide world of The Net: the invisible network of UNIX and other computers that extends worldwide. Check with your system administrator or other e-mail users to determine whether your organization is "on the net" (connected to the outside world).

Many interconnected networks informally exchange electronic mail. The largest and best known is the *Internet*, a network with hundreds of thousands of machines on every continent, including Antarctica. Furthermore, because many machines not directly connected to the Internet have made arrangements to have mail forwarded to and from the Internet, for the purposes of mail, they seem to be on the Internet. When we talk about someone being "on the net," we mean that you can use an Internet-style mail address to send mail to that person.

To send mail this way, you need a net address for the person you want to send mail to. Then you type it in exactly the way she wrote it. Internet addresses tend to look like this:

`ellenz@persimmon.abc.com`

The part in front of the @ is the person's user name. The rest of the address is the name of the computer and other information about where the computer is, usually the name of the organization. The computer name, company name, and so on are connected by periods. If the address ends with three letters, the letters tell you the type kind of organization it is: `com` for companies, `edu` for educational institutions, and `gov` for governments, for example. If the address

## Sending mail to people who use on-line services

You can send mail to people who don't use UNIX computers. By using the net, you can usually send mail to anyone who uses CompuServe, MCI Mail, and other services.

To send mail to a CompuServe user, do the following:

✓ Find out his or her CompuServe user ID. It is a nine- or ten-digit number with a comma somewhere in the middle, like this: 71234,5678. Most CompuServe user IDs begin with a 7, for reasons we don't claim to understand. Probably because of its mystical significance.

✓ For purposes of sending mail from UNIX, replace the comma in the CompuServe user ID with a period, like this: 71234.5678. Because net addresses aren't allowed to contain commas, you have to do this.

✓ Tack `@compuserve.com` to the end of the number and, voila! — you have the person's net address, like this:

`71234.5678@compuserve.com`

To send mail to an MCI Mail user, you do more or less the same thing as for a CompuServe user:

✓ Find out the MCI Mail account number. Your friend may not know it and may have to look on his or her MCI Mail bill to find out what

it is (MCI Mail is usually addressed by name rather than by number). The account number is a seven-digit number that looks like a phone number, like this: 123-4567.

✓ Take out the hyphen and tack `@mcimail.com` to the end of the number. Voila! — you have the person's net address, like this:

`1234567@mcimail.com`

✓ MCI Mail can also accept real names with periods between the parts:

`Richard.M.Nixon@mcimail.com`

For users of DELPHI, the address is the user name followed by `@delphi.com`, like this:

`service@delphi.com`

For users of AT&T Mail, the address is the user name followed by `@attmail.com`:

`rallen@attmail.com`

For users of America On Line, the address is the user name followed by `@aol.com`, like this:

`ab2873@aol.com`

Many other services, notably Prodigy and GEnie, have said that they soon will exchange mail with the net. You will have to check with them to find out the details.

ends with a pair of letters, it's a code for the country in which the mailbox is located. In the United States, the next-to-last pair of letters represents the state, and before that is the city; our address ends in cambridge.ma.us because the computer is located in Cambridge, Massachusetts. (The choice of geographic versus organization addresses depends on political issues that aren't worth recounting.) But the assignment of names is all very well organized, really.

If your computer is on the net, you can also exchange mail with users of commercial services such as MCI Mail and CompuServe. For details, see the sidebar "Sending mail to people who use on-line services."

When you type net addresses, keep these points in mind:

✔ Be sure that you don't type any spaces in the middle of the address. There are no spaces in user names or computer names, or on either side of the @ or period.

✔ Don't capitalize anything unnecessarily. Check the capitalization of the person's user name and computer name. Most addresses are entirely in small letters.

✔ Don't forget the periods that separate the parts of a net address.

If your computer is on the net and you want to try out network mail, send a message to the authors of this book, at dummies@iecc.cambridge.ma.us, and tell us what you think of this book. (If you can get that address right, you're already halfway to being a mail wizard.)

# A Mailbox with Cardinals and Pheasants on It

To receive mail, you need a mailbox. (Not one of those tasteful roadside mailboxes, in this case. It's an invisible mailbox made up entirely of electronic data.) Your system administrator can make (or already has made) one for you if your organization uses e-mail. The mailbox comes in the form of a file probably called /usr/mail/yourusername; it contains your unread mail and any mail you choose to leave lying around. You may also have a directory called mail or Mail (some systems capitalize it, some don't — sigh) in your home directory that you can use to sort your mail into piles and keep it for historical reference.

To read the mail in your mailbox and send mail, you use a program such as mail or elm. If you use Motif or OPEN LOOK, you can use fancy X Windows mail programs such as MailTool and xmail.

# *Playing Postman Pat with* mail

The basic mail program comes with every brand of UNIX and is an acceptable way to read and send mail. Not great, but acceptable.

Assuming that you want to send to send mail to your friend Nancy B., you can send a message with the mail program by typing this line:

```
mail nancyb
```

Some versions of mail prompt you to enter a subject line for the message; others respond by doing absolutely nothing. You can tell that something is afoot because you don't see a UNIX shell prompt such as $ or % anymore. The mail program is waiting for you to type the message. So, type something, as many lines long as you want, like this:

```
Yo, Nance! I think I've figured out how to use the e-mail on this thing!
Send a message back so that I can see if my mailbox works. Thanks...
```

Press Enter when the line reaches the right end of the screen (on the window) to make it easier to read. Otherwise, your line wraps around to another line, and UNIX may put the line break in the middle of a word.

When you finish typing the message, type a period on a line by itself to tell the mail program that you are finished. The mail program confirms that it has sent the message by doing absolutely nothing except displaying a UNIX prompt. (Some particularly ancient versions of mail don't understand the dot, so you have to tell it that you are finished by pressing Ctrl-D.)

Because the mail program is so helpful, you may want to consider using a better program, like elm, described later in this chapter. If you have to use mail, send yourself a test message to make sure that it is working. System V machines usually have a really old and awful mail program called mail and a somewhat better one called Mail. (These guys really had a lot of fun thinking up names for these programs.) If you can use Mail rather than mail, do so, because it is much more likely to work the way it's supposed to. (Often, mail doesn't even understand network mail addresses.)

## *What's in my mailbox?*

To read your mail, reply to letters, and do other mail-related stuff, type this on a line by itself:

```
mail
```

The mail program starts by showing you your unread mail. Some versions print the first unread message or show a list of incoming messages. Then the program displays a prompt:

?

The mail program understands many commands and is ready for you to type one. If it hasn't already showed you a list of messages, type h to tell mail to show you a listing of the messages in your mailbox (if there are any).

Figure 18-1 shows what you might see when you start the mail program. The little > shows you which message mail is working with.

```
3 letters found in /usr/mail/margy, 0 scheduled for deletion, 0 newly arrived
>   3    283   lydias    Wed Dec 23 11:51:57 1993
    2    365   jordany   Wed Dec 23 11:51:45 1993
    1   1738   johnl     Tue Dec 22 23:58:50 1993
?
```

**Figure 18-1:** An example of what you might see when you start the mail program.

## What's all this junk at the beginning of the message?

An e-mail message has a header that the mail program creates automatically. The message consists of the following pieces:

- ✔ The To address (the person to receive the mail)
- ✔ The From address (the return address)
- ✔ The cc addresses (the addresses to send copies to)
- ✔ The subject
- ✔ Optional information you rarely use, such as expiration date, priority, and addresses for blind copies

Don't worry if the header looks like gobbledygook — it is. On incoming mail, the header can have all sorts of extra reports on which systems have passed it along, which program was used to send the mail, and lots of other useless stuff.

You can specify cc addresses, subject, and other information for messages you send.

The `mail` program understands lots of commands, including these:

✔ Press Enter to see the current message (the one the > points to).

✔ To move to a different message, type the message number (the first thing on the line in the list of headers).

✔ Press d to delete the current message (usually after you have read it).

✔ Press u to undelete a message you didn't want to delete.

✔ Press m and type the address to send (mail) a new message.

✔ Press r to reply to the current message.

✔ Press z to see more message headers if there are too many to fit on-screen.

✔ Press p to print the current message.

✔ Press q to quit the `mail` program.

✔ Press ? for further help, including a list of other commands you can use.

## What does it say? What does it say?

To read a message, type its message number (the number at the beginning of the line). To read the current message (the one with the >), just press Enter. The `mail` program displays the message — or the first screen of it if it is a long message.

When you finish reading the message, you can do several things with it:

✔ Delete it (press d).

✔ Reply to it (press r ). Then type a message (like the one to Nancy, a few pages ago). End the message by typing . (a period) on a line by itself.

✔ Save it (see the next section).

If you don't make any other arrangements, messages you have read are saved in a file called `mbox`, which can get pretty big if you don't edit it now and then.

## Saving your letters for posterity

You can save a message in a text file to edit later or include in a word process-ing document. To save the current message (the one you are reading or have just finished reading), type this line:

```
s filename
```

Replace *filename* with the name of the text file you want to create. If the text file already exists, mail adds the current message to the end of the file; you can save a series of messages to a single text file in this way.

## *Run that by me again*

To print a message (on the screen, not on the printer) press p. You will want to do this when you are looking at a list of messages and you want to see the contents of one of them. If you want to see a message other than the current one, put the message number (shown in the list of headers) after the p:

```
p 5
```

To quit mail, press q. You will see the UNIX prompt.

# *Playing Postman Pat with* elm

The elm mail-reading program is a heck of a lot easier to use than is either version of the mail program. The elm program even tells you what is going on once in a while. It also helps you organize your mail into folders if you plan to save your messages.

To read your mail, send mail, or peruse mail you left lying around the last time, type this line:

```
elm
```

The elm program displays a list of your mail messages (see Figure 18-2).

This display is called the mail index. The first letter in every line tells you which ones are new (N), old and already read (blank), old and unread (O), and deleted (D). The listing also shows the date the mail was received, who sent it, the

```
    Mailbox is '/usr/mail/margy' with 3 messages [ELM 2.3 PL11]
  1  Dec 22 John R. Levine   (49)  a few troff hints
O 2  Dec 23 Jordan M. Young  (12)  junk
N 3  Dec 23 Lydia Spitzer    (10)
```

**Figure 18-2:** A list of mail messages in elm.

number of lines in the message, and the subject. Below the index are instructions, including the one-letter commands you use to read and send mail:

- ✔ Use the ↑ and ↓ (or press j and k) to highlight the message you want to read, reply to, delete, or whatever.

- ✔ Press Enter to read the highlighted message.

- ✔ Press d to delete a message after you have read it.

- ✔ Press u to undelete a message you didn't want to delete.

- ✔ Press m to send (mail) a message.

- ✔ Press r to reply to a message.

- ✔ Press f to forward a message to someone else.

- ✔ Press > or s to save the message in a folder or text file.

- ✔ Press p to print the message.

- ✔ Press q to quit the elm program.

- ✔ Press ? for more help.

## Just put a stamp on it

To use elm to send mail, press m. The program asks you for the address, the subject of the message, and addresses to send copies to. Then it runs a text editor, usually vi. (You can arrange for elm to run another editor if you loathe vi as much as we do — see the following Tip.) Use the editor to type the text of the message. When you finish, save the message and exit from the editor. (If you are forced to use vi, press Esc and type ZZ to save the message and exit from vi.)

## Tell the world!

Then elm gives you a chance to edit the message (perhaps to add a P.S.), fool with the header (useful if you decide that your message is so fascinating it should be sent to a wider audience), forget the whole thing, or send the message off.

Press h to edit the header for the message. elm displays all the components of the header, including the addressee and the subject line. You can change most of the them, or also add names of people to receive copies of the message (cc's).

To change each of these components, press the letter shown before the parenthesis. To add cc's, for example, press c. elm asks you for the list of addresses to send copies to. Enter the addresses, separated by at least one space, and press Enter. If elm recognizes the address as one in the local address book, it displays the person's actual name in parentheses after the e-mail address. Otherwise, it shows just the address you typed.

When you finish fooling with the header, press Enter to indicate that you are finished. elm asks what it should do with the message:

```
And now: s
  Choose e)dit message, !)shell, h)eaders, c)opy file, s)end, or f)orget.
```

Press s to send it. You can also press e to go back and edit some more, h to change the headers (To, Cc, and Subject, for example), and some less useful choices we won't worry about.

You can change the editor elm uses for writing and editing mail messages. (Thank goodness, because otherwise you might have to use vi!) When you are using elm and looking at the mail index, do the following:

1. Press o to look at the elm options.

2. Press e to change the editor you use.

3. Type the name of the editor you usually use to edit text files (we like emacs).

4. Press > to save this change.

5. Finally, press i to see the mail index again.

## Reading your mail

To read a message, highlight its line in the mail index and press Enter. The elm program displays the message — or the first screen of it if it is a long message.

When you finish reading the message, you can do several things with it:

- ✔ Delete it (press d).

- ✔ Forward it to someone else (press f and tell elm the address to forward it to).

- ✔ Reply to it (press r).

- ✔ Save it. To leave it hanging around in your mailbox, press spacebar to leave the current message and go to the next message, or press i to leave the current message and return to the mail index. In either case, the message remains unaltered. Alternatively, you can save the message in a folder or text file (see the following sections).

## Saving your mail for a rainy day

If you like to save mail messages, you can save them with elm in folders, one folder per topic or one folder per sender. You can have lots of folders — each one is just a text file in your Mail directory (note the initial capital letter).

To save a message to a folder, either highlight the message in the mail index or display the message. Then press > or s. The elm program asks for the name of the folder you want to save the message to. For some reason, folder names begin with = (an equal sign). The elm program suggests a folder with the name of the person who sent the message, assuming that you want to save messages organized by sender. But you can type any name you want (no space and no funny characters other than the = at the beginning).

To see the messages in a folder, return to the mail index and press c to change folders. Type the name of the folder you want to use (or press ? to see a list of your folders). Be sure to type the = at the beginning of the folder name. You see a list of messages just like the mail index of your original mailbox.

All the same commands that work in your regular mailbox work in a folder. After you highlight a message, for example, you can read it by pressing Enter, forward it by pressing f, or delete it by pressing d.

To return to your regular mailbox, press c again and type ! when elm asks for the name of the folder (don't ask us why).

## Mail for word processors

You can also save a message in a text file so that you can edit it later or include it in a word processing document. Use the > or s command to move the message, but, rather than type a folder name (which always begins with a =), type a filename (like message.text). The elm program creates the file in your home directory and puts the message there. If the file already exists, elm adds the message to the end of the existing file so that you can save a series of messages to a single text file.

## Taking it with you

To print a message on the printer, highlight the message in the mail index or display the message. Then press p to print it.

# Netiquette

E-mail has been around long enough for an etiquette to have sprung up around it, just as with real mail. Here are some tips:

✔ Be polite. The written word tends to sound stronger and more dogmatic than speech; sarcasm and little jokes don't always work.

✔ Don't write anything when you're annoyed. If you get a message that you find totally obnoxious, *don't answer it right away!* You will be sorry if you do because you will overreact and look just as obnoxious yourself. How do we know this? We used to do it, too. Everyone does at first, until they learn not to take e-mail too seriously. The exchange of needlessly obnoxious messages is so common that it has a name: *flaming.* Don't do it.

✔ Be brief.

✔ Be sure to sign your messages. The header shows where a message comes from, but your recipient may not remember who you are from your cryptic e-mail address.

✔ Use normal punctuation and capitalization. That is, DON'T CAPITALIZE EVERYTHING. It looks as though you are shouting, and that's not polite (see first tip in this list).

✔ Watch out for acronyms. E-mail is full of them, and you had better know what the common ones mean. A list of acronyms appears at the end of this sidebar.

✔ Don't assume that e-mail is private. Any recipient of your mail can easily forward it to other people. Some mail addresses are really mailing lists that redistribute messages to many other people. Glitches in the mail system may send your messages to various electronic dead-letter offices. In one famous case, a mistaken mail address sent a message to tens of thousands of readers. It began, "Darling, at last we have a way to send messages that is completely private...."

✔ To indicate emotion, most people use *emoticons,* little pictures made up of characters to look like faces. If you see : - ), for example, just look at it sideways: You see a little smiley face that usually means that whatever you just read was a joke. (You get a sad face if you use the other parenthesis for the mouth.) Some people — particularly those who use CompuServe — type <grin> or <g> or <smile>.

Here's a list of the most common e-mail acronyms:

| | |
|---|---|
| BTW | By the way |
| IMHO | In my humble opinion |
| IOW | In other words |
| PITA | Pain in the a** |
| ROF,L | Rolling on floor, laughing |
| RSN | Real soon now (ha!) |
| RTFM | Read the f'ing manual (that is, you could have looked it up yourself) |
| TIA | Thanks in advance |
| TLA | Three-letter acronym |

## It's Dead, Jim

If you get an address wrong, you usually get the message back within a few hours (for mail on your own computer or your own network), or within a few days (for mail that has bounced around the net). The dead letter usually has all kinds of cryptic, automated error messages in it, but the gist is clear — the message didn't get delivered. Check the address and try again. The safest way to address a message generally is to reply to someone else's message.

# Chapter 19
# My Files Are Where?

**In This Chapter**

▶ What are remote files?

▶ What is NFS?

▶ Tips and pitfalls of remote files

I f your UNIX system is attached to a network, in all likelihood some or all of your files are stored on a machine far away from where you are. If your system isn't networked — or if it has only slow telephone network connections — you can skip this chapter.

Quite a few different schemes let computers use files on other machines. They are named mostly with TLAs (*three-letter acronyms*) such as AFS, RFS, and NFS. This chapter talks mostly about NFS because that's the most commonly used scheme, even though, in many ways, it works the worst. If you didn't like the C Shell or the vi editor, you won't like NFS either; it also was written by Bill, the big guy with the strong opinions.

## You'll Never Find Your Stuff

The NFS (*Network File System*) program lets you treat files on another computer in more or less the same way you treat files on your own computer.

There are several reasons you might want to use NFS, which are discussed in this chapter.

## Share!

The most common reason for using NFS is that you have a bunch of similar computers scattered around, all running more or less the same programs. Rather than load every program on every computer, the system administrator loads one copy of everything on one computer (the *server*) so that all the other computers (the *clients*) can share the programs. This arrangement saves disk space and makes the administrator's job much easier — because, when a program is updated on the server, everyone gets the updated version immediately. The alternative is to update dozens of different machines over the network or even to run around to all of them with floppies or tapes in hand.

## One backup for all, and all for one backup

Centralizing the files on a server makes backup and administration easier. It's much easier to administer one disk of 1,000 megabytes than to administer 10 disks of 100 megabytes apiece. It's also easier to back up everything because everything is all in one place rather than spread around on a dozen machines.

## I think I'll work here today

Another use of NFS is to make a bunch of workstations function as a shared system. It is reasonably straightforward to set up a bunch of workstations so that you can sit down at any one of them, log in, and use the same set of files regardless of where on the network they physically reside. This capability is a great convenience. Also, by using programs like `rlogin` (discussed in Chapter 20), you can log in to another machine on the network and work from that machine (which is handy if the other machine is faster than yours or has some special feature you want to use).

## A penny saved is a network in use

In an extreme case, a system can have diskless workstations that use NFS for all their disk needs. For a while, diskless workstations were popular because one big disk on a server was much cheaper than several little disks on every workstation. They're less popular now: It turns out that sending every bit of disk action over the network is painfully slow. It helps a lot if you have a small local disk for scratch space; besides, little disks aren't very expensive these days. People also noted that the largest program they used on their workstation was the X Windows server program; they could instead use X terminals, which are cheaper than diskless workstations and get just as good performance at a lower cost.

## Talking with the "other" computer

A final use of NFS is in *heterogeneous networks,* a fancy term for networks with different kinds of computers. NFS is available for all sorts of computers from PCs to mainframes. It's common to run a version of NFS on PCs to let PC users use files physically located on UNIX or other systems, and there are NFS versions for many non-UNIX workstations, such as DEC VAX workstations running VMS, to let VMS users join the fun. Gateways connect NFS to other kinds of networks, particularly AppleTalk, for the benefit of Macintosh users.

The original version of NFS was written for Sun workstations, so NFS still works better on UNIX than it does on other systems. File formats vary a little from one kind of computer to the next, which makes things — in classic computer style — not quite as convenient as you want them to be. On DOS machines, for example, text files are stored with two characters at the end of every line: carriage return (Ctrl-M) and line feed (Ctrl-J); UNIX text files use just line-feed characters. The practical effect is that DOS editors and word processors treat UNIX files peculiarly, often treating the entire document as one enormous paragraph with hard carriage returns where the line-feed characters were; UNIX editors handle DOS files acceptably except that they show the carriage-return character at the end of every line as the ugly sequence ^M.

# Ignoring NFS

Except when NFS screws up, you don't have to worry about using it. Your system administrator did all the hard work when she installed it.

Files passed over the network act almost exactly like those on the local machine; in most cases, you can treat them the same. The primary difference is that access to files through NFS is about twice as slow as access to files on the local machine. This problem usually isn't a big one because, for most of the stuff you do, the machine doesn't spend much time waiting for the disk anyway.

When you do something really big and slow (like repaginating a 500-page document), it might be worth it to see whether you can log in to the machine on which the files reside and run the program there.

## Where are those files, anyway?

NFS works by mounting remote directories. To *mount* means to pretend that a directory on another disk or even on another computer is part of the directory system on your disk. Files that are stored in lots of different places can appear then to be organized nicely in one tree-structure directory.

Whenever UNIX sees the name of a directory — /stars/elvis, for example — it checks to see whether any names in the directory are *mount points*, directories in which where one disk is logically attached to another.

Your system might have the directory /stars mounted from some other machine, for example, and then the directory elvis and all the files in it reside on the other machine.

### This ain't the local Mounties

There are two kinds of directories you can mount:

- ✔ **Local directories.** These directories are on disks on your own machine. Being able to mount local directories is useful if your computer has several disk drives and you want them to appear connected.

- ✔ **Remote directories.** These directories are mounted by NFS and are on disks on some other computer.

Your computer might have two disks, /dev/sd0a and /dev/sd1b, for example. (Clearly, the people who came up with these names didn't have us in mind.) Your /usr directory, which contains your home directory — and maybe some other people's directories too — might be on /dev/sd0a, and other files you use may be in /budget on /dev/sd1b. It is more convenient for /usr to be a subdirectory of the same / (root) directory as /budget so that you can use the cd command to move between them.

### The df command

The easiest way to tell which files are where is with the df command. It prints the amount of free space on every disk and tells you where the disks are. Here's a typical piece of df output:

```
Filesystem       kbytes        used        avail     capacity    Mounted on
/dev/sd0a         30383         6587        20758     24%         /
/dev/sd0g         57658        24254        17639     88%         /usr
/dev/sd0h         64378        61795        66146     80%         /home
/dev/sd3a         15671          030        13074     7%          /tmp
/dev/sd3g       1175742       758508       299660     2%          mnt
server-sys:/usr/spool/mail
                 300481       190865        79567     71%         /var/spool/mail
server-sys:/usr/lib/news
                 300481       190865        79567     71%         /usr/lib/news
server-sys:/usr/spool/news
                 298068       243877        24384     91%         /var/spool/news
```

The Mounted on column shows you the directory name you are used to. In this example, the directory / resides on a local disk (a disk on your own computer) named /dev/sd0a; /usr resides on /dev/sd0g; /home resides on /dev/sd0h; and so forth. (We won't go into disk names other than to say that anything in /dev is on the local machine.) The directory /var/spool/mail is really the directory /usr/spool/mail on machine server-sys, /usr/lib/news is really /usr/lib/news on machine server-sys, and so forth.

Some of the local directory names are the same as the remote machine's directory names — and some aren't. This can and often does cause considerable confusion; unfortunately it's usually unavoidable. A system administrator with any sense will at least mount each directory with a consistent name wherever it's mounted so that `/var/documents/bigproject` is the same no matter which computer you're working on.

A database known as NIS (Network Information System) makes it easier to keep the naming process straight. It's discussed later in this chapter, but, in general, don't worry about it unless your system administrator messes up.

## What NFS cannot do

NFS sounds great so far. Files can be, here, there, and anywhere, and it all works automagically! Works great, right? almost.

The problem is that NFS is not very reliable. In particular, occasionally it just doesn't work. Data sometimes gets lost. This flaw in NFS is in its design — recent versions have largely but not entirely alleviated this problem. If you want to know what the problem is, read the sidebar "Why NFS is out of state" (even if you do, it won't help).

### I refuse to update these files

NFS is particularly bad at handling simultaneous updates — that is, when different computers update the same file at the same time. Some locking features are supposed to enable different computers to take turns updating stuff, but the locks don't work very well.

The most common instance of simultaneous update is in databases. NFS just isn't appropriate for databases. Fortunately, any database worth anything has its own provisions for remote-access and locking, so in practice it's not a problem.

The place where simultaneous updates can be an issue is when you have a directory full of files that several people update (such as log files that people add notes to as things happen). If you do this in the obvious way with NFS, sooner or later (probably sooner), data disappears into the void. You can circumvent this problem relatively easily by always running on the same computer the program that does the logging, probably by using the `rsh` command described in Chapter 20.

### Mommy, NFS won't share

The other thing NFS cannot do is handle devices, such as tapes, printers, and terminals. Most systems that have a tape drive hook up the tape drive as a file called something like `/dev/tape`; that makes it easy to back up stuff by running a backup program and telling it to write the backup to `/dev/tape`. If your machine doesn't have a tape drive and the one in the next office does, you might think that the obvious way to make a backup is to mount the other machine's `/dev/tape` with NFS and tell the backup program to use the remote tape. That doesn't work.

Why doesn't it work? It just doesn't. NFS doesn't do tapes — or printers or anything else, except disks. To make the backup, you must do things the other way: Run the backup program on the machine with the tape drive and get to your files through NFS. Most system administrators and all wizards are painfully aware of the limitations of NFS and can help you make tapes on other people's machines if that's what you need to do.

## Why NFS is out of state

We discuss the technical theology of remote file access here. Still reading? Jeez, what a glutton for punishment.

There are two general ways to handle the communication between the server (the machine with the files) and the client (the machine that wants to use them). One approach is known as *stateless* and the other (for lack of a better word) is called *stateful*.

The stateful approach is more straightforward: The two machines have a conversation, the gist of which runs something like this:

"I want to read a file called `/usr/elvis/current-whereabouts`."

"Very good, sir — an excellent choice."

"Can I have the first piece of that file I just asked about?"

"Certainly, sir. It's so-and-so."

"Thank you so much. May I have the next piece?"

"My pleasure. It's such-and-such."

The only problem here occurs if one or the other machine crashes during the conversation. When it comes back, that machine has no recollection of what it was talking about, the conversation cannot be reestablished easily, and all sorts of special recovery schemes are necessary to get things back in sync. ("Beg your pardon, old boy, I've had a spot of amnesia. Can you remind me what we were chatting about?")

Back when Bill was writing NFS, he didn't feel like writing all that recovery code (it's difficult to write and boring, to boot) so he made NFS stateless. This decision gave NFS a severe case of amnesia on the part of all the servers. Rather than keep track of which client is asking for which file, NFS couldn't care less. The NFS servers don't have the faintest idea who their clients are, and they forget everything about a client from one request to the next. The conversation goes more like this:

"I want to read `/usr/elvis/current-whereabouts`."

"It's all the same to me. On my disk, it's file number 86345."

"Send me the first piece of file 86345."

"Well, OK, if you insist. It's so-and-so."

"Send me the second piece of file 86345."

"Who the heck are you? Hardly matters — I wouldn't remember, even if you told me. Anyway, the answer is such-and-such."

*(continued)*

*(continued from previous page)*

The advantage here is that, if the server crashes, when it comes back up it can pick up where it left off. Because it didn't know anything about its clients anyway, it doesn't forget anything. The disadvantage is that it's difficult to determine whether a request got lost or, because of network glitchery, got handled twice. In a stateful setup it's easy to tell: Every message has a number. If messages 106 and 108 arrive without 107 between them, you know that something got lost. Stateless messages don't have numbers (it wouldn't matter if they did, because the stateless server doesn't remember the number from one message to the next), so there's no way to tell whether a message got lost. In practice, if a client doesn't get an answer to a request within a few seconds, it repeats the request because NFS requests are supposed to be *idempotent* (this 25-cent word means that it doesn't hurt if the server does them more than once).

Most requests are indeed idempotent (it doesn't matter whether you write the same stuff to the same part of a file twice in a row) — but not all of them are. If the request was something like "delete the `furble` file" and the server in fact received the request but lost the response, the second time the client sends the request, the server complains that the file is not there and sends back an error (even though, from the client's point of view, the file was there when it asked to delete it). Are you confused yet? We certainly are.

There are more complex sequences of repeated and lost messages that can cause the contents of a file to be thrown away by mistake. (No, we don't go into detail — we know that you have already stopped reading this part.) Fortunately, such sequences are rare, although they have been known to happen.

If you are wondering why NFS doesn't handle tapes, printers, and the like, it's because even Bill couldn't figure out how to make an idempotent printer — one in which printing a page twice was the same thing as printing it once. Perhaps he could have used transparent ink?

# NFS and System Crashes

What happens if you're working with NFS, your files are stored on a server, and the server crashes? The answer is, you wait. Eventually, when the server comes back, you continue from where you left off. If it's a severe crash, you may wait a long time. In one extreme case (so we have heard), a program on an NFS client system waited more than six months while the server crashed, was dismantled and shipped back to the manufacturer and then was refurbished, shipped back, reloaded from tape, and rebooted — at which point the client program continued. You probably won't be so patient.

The worst practical problem is that, if a program stalls while it is waiting for a dead NFS server, there is no way to stop or kill the program, short of rebooting your UNIX computer.

Recent versions of NFS have features called *soft* and *hard mounts* (not as indecent as they sound, but close) that make it possible to stop a program that has stalled while waiting for a dead server. The problem is that if a server is merely slow and not dead (and believe us, a server loaded with hundreds of clients can be impressively slow), a client may assume that the server is dead and stop a program. Had the client been a little more patient, the server would have responded and the program could have completed its task.

## What's in a name?

One of the trickiest problems in networked computing is giving consistent names to everything. If user `melvin`, for example, has internal user number 1234 and home directory `/usr/drones/melvin` on one computer in a network, he probably should also have the same internal number and same home directory on all the other computers in the network. With this type of an arrangement, no matter which computer he logs in to, he can access the correct files. Similarly, every machine on the network has a name that must be known consistently by all the other machines, NFS directories should be mounted using the same names on all machines, and so forth.

In a network with more than two or three machines, keeping all the naming information complete and up to date can become a major challenge for the system administrator. The user names and user's directory names are in a file called `/etc/passwd`, the machine names are in `/etc/hosts`, NFS directory names are in `/etc/fstab`, and four or five other files should be kept consistent among machines.

Originally, the administrator had to update all those files by hand. (You can't just share them through NFS because it turns out that the system needs some of the information in those files to start NFS.) When a new user was added, all the `/etc/passwd` files had to be updated, and so forth. It was, to put it mildly, a pain.

An answer to this confusion is *NIS*, the *N*etwork *I*nformation *S*ystem. NIS keeps nearly all the name information in a central database on one or two machines called the *NIS servers*. (The NIS servers can also be NFS servers, although they don't have to be.) Every machine's copy of `/etc/passwd`, `/etc/hosts`, and so on contains just enough information to get NFS and NIS started; thereafter, all the user names, machine names, NFS directory names, and so forth come from NIS. To add a new user, the administrator has to update only the central NIS database; all the machines on the network then can retrieve from NIS the new user name, number, home directory, and any other relevant information.

It is a pain for the administrator to get NIS set up in the first place, but, after it's set up, it works well. Some administrators resist using it because they don't want to go to the trouble of setting it up. On a network of more than two or three machines, however, NIS is well worth the trouble.

NIS was originally called Yellow Pages, but the British phone company owns the exclusive trademark rights for that term in Britain, so the name was changed to NIS (a trademark no one else wanted). Some people still call it Yellow Pages, and some commands that control NIS databases still begin with the letters `yp`.

# What Other File Systems Do I Have To Contend With?

Although NFS is the most widely used network file facility, you may run into some others. Many of these systems can coexist — it is common to have a single machine running both NFS and RFS or both NFS and AFS. Here are other file facilities you may run across:

✔ RFS (Remote File Sharing) is an NFS competitor that originally was written at AT&T. (NFS is originally from Sun Microsystems.) RFS avoids NFS's reliability problems and flakiness, but works only on UNIX System V systems — not BSD, DOS, Macs, or anything else. If your entire network runs System V, your administrator may use RFS rather than NFS (then you can ignore all the rude things we said about NFS).

✔ AFS (Andrew File System), written at Carnegie-Mellon University, is designed to support thousands of clients that share more or less the same set of files. Unlike NFS and RFS, AFS works reasonably well over long-distance network links to enable machines thousands of physical miles apart to share files.

✔ Novell NetWare, the most common network for DOS PCs, also works on UNIX systems, generally with one or two UNIX systems as servers and zillions of PCs as clients. Now that Novell owns the company that supports System V, we expect to see much more NetWare on UNIX systems.

# Chapter 20

# Stealing Computer Time and Files — Network Bandits

*I*f your computer is on a network, sooner or later you have to use computers other than your own. You can do lots and lots of things over a network, but the two most widely used are remote login and file transfer.

*Remote login* is no more than logging in to some other computer from your own. While you're logged in to the other computer, whatever you type is passed to the other computer; whatever responses the other computer makes are passed back to you. In the great UNIX tradition of never leaving well enough alone, there are two slightly different remote-login programs: `telnet` and `rlogin`. A variant of `rlogin` called `rsh` lets you do commands one at a time on other computers.

A *file transfer* copies files from one system to another. You can copy files from other systems to your system, and from your system to others. There are two different file-transfer programs (how did you know that?): `ftp` and `rcp`.

## Logging In and Out

Telnetting (in English, you can verb any word you want) involves no more than typing `telnet` and the name of the computer you want to log in to:

```
telnet pumpkin
```

UNIX tells you that it is making the connection and then gives the usual login prompt:

```
Trying...
Connected to pumpkin.bigcorp.com.
Escape character is '^]'. SunOS UNIX (pumpkin.bigcorp.com)
login:
```

At the login prompt, you type your user name and then your password. After the other computer connects, you log in exactly as though you were sitting at the other computer. In the following example, we typed john1 as our user name and then gave our secret password:

```
login: john1
Password:
Last login: Thu Jan 7 23:03:58 from squash
SunOS Release 4.1.2 (PUMPKIN) #3: Fri Oct 16 00:20:44 EDT
1992 Please confirm (or change) your terminal type.
TERM = (ansi)
```

If the other computer asks you what type of terminal you're using, give the answer appropriate to the terminal you're using. If you're using an X terminal window from a GUI system, it's xterm. Try VT100, ANSI, or TTY if you're using a dumb terminal or PC.

The normal way to leave telnet is to log out from the other computer, like this:

```
logout
```

UNIX gives you the following message to tell you that the other computer has hung up the phone, so to speak:

```
Bye Bye
Connection closed by foreign host.
```

Sometimes the other computer is recalcitrant and doesn't want to let you go. Remember that you're in control. To force your way out, you first must get the attention of the telnet program by pressing Ctrl-] (that's a right square bracket). A few versions of telnet use a different escape character to get telnet's attention (it tells you which character when you first connect to the other system). After you get telnet's attention, type quit to tell telnet to wrap things up and return to the shell:

```
Ctrl-]
telnet> quit
```

# The Lazy Man's Remote Login

The `telnet` command is general. You can use it to log in to all sorts of machines — whether or not they're running UNIX. If you want to log in to another UNIX system, the `rlogin` command is usually more convenient because it automates more of the process. You use `rlogin` in much the same way you use `telnet`:

```
rlogin pumpkin
```

UNIX responds with the following:

```
Last login: Fri Jan 8 14:30:28 from squash
SunOS Release 4.1.2 (PUMPKIN) #3: Fri Oct 16 00:20:44 EDT
1992 Please confirm (or change) your terminal type.
TERM = (ansi)
```

Hey! It didn't ask for the user name or password. What happened? You frequently have a setup in which a bunch of machines use the same set of user names. (We mention this in Chapter 19. There's even a database called NIS that helps keep all the names consistent across all the machines.) In that case, after you log in to one machine, all the others can safely assume that, if you log in to one of them, you will use the same user name to log in to others.

The `rlogin` command also passes along the type of terminal you're using so that, even if the other system asks you to enter your terminal type, it always guesses correctly if you don't tell it explicitly.

If the remote system doesn't recognize your user name, it asks you to type a user name and password, just as `telnet` does.

## Escaping from `rlogin`

One place where `rlogin` is quite different from `telnet` is in how you escape from a recalcitrant remote system: You type ~. (a tilde followed by a period) on a line by itself. What you have to press is Enter (or Return), tilde, period, Enter.

## User-name matching for `rlogin`

This section is pretty nerdy. If you work in an office with a bunch of workstations, you can assume that they generally all share user names and skip this section.

Two files control rlogin's assumption that you want to use the same user name when you are logging in to other machines. The first is called /etc/hosts.equiv. On every machine, this file lists all the other machines it can "trust" to have matching user names. If you look at the file and find lines with + and @ signs, they mean that NIS is providing its own list of trustworthy machines (generally, all the machines in the department or in the entire company).

Individual users may have accounts on machines outside the local group or department. If you are in this situation, you can have your own file called .rhosts, which is sort of a private trusted-machine list. .rhosts has a list of machine names, one per line. If you log in with rlogin from any of those machines, rlogin forgoes asking for your name and password. If you have different user names on different machines, edit the file and put the appropriate user name after the machine name, as shown in this example:

```
pumpkin
squash
gerbil steph
```

Translation: You have accounts on pumpkin and squash with the same user name as on the machine you're using now. You also have an account on gerbil, but your user name there is steph.

When you have a different user name on the system you're logging in to, you have to use -l to tell rlogin the name to use. Suppose that you want to log in to prune, where your login name is sdl:

```
rlogin prune -l sdl
```

TIP

## Dialing out

Another command that acts sort of like telnet is cu (for call UNIX). It activates a simple "terminal emulator" program that uses a modem attached to the local computer to call out over the phone. Despite its name, cu can call *any* system that has a modem compatible with the one on your computer. The program is useful for calling on-line services like MCI Mail and CompuServe.

Your system administrator probably has set up the list of system names and phone numbers that cu uses. After they are set up, you call out by simply typing the following line:

cu *systemname*

You escape from cu and hang up the phone in the same way you escape from rlogin: by typing ~. (a tilde followed by a period on a line by themselves). You can give a phone number with no spaces between the digits rather than a system name to call a system not already in cu's list.

Notice that the system name comes first. If you have a .login file on prune that lists both the machine from which you are logging in and your user name on that machine, it doesn't ask you for a password.

# One Command at a Time

Sometimes rlogin is overkill for what you want to do — you just want to run one command on the other computer. In this type of situation, the rsh command (for *remote sh*ell) does the trick:

```
rsh pumpkin lpq
```

You give rsh the name of the system you want to use and the command you want to run on that system. This example runs the command lpq on system pumpkin (remember that lpq asks what's waiting for the printer on pumpkin).

The rsh command uses the same user-name strategy rlogin does, so if you can use rlogin to access a system and not give a user name or a password, you can use rsh also. But because rsh doesn't handle the terminal very cleverly, you can't use full-screen commands like vi and emacs. You can use ed, however. Wow.

An old program, also called rsh, sometimes conflicts with the rsh we're talking about here. The old rsh is the *restricted sh*ell: a version of the Bourne Shell that is of no use to you. If you type rsh and UNIX responds by displaying pumpkin: pumpkin: cannot open or displays a $ and sits there, you have the old rsh. If UNIX displayed the $, type exit to make it go away. If you have the old rsh, what we're calling rsh is probably called remsh or rshell, so try those names instead.

# Blatting Files Across the Network

Although telnet and rlogin may be the next best thing to being there, sometimes there's no place like your home machine. If you want to use files that are on another machine, often the easiest thing to do is to copy them back to your own machine. There two programs to do this: rcp and ftp. We discuss rcp first (because it's much simpler to use).

# The sweet-and-simple file-transfer program

The idea behind `rcp` is that it works just like `cp` (the standard copy command) — except that it works on remote files that you own or that you at least have access to. To refer to a file on another machine, type the machine name and a colon before the filename. To copy a file named `mydata` from the machine named `pumpkin` and call it `pumpkindata`, you type the following:

```
rcp pumpkin:mydata pumpkindata
```

To copy it the other way (from a file called `pumpkindata` on your machine to a file called `mydata` on a machine called `pumpkin`), you type this line:

```
rcp pumpkindata pumpkin:mydata
```

The `rcp` program uses the same user-name rules as do `rlogin` and `rsh`. If your user name on the other system is different from that on your own system, type the user name and an @ sign before the machine name:

```
rcp steph@pumpkin:mydata pumpkindata
```

If you want to copy files from another user's directory on the other system (suppose that `tracy` is the other user's name whose directory you want to pilfer), place that user's name *after* a ~ (a tilde) but *before* the filename you want to copy.

```
rcp pumpkin:~tracy/somefile tracyfile
```

To copy an entire directory at a time, you can use the `-r` (for *recursive*) flag to tell `rcp` to copy the entire contents of a directory:

```
rcp -r pumpkin:projectdir .
```

This command says to copy all the files from the directory `projectdir` on machine `pumpkin` into the current directory (the period is the nickname for the current directory) on the local machine.

You can combine all this notation in an illegible festival of punctuation:

```
rcp -r steph@pumpkin:~tracy/projectdir tracy-project
```

Translation: Go to machine `pumpkin`, where my user name is `steph`, and get from user `tracy` a directory called `projectdir` and copy it to a directory on this machine called `tracy-project`. Whew!

In the finest UNIX tradition, rcp is extremely taciturn: It says nothing unless something goes wrong. If you are copying a lot of files over a network, it can take a while (a couple of minutes), so you may have to be more patient than usual while waiting for it to do its work. It is finished when you see the UNIX prompt. We usually use Ctrl-Z and put rcp in the background, and then we know that it's done when the shell reports that the background rcp command has terminated.

If you copied stuff *to* another machine and want to see whether it worked, use rsh to give an ls command afterward to see which files are on the other machine:

```
rcp -r projectdir pumpkin:squashproject
rsh pumpkin ls -l squashproject
```

Although rcp is pretty reliable (if it didn't complain, the copy almost certainly worked), it never hurts to be sure.

## *The he-man's file-transfer program*

Sometimes rcp isn't studly enough to satisfy your file-transfer needs, particularly if you want to copy to or from a non-UNIX machine or if you want to retrieve files from a public file archive on a machine on which you don't have a personal account.

When you need more file-transfer power, you run ftp and give it the name of the machine to which you want to connect:

```
ftp pumpkin
```

The ftp program responds by giving a login prompt similar to what telnet does:

```
Connected to pumpkin.fruit.com.
220 pumpkin.fruit.com FTP server (SunOS 4.1) ready.
Name (pumpkin:johnl):
```

You always have to log in. The ftp program suggests that you use your own user name (as good a guess as any). Press Enter — if the user name it suggests is the one you want to use — or type the user name you do want to use and press Enter. It then asks for your password (the same one you use when you log in):

```
331 Password required for johnl.
Password:
230 User johnl logged in.
```

If you don't have a user name on the machine you're trying to access, you may still be able to use `ftp`. See the sidebar "Anonymous FTP" for details.

After you're logged in with `ftp`, you can use lots and lots of commands — far more than we have any intention of explaining. But, first things first: To leave `ftp`, type `quit`:

```
ftp> quit
```

The program probably responds politely:

```
221 Goodbye.
```

If `ftp` is in the middle of a long transfer and you decide that it's not worth waiting for, press Ctrl-C or whatever your interrupt character is (it's the Delete key in some places) to get back to `ftp`. Then you can either quit or try another command. When the network connection is slow, it can take the better part of a minute to stop a transfer. Pressing Ctrl-C over and over is a good way to pass the time while you wait. Perhaps a nice bossa nova beat is appropriate.

### Listing remote directories

An `ftp` command you use a lot is `dir`: It lists the directory on the remote machine by using `ls` (or an equivalent program if the remote machine is not running UNIX):

```
ftp> dir
```

The result of the `dir` command is that your basic `ls -l` report is displayed (see Chapter 4) with some junk from `ftp` that tells you what it's doing (see Figure 20-1).

The `ftp` command is the opposite of `rcp`, chattiness-wise. You just can't shut it up: It insists on telling you all about what it's doing.

### Copying files to and from the other system

To use `ftp` to retrieve files from the remote system, use the `get` command:

```
ftp> get .plan pumpkin-plan
```

You give `get` the name of the file on the other machine and the name of the file you want it to make on your machine. If both names are the same (they usually are), you can omit the second name. The `ftp` program gives the usual chatty report as it copies the file:

```
200 PORT command successful.
150 ASCII data connection for /bin/ls (140.186.80.3,1398) (0 bytes).
total 52
-rwxr-xr-x 1 johnl   staff      1066 Oct 21 16:23 .login
-rwxr-xr-x 1 johnl   staff       283 Feb 14 1990  .logout
-rw-rw-rw- 1 johnl   staff         2 Jul 31 00:03 .msgsrc
-rw------- 1 johnl   staff      1282 Jan 27 1992  .netrc
-rw-r--r-- 1 johnl   group       100 Jan 6 20:50  .plan
-rwxr-xr-x 1 johnl   staff       232 Feb 14 1990  .profile
-rw-r--r-- 1 johnl   group        57 Jan 8 14:31  .rhosts
drwxr-xr-x 2 johnl   staff       512 Jul 14 16:07 News
drwxr-xr-x 2 johnl   staff       512 Dec 22 18:15 bin
drwx------ 2 johnl   group       512 Jan 8 14:28  mail
226 ASCII Transfer complete.
1454 bytes received in 1.1 seconds (1.3 Kbytes/s)
```

**Figure 20-1**: An example of the result of typing the `dir` command in `ftp`.

```
200 PORT command successful.
150 ASCII data connection for .plan (140.186.80.3,1403) (100 bytes).
226 ASCII Transfer complete.
local: pumpkin-plan remote: .plan
102 bytes received in 0.051 seconds (2 Kbytes/s)
```

To copy files to the remote system, use `put`, which is much like `get`:

```
ftp> put letter-to-fred
```

The `ftp` program gives the same sort of output:

```
200 PORT command successful.
150 ASCII data connection for letter-to-fred
(140.186.80.3,2702).
226 ASCII Transfer complete.
local: letter-to-fred remote: letter-to-fred
2831 bytes sent in 0.067 seconds (41 Kbytes/s)
```

You can provide a second filename if you want to call the file something else on the other system.

ftp normally doesn't say anything between the time it starts to copy a file and the time it finishes. If you get nervous waiting for a large copy that takes a long time, type the hash command before you do a get or put. That tells it to print a hash mark (#) every time it copies a thousand characters so that you know that it's doing something. **Warning:** Watching those #s crawl across the screen is really boring.

### Changing directories

If the files you want are in some other directory on the remote system, ftp has a cd command that works just like the regular shell cd command — except that it is effective on only the remote machine:

```
ftp> cd mail
```

Of course, ftp, voluble as ever, tells you that the command worked:

```
250 CWD command successful.
```

If you're not sure which directory you're in, ftp also has a pwd command that works like you expect it to:

```
ftp> pwd
```

You get the obvious response:

```
257 "/mnt/users/johnl/mail" is current directory.
```

### Copying lots of files

If you want to use ftp to copy a bunch of files, typing all those get and put commands can be mighty tedious. You can copy a group of files with mget and mput. The mget command gets many files; mput puts many files. You list all the files you want to put or get on one line (you can even use * and ? wildcards). The files are copied with the names they already have. (You can change the names as you copy them, but the method is so arcane that even most wizards don't use it.) Each command asks, before it copies each file, whether you want to copy that particular file. Press y if you want to copy and n if you don't.

Suppose that you want to copy some files from the remote system's current directory to your current directory. To work with ftp interactively in selecting the files you want to copy, type this line:

```
ftp> mget *
```

```
mget budget? y
200 PORT command successful.
150 ASCII data connection for budget (140.186.80.3,2752)
(14657 bytes).
226 ASCII Transfer complete.
local: budget remote: budget
14750 bytes received in 0.27 seconds (53 Kbytes/s)
mget budgerigar? n
mget letter-to-fred? n
mget saved-messages? y
200 PORT command successful.
150 ASCII data connection for saved-messages
(140.186.80.3,2754) (0 bytes).
226 ASCII Transfer complete.
```

**Figure 20-2:** An example of the result of working with ftp interactively.

For every file you tell ftp to copy, it gives the usual report (see Figure 20-2).

To copy most of the files in a directory, the easiest thing to do is to type mget * or mput * and then pick the files you want as ftp asks the questions.

To shut ftp up so that it doesn't ask questions (a method more in line with the UNIX "you asked for it, you got it" philosophy), type the command prompt on a line by itself before you give the mget or mput command. Then ftp copies all the files you asked for without stopping. Be sure that you type the command correctly: This is a good way to generate a lot of useless network traffic.

### ftp*ing files that don't contain text*

Normally, ftp assumes that the files you're copying contain plain ASCII text. If the remote machine isn't running UNIX, ftp usually automatically adjusts the file contents as they come or go to account for the various ways other computers store text files.

As often as not, the files you're transferring don't contain text. They can be programs, databases, word processor files, or compressed files. (Even though word processor documents contain mostly text, they also contain nonprinting glop to specify page sizes, fonts, and the like.) Before you copy anything that doesn't contain text, give the binary command to tell ftp not to mess with the files and to copy them verbatim:

```
ftp> binary
```

## Anonymous `ftp`

If your computer is on the Internet, there are hundreds — maybe thousands — of machines from which you can `ftp` files by using *anonymous* `ftp`. Available material ranges from scanned images of girls in bathing suits (all G rated, so let's not be tasteless here) to transcripts of Supreme Court decisions. These machines let anyone use `ftp` and the user name `anonymous` to log in. You can usually use any password you want, but convention says that you use your full network e-mail address, including the @ and machine name (see Chapter 18 if you don't know what it is).

One large `ftp` repository is run by UUNET, a nonprofit service that handles enormous amounts of e-mail and netnews for UNIX systems. Their repository is on a machine called `ftp.uu.net`. Here's what it looks like when you log in.

After you log in, use lots of `cd` and `dir` commands to find out what's available. Most directories contain files called README that you can retrieve to see an explanation of what the directory contains. In many cases (not in UUNET, however), all the interesting files are in a directory called pub; type cd pub if the first directory you see doesn't look promising.

Most ftp archives are run informally by individuals at schools and companies; when you log in, they ask you to limit the amount you retrieve or the times of day you retrieve stuff. Please honor these requests or the archives will simply go away.ftp ftp.uu.net

```
Connected to ftp.uu.net.
220 ftp.UU.NET FTP server (Version 6.34 Thu Oct 22 14:32:01 EDT 1992)
ready.
Name (ftp.uu.net:johnl): anonymous
331 Guest login ok, send e-mail address as password.
Password: type your e-mail address here
230-
230-          Welcome to the UUNET archive.
230-   A service of UUNET Technologies Inc, Falls Church, Virginia
```

As you expected, `ftp` can't help itself; it says:

```
200 Type set to I.
```

(If you care, I stands for Image. But you probably don't.) You can use binary mode to copy text files from one UNIX system to another because `ftp` doesn't need to make any adjustments to text files between one UNIX system and another.

If you're copying large files (longer than 20,000 characters or so), you can save time if you first compress them to make them smaller (see Chapter 13), copy the compressed versions, and then uncompress them on the other machine. The time it takes to compress and uncompress can be considerably less than the time you save using `ftp` on the smaller compressed versions. When you retrieve files from a public archive, they're almost always in a compressed form to save disk space and transfer time, so you should read up on compressing anyway.

# Part VII

## Help!

The 5th Wave          By Rich Tennant

NETWORK JONES AND THE LOST FILE OF WENDY

Oh Nety—
be careful!

## In this part...

The point of this book is to help you when things go wrong. That's what makes it so different from "good news" books that talk only about how everything works in a perfect world. This part contains lists of things that can go wrong and error messages you might see, and things you can do about them.

# Chapter 21

# Disaster Relief

. . . . . . . . . . . . . . . . . . . . . . . . . . . . . . . . . . . . . . . . . . . . . . . . . .

## In This Chapter

▶ My computer won't turn on

▶ My mouse is acting glitchy

▶ The network is gone

▶ These aren't my files!

▶ It's not listening!

▶ I give up....

. . . . . . . . . . . . . . . . . . . . . . . . . . . . . . . . . . . . . . . . . . . . . . . . . .

*T*here is always the tiny, infinitesimal chance that you may run into some kind of problem with your computer. It can be something major (like losing the funniest interoffice memo you have seen in years) or minor (like accidentally deleting the analysis you have spent two months creating).

Some computer problems you can fix — some you can't. It's similar to cars: You can pump gas yourself and maybe change the oil, but, when it's time to rebuild the engine, call for help. (We do, anyway.)

This chapter describes some problems you may run into, with suggestions for what to do.

## My Computer Won't Turn On

You come in to the office one morning, flip the switch on your computer, and nothing happens. No friendly whir, nothing on-screen. Uh-oh. Lots of things could have happened, so check these possibilities:

> ✔ **Is the computer plugged in?** It sounds stupid, but we have had computer problems when the people who clean the office bumped their vacuum cleaners into the outlet that all our equipment was plugged in to. If you're using a terminal or X terminal, this check applies to both the terminal and the computer.

- ✔ **Check the switch.** If the computer is plugged into a power strip that has its own on-off switch, people have been known to turn off the switch inadvertently with their toes.

- ✔ **Is the computer still attached?** Are the cables that connect the computer, keyboard, screen, and whatever else still connected? If your terminal is connected to a network, is the network cable firmly attached to the computer? Try wiggling it a little even if it looks OK.

- ✔ **Is there power in the rest of the office?** Plug a lamp into the same outlet as the computer and make sure that it turns on. (True story: "Hello, help desk? My computer won't turn on." "Is it plugged in correctly?" "I can't tell. The power failed and none of the lights work.")

- ✔ **Is the picture on the screen turned off?** The computer can be on, and the screen can even be on, but the picture on the screen can be dimmed. Fool with the brightness knob (remember where the knob was positioned when you started fiddling with it).

- ✔ **Does your computer have a screen-blanker program?** Press a key (we like to press the Shift key because it has no effect on the computer) to make sure that a screen-blanker program didn't black out your screen as a favor to you. Moving the mouse a little also unblanks the screen.

If it's not a power problem, it's probably not something you can fix yourself. Call your system administrator for help. Some component may have burned out. Stay calm — this does *not* mean that the files stored on your disk are gone. They are probably fine: Disks remember data perfectly well with the power off.

# My Mouse Is Acting Glitchy

If you have a computer with a male mouse (see Chapter 8 for details on mouse gender), dust or crumbs inside it can prevent the ball from rolling smoothly. Most mice with balls have a way to remove the ball for cleaning, usually by turning a plastic ring that surrounds the opening for the ball. (We won't begin to suggest appropriate names for that ring.) Turn the mouse over so that the ball falls into your hand and not on the floor, gently wipe off the grit, and snap it all back together. Female mice appreciate it if you occasionally wipe off the mouse pad with a tissue. Also, look at the bottom of your female mouse: If it's turned on and working, you should be able to see a little, red lamp through one of the openings.

# The Network Is Gone

You can't print on the printer down the hall and you can't run certain programs. The problem may be that your computer is not communicating properly
with the network to which it is normally attached.

Most network problems are not for the faint of heart. You can try to check the
cables in the back of your computer. Is the network cable firmly attached to the
computer? Try wiggling it a little even if it looks OK. (See Chapter 7 for more
details.) Otherwise, it's time to call in the experts.

# These Aren't My Files!

Normally, when you log in, you start working in your home directory. If you
type the following line, you return to the home directory from whichever directory you may have roamed to:

```
cd
```

If `cd` doesn't get you back home, you may not be who you think you are. Try
typing `whoami` or `who am i`. If someone else's user name appears, your computer thinks that that's who you are! A co-worker may have logged in to your
computer to do some work for a moment.

You then have several options:

- ✔ Send some malicious e-mail; it appears as though your co-worker sent it.
  Delete all her files that look important, and then log out and pretend that
  nothing happened.

- ✔ Log out without fouling anything up, and then log in as yourself. Type this
  line:

```
logout
```

Maybe you have to type `exit` or just press Ctrl-D. At any rate, when you
see the login screen, log in as yourself.

Most courses in business ethics tell you that option 2 is preferred by all but the
slimiest of bottom-feeding MBAs, but the urge to send goofy e-mail is sometimes irresistible. Remember: You might be caught.

# *It's Not Listening!*

The computer is on, you are working away, and suddenly it doesn't respond to anything you type. It's the Abominable Frozen Computer.

The computer is probably fine — it's a program that has frozen up. Here are some things to try to get the program's attention:

- Press Esc a bunch of times.

- Press Ctrl-C a bunch of times.

- Press Ctrl-D a bunch of times. (You never know what will work.)

- If you are running X Windows, Motif, or OPEN LOOK, see whether you can use the mouse to select another window or whether you can type a command or two in a shell window. If you can, you can probably arrange to murder the frozen program and start it up again (see below).

- If your window system is completely stuck, you can usually murder the window system and start it over again and not have to restart your computer (see below).

If your computer is on a network or has more than one terminal, you can ask a computer guru to kill the program. If you're feeling brave, you can kill it yourself. When you kill a program, you lose any work you were doing in that program since the last time you saved data to the disk.

Tell the wizard what happened (in order), which programs were running, and what you did. She will probably kill the process (see Chapter 23). If you have a number of processes running, she may kill one after another until your computer feels better.

# *I Give Up....*

Sometimes discretion is the better part of valor (whatever that means). If you need to call for help, be sure to do the following:

- **Don't turn off the computer**. Unless flames are coming out of the screen and threatening to engulf your entire office, this is not a good idea. Even then, you might be better off waiting for it to trip the circuit breaker than facing your wizard, who will surely ask, "Did you turn if off?"

- **Know the symptoms**. Be ready to tell someone what happened and which actions you took to fix the problem.

✔ **Know what has changed recently.** Did you install new software? Did you run something you have never run before? New things are always suspicious. A claim of "I didn't change anything" does not endear you to your wizard. Something, somewhere, *must* have changed.

✔ If you call for help by phone, call from within reach of the computer. Your savior may want you to try a few maneuvers at the keyboard.

# Chapter 22
# The Case of the Missing Files

· · · · · · · · · · · · · · · · · · · · · · · · · · · · · · · · · · · · · · · · · ·

· · · · · · · · · · · · · · · · · · · · · · · · · · · · · · · · · · · · · · · · · ·

S ooner or later, you will delete a file by mistake. Scratch that *later*. Sooner than you think, you will delete a file by mistake. In far too many cases, you are out of luck, but there are a few things you can do to avoid disaster.

## How To Clobber Files

Contrary to the usual image of UNIX users being radically technical and without a creative bone in their bodies, we submit that typical UNIX users are immensely creative: They can come up with a zillion inventive ways to avoid the computer altogether and, when they are forced to sit down to stare the computer in the face, can come up with a dozen more inventive reasons for why things went wrong. There are lots of ways you can make files disappear (either intentionally or accidentally). The following sections list the three main ways you can trash files — although you can probably come up with a dozen new and creative ways to do the vanishing act with your files.

### Clobbering files with rm

Because disks are not infinitely large, sooner or later you have to get rid of some files. (Some wag once commented that the only thing standard among all UNIX systems is the message-of-the-day reminding users to delete unneeded files.)

The normal way to get rid of files is the rm (for *rem*ove) command. Until (notice that we didn't say *unless*) you screw up, rm removes only what you want it to. Recall that you tell rm the names of the files you want to remove like this:

```
rm thisfile thatfile somedir/anotherfile
```

You can remove more than one file at a time, and you can specify files in other directories (rm removes just the file and not the directory).

This method is usually pretty safe. The tricky part comes when you use wildcards. If you use a word processor that leaves backup files with names ending in .bak, for example, you can get rid of all of them with this command:

```
rm *.bak
```

That's no problem — unless you put in an extra space (DON'T TYPE THIS LINE!):

```
rm * .bak
```

Note that there is a little, tiny space between the asterisk and the dot. In response to this command, UNIX says this:

```
rm: .bak non-existent
```

Uh-oh. UNIX decided that you wanted to delete two things: * and .bak. Because the asterisk wildcard matches every single filename in the working directory, every single file in the working directory is deleted. Then UNIX tries to delete a file called .bak, which isn't there. Bad move.

At this point, we recommend that you panic, gnash your teeth, and throw Nerf balls at the computer. After you calm down a little, read the rest of this chapter for some possible ways to get your files back.

You can also make slightly less destructive but still aggravating mistakes when you forget just which files you have. Suppose that you have files called section01, section02, and so forth up to section19. You want to get rid of all of them and type this line:

```
rm sec*
```

Now suppose that you forgot you also have a file called second.version that you want to keep. Oops. Bye-bye, second.version.

The obvious solution is to delete things one at a time. But, unless you are an extremely fast and steady typist, that's not very practical. In the following sections, we make some suggestions about that too.

TECHNICAL STUFF

## Links, copies, moves, truncation, and other details about file destruction

Clobber-wise, copying files works a little differently from moving and linking files. More often than not, the practical difference is unimportant although, in a few cases, it can be worth knowing about.

The cp command does one thing as it clobbers a file; mv and ln do another. The difference is noticeable only if additional names or links were created for that file with ln. (See Chapter 26 for how to create links, or additional names, for files using the ln command.)

**Clobbering a file with** cp: Suppose that you have two files, first and second. You give second an additional name by using this ln command:

ln second extra.name

Now suppose that you accidentally (who knows why) type cp first second (remember that you already have a file called second). What happens to the file named second? The cp command replaces the current contents of second with a copy of first. That is, it replaces the text (or whatever) that second contains with whatever the file first contains. This change affects the file named extra.name too because this is another name for the file second. If you use cat or a text editor to look at either second or extra.name, you see a copy of first. The original contents of second and extra.name are gone with the wind.

**Clobbering a file with** mv **or** ln: "So what?" you ask, to cut to the heart of the matter. Here's the interesting part (interesting to us, anyway). If you had used mv or ln rather than cp, the second file would not be gone. The mv and ln commands don't fool with the contents of the file — they just change what filename is connected with what contents. Suppose that you type this line:

mv first second

The mv command disconnects the name second from its current contents. The contents are still linked to the name extra.name, so that file is still safe and sound. The mv command then connects the name second to the contents of first, and finally disconnects the name first from the file. Now there is no file called first.

As a result, the contents of the second file are not clobbered (you can use the other name for the file to see them). The ln command works the same way as mv to disconnect filenames and not touch the contents of files.

The message here is that if you have just fouled up an mv or ln command, you may still have hope of retrieving the old file (if it had other links).

**Clobbering files with soft links:** To add more confusion, the story is a little different if you use soft links rather than regular hard links. (See Chapter 26 to learn how soft links can link files from different file systems.) Because soft links are just aliases for the true file name, if you do something to the original file, all the links refer to the changed file because it has the same name. On the other hand, if you use cp to change one of the links, the cp command replaces the contents of the original file; mv and ln affect just the link.

Confused? The moral is the same with soft links: After a botched mv or ln, you may still be able to find the original file if it had another name. It can't hurt to look.

## Clobbering files with cp, mv, and ln

Are you feeling paranoid yet, as though every time you press the R and M keys you're going to blow away a year's worth of work? Wait — it gets worse.

The cp, mv, and ln commands can also clobber files by mistake: If you use one of these programs to copy, rename, or link a file and there is already a file by the new name, the existing file gets clobbered. Suppose that you type this line:

```
mv elbow armpit
```

If you already had a file called armpit — *blam!* It's gone! The same thing happens if you copy or link. (Copying is a *little* different: See the sidebar if you care.) Here's an example of the most annoying case of blasting away good files with trash when you use the copy command:

```
cp important.file.save important.file
```

As a responsible and paranoid computer user, you want to save a copy of an important file before you make some changes. But your fingers work a little faster than your brain and you get the two names switched (left-handed users are particularly prone to getting names sdrawkcab) — and *blam!* (again) you've just copied an obsolete saved version over the current version. Fortunately, you can arrange your file-saving habits to make this kind of mistake harmless, or at least mostly harmless.

## Wrecking files with text editors

The third way you're likely to smash files is in a botched editor session. The problem usually comes up after you have been editing a file for a while and realize that you have completely screwed up: The changes you have made are not what you want, so you decide to leave the editor. On the way out, however, you write the botched changes to the disk and wreck the original file. A similar problem occurs when you use an editor to look at a file; although you may not intend to change anything, you may make some inadvertent changes anyway. (This can easily happen in emacs, where pretty much anything you type goes straight into the file.) If you're not careful, you can write the changes to the disk by mistake.

If you use vi, you can avoid the accidental-clobber problem by typing view rather than vi. The view editor is the same as the vi editor (vi and view are links to the same program); view works the same as vi except that it doesn't let you write changes to the file. Keep it in mind.

Some versions of `emacs` can mark files as read-only so that you can't make changes to the files, but the methods of doing this aren't standardized so that we can give you any general rules. Ask your wizard as you pass in the hall.

# Ways To Try To Get Files Back

Well, now you've done it: You've clobbered something important, and you really, *really* want it back. Let's see what we can do.

If you're used to other systems, like DOS, in which you can magically "unerase" stuff, we're sorry to tell you that UNIX doesn't let you do that. If it's gone, it's gone. (A version of the Norton Utilities that includes an unerase command is available for some versions of UNIX, but it isn't widely used.)

## Copies, copies, everywhere

Maybe you have stashed away in a different directory other copies of the file you deleted. For our important files, we stick copies in a directory called `save` (or something similar). Also, sometimes you can reconstruct the information from a different form. If you clobber a word processor file, for example, you might have a backup version (the `.bak` files mentioned earlier in this chapter) that's pretty close to the current version; you might have printed the deleted file to a file (rather than directly to the printer) and can edit the print file back into document form.

If you share your computer with other people or use a network, see whether someone else has a copy. It's a rare file that really exists in only one place.

## Call in the backup squad

It's really gone, huh? Now it's time for the final line of defense: backups. You *do* have backups, don't you?

We interrupt this chapter for a stern lecture: *Always make backups.* If your system administrator is on the ball, tape backups are made automatically every night; all you have to do is go to the administrator, with chocolate-chip cookies in hand, and ask very politely for some help getting your valuable file back from the previous night's backups. If no backups exist, it's fair to jump up and down and scream that someone had better get on the ball.

Seriously, backups are a standard part of any administrator's job, either by making the backups personally or by overseeing operators who do the backing up. After the procedures are set up, making backup tapes is so simple that you can practically train your dog to do it. (One reason that it sometimes doesn't get done is that backing up is boring.)

If your system administrator doesn't make backups, you better learn how to do it. If you have a tape unit on your machine, the procedure is usually as follows:

1. Put a tape in the tape unit and flip the latch to seat the tape firmly.

2. Give a command to copy files to the tape, usually the tar (*t*ape *ar*chive) program; on Sun workstations, the program is bar (*b*ackup *ar*chive), and some System V administrators prefer cpio (*c*opy *i*n and *o*ut). The exact things you have to say to the tar program vary from one system to another, mostly because of the peculiarities of different kinds of tape units. You can't use the regular cp command because tapes aren't logically organized the same way disks are.

3. Take the tape out of the tape unit.

4. Write the current date on the label so that you know that it is a current backup. (The sensibly paranoid alternate several tapes, in case one of them goes bad. We describe this subject in more detail in the next sidebar.)

5. Put the tape back in its box and put the box back on the shelf.

If you have a lot of files, copying everything to tape can take a while (like an hour or so). You might want to do the backup over lunch. Or, do what we do and have your administrator arrange to run the tar program automatically every night at about 3 A.M. We leave a tape in the tape unit every night; when we come back the next morning, the backup has been done, and we take the tape out and put it away. The tar command creates a report that is e-mailed to us so that we can check to see whether the tape was written correctly.

Getting stuff back from a tape also involves the use of tar but is a little trickier because you want to restore just the files you clobbered. Ask for help — at least the first time. Generally speaking, you put the tape in the drive the same way as you did to make the backup and then type a tar command similar to this one:

```
tar xvf /dev/tape somedir/clobberedfile
```

The xvf option stands for *e*xtract *v*erbosely *f*rom, followed by the name of your tape drive (which may be different from /dev/tape), followed by the name of the file to get back. The tape spins as tar looks for the file. When it finds the file you want, it copies it to the disk and reports that it did so. If you clobbered a bunch of files, you can get them all back by using shell-style wildcards in the `tar` command, like this:

```
tar xvf /dev/tape "somedir/*"
```

We enclose the wildcard pattern in quotation marks here because, in this particular case, the `tar` program rather than the shell handles the wildcard character.

There may be other minor differences. In particular, before you try to get files back, you should change to the same directory in which the backup `tar` command was run, probably the root (/) if the system administrator backed up the entire system.

Some systems don't have tapes; they have floppy disks. Floppies are a major pain for backup use for two reasons: You need a stack of them, and you must format them first.

# Why you need backups

Making backups is a pain. But the question isn't whether you will lose data, it's *when*. Here are some events that have sent us heading for the backup tapes:

✔ The obvious one: We deleted a file by mistake.

✔ Just as we were saving a file, the power failed and scrambled both the old and new version of the file. Yikes!

✔ One day, while working on the insides of the computer (one of us is a closet nerd), we accidentally dropped a screwdriver on the disk controller card that attaches the disk to the rest of the computer. Exciting sparks came out and fried the card. We got a new controller card and found that, although the disk was physically fine, the new controller wasn't quite compatible with the old one and we had to reformat the disk and restore everything from tape.

✔ We remembered hearing that we should absolutely, positively run a "disk-head parking" program before moving our hard disk, so we ran one. Unfortunately, it was a version that was incompatible with the hard disk, so it parked the disk head right off the edge of the disk, way out past what you might call the Long-Term Parking Area. We could hear the disk head banging on the side of the hard disk as it tried to get back on. Rats!

✔ Back in the good old days, computers weighed about 15,000 pounds and you needed a fork lift to move one. Now they weigh about 25 pounds, which means that if the cleaning people bump into one with a vacuum cleaner, they can knock it over with a clunk that can put an unreadable ding into the disk. Oops — sorry, lady.

You probably have horror stories of your own, but they all have the same moral: Make those backups.

Before you can use a floppy disk, you must format it, which means that the computer writes some bookkeeping junk on it to mark where to put the data, and in the process checks to be sure that no bad spots are on the floppy. Fortunately, you only have to do this one time per disk. Formatting disks is easy but tedious, and, of course (sing along with us as we say this), varies from one system to another. You stick the blank disk in the computer, type the formatting command, and UNIX does it.

On Sun workstations, the command is `fdformat`. On PC UNIX systems, the command is `format`, but you have to give it the device name for the floppy drive. (The device name is something like `/dev/rdsk/f0q15dt`. Is this user friendly or what?) Ask for help. We usually stick a blank disk label on each floppy after it's been formatted to differentiate between floppies that have been formatted and those that haven't.

After you have an adequate stack of disks, you use the `tar` program to do the backup. Then you feed in the disks one at a time. Each disk takes only a minute or so to write, so feeding in the disks is an incredible waste of time because you don't change disks often enough to keep busy doing just that, but there isn't enough time between changes to do anything else. Maybe you could read the newspaper.

## My own backup cheat sheet

We've been dismayingly vague in our backup instructions because the details of tape and disk names vary from system to system. After you have pestered your local wizard or administrator one time, though, to get the command and file names, backing up is pretty easy. This sidebar provides a place to write down what you need to know to back up your stuff.

Backup device: ___ Tape ___ Floppy

Command to format a floppy
(not necessary if you back up to tape): _____

Directory from which to make backups: cd _____

Command to use to make backups: _____

You probably will want to store the preceding command in a shell script because it's a pain to type all that punctuation. See Chapter 14 for details on how to make a shell script.

The name of my backup script: _____

After each disk is written, be sure to write on the disk the date and the sequence number in the backup (if you need to restore stuff from these disks, you have to be able to go through the disks in sequence). In all, floppy backup is a poor second to tapes unless the amount you have to back up is small enough to fit on a single floppy. Tape drives don't cost much, so you may want to think about buying one.

## Backup strategies

The obvious way to do tape backups is to copy the entire contents of the disk to a tape every night. But here are a couple reasons that it might not be the best approach:

- ✔ The disk might contain too much stuff to fit on a tape. Tape and disk manufacturers continually battle to see who can outstrip the other. The battle is pretty evenly matched — as we write, they're both in the 2 gigabyte (2,000 megabyte) range, although most people are still using 150M tapes, which are smaller than most disks on UNIX systems.

- ✔ You might not notice for a day or two that you clobbered something important, so a scheme that gives you a few days' grace to get your data back would be nice.

- ✔ Murphy's law says that the system will fail as it's writing a backup tape, so you better not depend on one tape.

The best scheme is a combination of rotating and incremental backups. With *rotating backups,* a set of tapes is used in rotation; five tapes, for example, one written every Monday, one every Tuesday, and so on. Because each tape is written only once a week, if you delete a file by mistake on Tuesday, for example, the file is still on the Monday tape until the following Monday. You then have nearly a week to realize that it's gone and get it back. The number of tapes you use depends on your budget and your paranoia. Some people use as few as two, some as many as seven. (We use four because we bought a four-pack of tapes.)

With *incremental backups,* you back up only what's changed. Generally, you do a full backup of everything on the disk at infrequent intervals — once a month, for example. This process may take five or six tapes, but because you do it only once a month, it's not that bad a job. For the daily incremental backup, you back up only what has changed since the last full backup (it should fit on a single tape). Any given file then is either on the full backup (if it hasn't changed in a long time) or on the current backup, so there are only two places to look.

If you have a large tape budget, you may want to have two sets of tapes you use alternately for full backups, in case your system fails while it is writing the full backups. Sometimes, full backups are stored off-site in a bank vault or other safe place, but there's a trade-off: the security of the vault versus the inconvenience of going to the bank when you need to recover a file. If you're really paranoid, you can have two full backups, one off-site and one on-site.

Your system administrator should handle all of this, of course. It's useful to understand at least the rudiments of backup theory, however, so that, when the administrator hands you several different tapes that might contain your file, you will understand why.

# Three Ways Not To Lose Files

Now you're probably quaking in your boots (or sandals, depending on where you live). You figure that, if you so much as touch the keyboard, you will do horrible, irreparable damage and spend the next week spinning tapes. It's not that bad. Here are some tricks to avoid deleting files by mistake in the first place.

## Are you sure that you want to clobber this one?

When you delete files with rm, use the -i (for *interactive*) switch, like this:

```
rm -i s*
```

This line tells rm to ask you before it deletes each file. You answer Y if you want to delete it, and N to tell UNIX not to delete. (Remember that the question UNIX asks is, "Should I delete this?" and not "Do you want to keep this?")

The main problem with -i is that it can get tedious when you want to delete a lot of files. When you do that, you probably use wildcards. To be safe, check that the wildcards refer to the files you think they do. To make that check, use the ls command with the same wildcard. If you want to delete all the files that start with *section*, for example, and you think that you can get away with typing only *sec* and an asterisk, you had better check what *sec*\* refers to. First give this command:

```
ls sec*
```

UNIX responds with an appropriate list:

```
second.version  section04  section08  section12  section16
section01       section05  section09  section13  section17
section02       section06  section10  section14  section18
section03       section07  section11  section15  section19
```

Hey, look! There's that file second.version. You don't want to delete that; looks like you will have to type out section* to get the correct files in this case.

# Idiot-proofing save files

The best way to make temporary backup copies of files is to make a directory called save and put all saved copies of files there, as shown in this example:

```
mkdir save
cp important.file save
```

These commands tell UNIX to make a directory called save and then to make a copy of important.file to save/important.file. If you reverse the order of the names, nothing happens. Suppose that you type this line instead:

```
cp save important.file
```

UNIX makes this observation:

```
cp : <save> directory
```

UNIX is saying that you can copy a file to a directory but that you can't copy a directory to a file. As a result, it doesn't copy anything. To copy a file back from the save directory, you have to use its full name: save/important.file.

Here's a variation. Suppose that you have a bunch of files you want to get rid of but there are some good files mixed in the same directory. Make a directory called trash and then use mv to move to the trash directory the files you plan to delete:

```
mkdir trash
mv thisfile thatfile these* trash
mv otherfile somefile trash
```

Then use the ls command to check the contents of trash. If there's something in that directory you want, move it back to the current directory:

```
mv trash/these.are.still.good .
```

(The dot at the end there means to put the file back in the current directory.) After you're sure that there's nothing but trash in trash, you can use rm with the -r option:

```
rm -r trash
```

This line tells rm to get rid of trash and everything in it.

# Don't write on that!

Another thing you can do to avoid damage to important files is to make them read-only. When you make files read-only, you prevent cp and text editors from changing them. You can still delete them, although rm, mv, and ln ask you before doing so. The chmod command changes the "mode" of a file (as explained in Chapter 28). Here's how to use chmod to make a file read-only:

```
chmod -w crucial-file*
```

The -w means *not writable*. To make changes to the file later, do another chmod but use +w instead. (This isn't inspired command syntax, but the old syntax was even worse and used octal digits.) After a file is made not writable, editors can't change it. The vi program and some versions of emacs even display a note on-screen that the file is read-only. If you try to delete it, rm, mv, or ln asks you in a uniquely user-hostile way whether that's really what you had in mind. Suppose that you type the following line and crucial-file is a read-only file:

```
rm crucial-file
```

UNIX responds with this line:

```
crucial-file: 444 mode ?
```

The number may not be 444: it may be 440 or 400 (depending on whether your system administrator has set things up so that people can normally see the contents of other people's files). As with rm -i, you type Y if you want to delete the file, or N to say that you don't want to delete this valuable data.

# Chapter 23

# IDing and Killing Processes

## In This Chapter

▶ What processes are

▶ Where processes come from

▶ Where processes go and how to hurry them on their way

*A*ll the work UNIX does for you is done by UNIX *processes*. When you log in, the shell is a process. When you run an editor, the editor is a process. Pretty much any command you run is a process.

Processes called *daemons* lurk in the background and wait to do useful things without manual intervention — when you use lp or lpr to print something, for example, a daemon does the real work of sending the material to the printer.

Normally, all this process stuff happens automatically and you don't have to pay much attention to it. But sometimes a program gets stuck and you can't make it go away. If you use a personal computer running DOS or a Macintosh, the usual response to a stuck program is to restart the computer. When you run UNIX, restarting the computer is a little extreme for a single stuck program. For one thing, other running programs and other people who are logged in do not appreciate having their computer kicked out from underneath them. Also, it can take UNIX a while to restart from a forced reboot (it takes our system about 20 minutes to check all the disks), and you run the risk of losing files that were being updated.

You can almost always get rid of recalcitrant programs without rebooting. In this chapter, we talk about how to figure out which processes you have and how to make unwanted ones go away. Also, look at Chapter 15, where we talk about how you can juggle processes yourself and do neat tricks like stop one program, run another one, go back to the first one, and pick up exactly where you left off.

## Why processes are not programs and vice versa

Programs and processes are similar, but they're not the same. A process is, more or less, a running program. Suppose that you're using OPEN LOOK or Motif, have two windows on-screen, and are running vi in both of them. Although the same program is running in both windows, they're different processes doing different things (in this case, editing different files).

To add to the confusion, some programs use more than one process apiece. The terminal program cu, for example, uses two processes: one to copy what you type to the remote computer, and the other to copy stuff from the remote computer back to your screen. Sometimes there are "hidden" processes: Many programs have a way you can execute any UNIX command from inside the program. (In ed, for example, you type ! and the command you want to run.) In addition to the command, a shell process usually interprets the command.

In most cases, when you are looking at a list of processes from the ps command, it is easy enough to tell which process is which because each one is identified by the command that started it.

# Any Processes in the House?

The basic program you use to find out which processes are around is ps (for *process status*). The details of ps (wait! — how did you know?) vary somewhat from one version of UNIX to another, but there are two main kinds of ps: the System V kind and the BSD kind. (SVR4 uses the System V kind of ps, even though SVR4 has a lot of BSD mixed in.)

## Mind your ps (and qs)

If you run plain ps, no matter which version of UNIX you have, you get a list of the processes running from your terminal (or window, if you're using a window system). The list looks something like this:

```
    PID TTY    TIME COMMAND
  24812 ttyp0  0:01 csh
  25973 ttyp0  0:00 ps
```

The PID column gives the *process identification*, or *process ID*. To help keep processes straight, UNIX assigns every process a unique number as an identifier. The numbers start at 1 and go up. When the PIDs get inconveniently large (about 30,000 or so), UNIX starts over again at 1 and skips numbers that are still in use. To get rid of a stuck process, you need to know its PID to tell the system which process to destroy.

The TTY column lists the terminal from which the process was started. In this case, ttyp0 is the terminal, which happens to be pseudo-terminal number 0. (Because UNIX systems were written by and for nerds, they tend to start counting at 0 rather than at 1.) A *pseudo-terminal* is what UNIX uses when you're logged in from an X window or from a remote system through a network rather than through a real, actual, drop-it-on-your-foot-and-it-hurts terminal. For our purposes, all terminals act the same, be they real, pseudo, or whatever.

The TIME column is the amount of time in minutes and seconds the computer has spent running this process. (The time spent waiting for you to type something or waiting for disks and printers and so forth doesn't count.)

The COMMAND column shows the name of command that started the process, more or less. If the process is the first one for a particular terminal or pseudo-terminal, the command name starts with a hyphen. In this example, one process is running csh (the C Shell), and another is running the ps command.

## *Fancier* ps *(and* qs*)*

The System V version of ps has lots of options, most of which are pretty useless. One of the more useful is -f, which produces a "full" listing:

```
UID   PID    PPID   C  STIME     TTY     TIME COMMAND
john1 11764   3812  0  14:06:02  ttyp3   0:00 /usr/bin/emacs
john1 11766  11764  0  14:06:05  ttyp3   0:00 /bin/sh -i
john1 11769  11766  10 14:06:15  ttyp3   0:00 ps -f
john1  3812   3804  0  Jan 18    ttyp3   0:04 -sh
```

This listing has a few more columns than does the basic ps listing, and a few columns are different. The UID column is the user name, just what it looks like. PPID is the *parent PID,* the PID of the process that started this one. We had run emacs from the shell and then had told emacs to start another shell to run a ps command.

The parent PIDs reflect the order in which the processes started each other: The login shell process (number 3812) is the parent of emacs, which in turn is the parent of the shell /bin/sh, which is the parent of ps. (We could explain why the processes aren't listed in order, but, trust us — you don't want to know.) All processes in a UNIX system are arranged in a genealogical hierarchy based on which process started which. The grand ancestor of them all is process number 1, which is named init. You can trace the ancestry of any process back to init. "Hark! I am yclept Ps, son of Bourne Shell, daughter of Emacs, son of Dash-shell (or is that Dashiell?), great-great-grandson of the ancient and holy Init!"

The C column is a totally technoid number relating to how much the process has been running lately. Ignore it. STIME is the *start time*, the time of day the process began. If it began more than 24 hours ago, this column shows the date. TTY is the name of the terminal the process is using. If you run a GUI, like X Windows, Motif, or OPEN LOOK, and you run the xterm program in a window (as we did here), the entry for TTY doesn't show the terminal you are using. Instead, it lists the "pseudo-terminal" that connects the shell in the window to the xterm in charge of displaying the window on-screen (a largely useless piece of information). Sometimes the TTY column shows a ?, which means that the process is a daemon that doesn't use a terminal.

The COMMAND column shows the full command that began this process, including (in some cases) the full path name of the program. (Standard system programs live in the directories /bin and /usr/bin, so you see them a lot in ps listings.)

If you're logged in on several terminals or in several windows, you may want to see all your processes, not just the ones for the current terminal. With the System V version of ps, you can ask to see all processes for a given user:

```
ps -u tracy
```

This command lists all processes belonging to user tracy. You can ask to see any user's processes, not just your own. You can get a full listing for that user too:

```
ps -fu tracy
```

System V has other, less useful switches for ps, notably -e, which shows every process in the entire system.

## *Berkeley* ps *(and* qs*)*

The basic report from the BSD version of ps looks like this:

```
  PID TT STAT TIME  COMMAND
 7335 p4 S    0:00  -csh (csh)
 7374 p4 R    0:00  ps
```

The PID, TIME, and COMMAND columns are the same as those you already know about. (In the COMMAND column, the true name of the program is listed in parentheses if a dash or something is in the regular name.) The TT column lists a short form of the terminal name (pseudo-terminal 4, in this case). STAT lists the status of the process: R means that the process is running right now; anything else means that it isn't. Usually you don't care unless you have a stuck process and you wonder whether it's sitting there waiting for you to type something (then its status is I or IW) or running off into the woods (then its status is R).

Adding the -u switch gives a user-oriented report, although perhaps they had a different kind of user than you and us in mind:

```
USER    PID  %CPU %MEM   SZ RSS TT STAT START TIME COMMAND
johnl  7375  0.0  0.9  196 436 p4 R    14:59 0:00 ps -u
johnl  7335  0.0  0.6  196 316 p4 S    14:56 0:00 -tcsh (tcsh)
```

The %CPU and %MEM columns list the percentage of the available central processor time and system memory the process has taken recently (these numbers are usually close to 0). RSS is Resident Set Size, a measure of how much memory the process is using right now, measured in thousands of bytes (abbreviated as K). The ps command, for example, is taking 436K bytes (which is horrifying when you consider that the entire UNIX system used to fit into 64K total bytes). The START column lists the time of day the process began.

You can ask for a particular terminal's process list by using -t, as in this example:

```
ps -tp4
```

With the -t switch, you have to use the same two-letter terminal abbreviation ps uses. Have fun guessing it. Try the two-letter abbreviations that appear in the TT column in the ps listing.

There are lots of other useless options for the BSD version of ps, including -l for a *long* technoid listing, -a for *all* processes (not just yours), and -x to show processes not using a terminal. There's no way to ask for all processes that belong to a particular user.

To see all the processes you started, type the following incantation:

```
ps -aux | grep tracy
```

Replace Tracy's name with your own user name. This line redirects the output of the ps command to the grep command (described in Chapter 26), which throws away all the lines except those that contain your user name.

## Why cd isn't a process

People always ask us (well, someone asked once) why the cd command doesn't always act the way they expect it to. The problem is what is called in erudite circles *Lamarckian Heritability* but what we call "you look like your mother."

When a parent process creates a child process, the child inherits many characteristics from its parent, such as the user name, the terminal, and (this is important) the current directory. The child, ungrateful for its heritage as all children are, can change many of these things. Inheritance goes only one way, so changes in the child don't affect the parent. Suppose that you create a new process (type sh to start a new shell as the second process). Then go to some directory other than the one you were using, like /tmp, by typing cd /tmp. Then type pwd to make sure that you are in /tmp. Leave the new shell by typing exit and type pwd back in the old shell to prove that you're back in the original directory.

This example proves that cd can't be a normal command executed in its own process. If it were,

the new directory would apply only to that process; as soon as the process was finished, you would be back in the shell with the directory unchanged.

The authors of the various shells finessed this problem using what's technically known as a *kludge* (something that works but that you're not proud of; it rhymes with "huge," not with "fudge.") The kludge checks especially for the cd command and handles it itself in the shell. The exit and logout commands also are handled in the shell for the same reason.

Here's the example where you may run into this: If you make a shell script (see Chapter 14) that contains a cd command, the cd affects only subsequent commands in that script. After your shell script finishes running, you find yourself back in the original directory as though the cd had never occurred. Although it's possible to write a script that does change the directory, it's so complicated that even wizards shrink from the task.

# Murder on the Process Express

Suppose that you're running along, minding your own business, and you find that you have a program that just won't stop. Vell, vee haff vays to make eet stop. First, we discuss the normal ways to kill a process and then we get into some serious artillery.

## Fifty ways to kill your process

The usual way to get rid of a process is to press the interrupt character, which is usually Ctrl-C, although sometimes it's Del or Delete. In most cases, the rogue program gives up peaceably and you end up back in the shell. Sometimes, though, the program arranges to handle Ctrl-C itself. If you use the ed editor (if you're a masochist) and you press Ctrl-C, for example, ed returns to command mode rather than give up and throw away any work you have done. To exit ed, you have to use the q command.

If the interrupt character doesn't work, you can up the ante and use the *quit character,* generally Ctrl-\ (a reverse slash or backslash — not the regular forward slash). The quit character not only kills the program but also saves the dead body of the process (this description is awfully morbid, but we didn't invent these terms) in a file called, for arcane historical reasons, core. The shell then gives this requiem:

```
Quit (core dumped)
```

This message tells you that the process is dead and that its body has been put on ice with the filename core.

Most programs that catch Ctrl-C give up under the greater onslaught of Ctrl-\. If the program you were running is one written locally, your system administrator may appreciate it if you save the core file because it includes clues about what was going wrong when you killed the program. Otherwise, delete any core files with rm because they're a waste of space.

It is possible for a program to immunize itself to Ctrl-\ (ed, for example, just ignores it), so the next possibility is the *stop character* (always Ctrl-Z). The stop character doesn't kill the program, it just puts it to sleep and returns you to the shell. (See Chapter 15 for more information about what Ctrl-Z really does and how it can be useful even with programs you like.) After you're back in the shell, you can apply the stronger medicine described in the next section.

For Ctrl-Z to work, your shell must do some of the work. Many versions of the Bourne Shell aren't up to it and ignore Ctrl-Z. The C Shell and Korn Shell are Ctrl-Z-aware.

## Dirty deeds, done dirt cheap

No more Mister Nice Guy: It's time for merciless slaughter. If you were successful in the preceding section at putting the process to sleep with Ctrl-Z, go ahead and kill it with the procedure in this section.

All the following techniques require that you have a terminal or window in which you can type some commands to do the dirty deeds. If Ctrl-Z didn't work to put the process to sleep, you may not have a shell prompt at which to type the requisite commands. Here are other places you can use to type the commands to kill the process:

- ✔ If you're running a window system, any window other than the one with the stuck program will do.

- ✔ Otherwise, you may have to find another terminal attached to your computer or go to another computer on the network and use telnet or rlogin to get into your computer.

- ✔ If there's no other terminal or window and no other way into the machine, you're out of luck and probably will have to reboot. Before you reboot, check with your system administrator, who may know some other tricks.

Here is a simple two-step procedure for murdering a rogue process:

1. Find out the rogue process's true name.

2. Utter the true name in an appropriate spell to murder it.

The true name of a process is its PID, one of the things ps reports. First give a ps command to find out the PID of your victim. To determine the PID, follow these steps:

1. If you pressed Ctrl-Z to put the rogue process to sleep and you are using the same terminal to kill it utterly, type a plain ps.

2. Otherwise, if you use System V, type ps -u or ps -e; if you use BSD, type ps -a.

Suppose that you saw this listing after typing ps -fu john1, which lists all processes for user john1 (the listing is shortened to save space):

```
 UID  PID   PPID  C  STIME T TY   TIME COMMAND
john1 24806 24799 0  Jan 18  ?    0:39 xclock_
```

The PID of the process we want to kill is 24806. You kill it by typing the kill command:

```
kill 24806
```

The normal kind of kill sends a request to a process: "Please, nice Mr. Process, would you be so kind as to croak?" This method usually works, but occasionally a program won't take the hint. Another kind of kill, the ominously named Number-Nine kill, offers the victim no choice:

```
kill -9 24806
```

If you stopped a particularly uncooperative program with Ctrl-Z, a regular `kill` may provoke it to retaliate by trying to take over your terminal (something the shell fortunately prevents). Here's a true-life transcript of our attempts to murder our old text editor pal, `ed`. First we pressed Ctrl-Z, which put it to sleep. Then we tried a regular kill; when `ed` tried to strike back, we did a Number Nine. Sayonara, Bud:

```
% ed badfile
?badfile
Ctrl-Z
Stopped
% ps
   PID TTY    TIME COMMAND
 12746 ttyp1  0:00 ed
 12747 ttyp1  0:00 ps
 11643 ttyp1  0:02 -csh
% kill 12746
?
[1] + Stopped (tty input)  ed badfile
% kill -9 12746
[1]  Killed              ed badfile
```

# Resuscitating a Terminal

If you blow away a program that reads a character at a time from your terminal, such as `vi` or `emacs`, the dead process leaves your terminal in a rather peculiar state that makes it hard to get any work done. This three-step method usually brings the terminal back:

1. Press Ctrl-J. The shell may complain about strangely named nonexistent commands. Ignore its whining.

2. Type `stty`, a space, and `sane` (as opposed to the insane state your terminal is in). You may not see anything on-screen. Remain calm.

3. Press Ctrl-J again. This should put your terminal back in a usable state. For more about the mysterious `stty` command, see Chapter 28.

# When X Goes Bad

If you're using X Windows in any of its multiple guises (particularly Motif and OPEN LOOK) and are especially unlucky, X itself may freeze the entire screen. If you can get into your computer through another terminal or a network, you can get rid of X itself; this makes all the programs using X go away so that you have to log in all over again. The trick is to figure out which program is X. Here's an edited ps report from a System V system:

```
UID   PID   PPID  C  STIME  TTY   TIME COMMAND
johnl 24788 19593 0  Jan 18 vt01  0:00 /usr/bin/X11/xinit
johnl 24789 24788 5  Jan 18 ptmx  38:10 Xgp :0
```

In this case, X is called Xgp because the particular computer happened to have a graphics processor running the screen.

Here's the equivalent from a Sun workstation:

```
PID TT STAT TIME COMMAND
224 co IW  0:00 /bin/sh /usr/openwin/bin/openwin
228 co IW  0:00 /usr/openwin/bin/xinit — /usr/openwin/bin/xnews :0
229 co  S 149:23 /usr/openwin/bin/xnews :0 -auth /usr/johnl/.xnews
```

There are two easy ways to know which process is X:

- ✔ The command line has the strange code :0, which turns out to be X-ese for "the screen right there on the computer."
- ✔ The amount of computer time used is large because X is, computationally speaking, a pig.

After you figure out which process is X, you can give it the old Number-Nine kill and probably be able to log back in.

If you're using an X terminal, the Number-Nine kill doesn't apply because X itself runs in the terminal and not in the main computer. In this case, you kill X by restarting the X terminal. In the worst case, you turn the terminal off and back on, although your system administrator can probably tell you an easier way.

# Chapter 24

# My Computer Says
# It Hates Me

● ● ● ● ● ● ● ● ● ● ● ● ● ● ● ● ● ● ● ● ● ● ● ● ● ● ● ● ● ● ● ● ● ● ● ● ● ● ● ● ● ● ● ● ● ●

## In This Chapter

▶ Lots of error messages

▶ What they mean

▶ What to do about them

● ● ● ● ● ● ● ● ● ● ● ● ● ● ● ● ● ● ● ● ● ● ● ● ● ● ● ● ● ● ● ● ● ● ● ● ● ● ● ● ● ● ● ● ● ●

*Y*ou type a command. UNIX says something incomprehensible. What does it mean? And what should you do?

**Answer:** Look in this chapter for the error message. We tell you what it means and what you can do to fix the problem.

Most error messages start with the name of the command you tried to use. If you want to use the `cp` command to copy a file, for example, but you spell the name of the file wrong, `cp` can't find a file with the name you typed. So it says something like this:

```
cp: No such file or directory
```

At the beginning of the line is the name of the command that failed to work. After the colon comes the UNIX error message — UNIX's attempt to explain the problem.

This chapter contains the most common error messages, in alphabetical order. In some of the explanations, we refer to things called *arguments,* not because we are feeling argumentative but because it is the technical name for the information you type on the command line after the command. Suppose that you type this line:

```
cp letter.to.santa save
```

cp is the command, letter.to.santa is the first argument, and save is the second argument. You can have lots of arguments on the line: The number you need depends on the command you use (cp requires two). Type a space between arguments.

There are also things called *options,* which tell the command how you want it to work. Options always start with a hyphen (-). Suppose that you type this line:

```
ls -1
```

The -1 tells the ls command how you want it to display the files. Options don't count as arguments. If you type this line:

```
ls -1 *
```

the -1 is an option, and * is the first (not the second) argument.

This is really nit-picky stuff, but, if UNIX complains about a particular argument or option, it is handy to know exactly which item it doesn't like.

And now (drum roll, please) the error messages!

# Arg list too long

**Meaning:** The list of arguments (stuff on the command line after the name of the command) is too long.

**Probable cause:** When you type a wildcard character as part of a filename or path name, UNIX replaces it with the list of filenames and then calls the command. If you go wild with the asterisks, the result is a very long list. The list can be more than 5,000 characters long, so it is unlikely that you typed too long a list of filenames yourself unless you are an unusually fast typist.

**Example:** You are in the root directory (/) and you type this line:

```
ls */*
```

If there are a lot of files in the root directory and its subdirectories, */* turns into a really long list.

**Solution:** Check the wildcards you used in the command and use fewer of them.

# Broken pipe

**Meaning:** You are running two programs connected by a pipe ( | ), and the program at the receiving end of the pipe exited before it received all its data (see Chapter 6).

**Probable cause:** You get this error occasionally when you use a pipe to redirect the output of a program into the more program and then press q to cancel the more program before you see all the output. The program has no place to put its output because you canceled the more program, so you get this error. In this case, it's harmless.

**Example:** You type this line:

```
furgle | more
```

The furgle program (whatever it is) gives you screen after screen of boring information. You press q to cancel the more program, but the furgle program gives you the error message.

**Solution:** Nothing to do — it's not really an error!

# Cannot access

See the message No such file or directory.

# Cross-device link

See the message Different file system.

# Device or resource busy

**Meaning:** A device such as a terminal or printer is in use by another program.

**Probable cause:** Sometimes you see this message when you try to use cu to access a remote system by way of a local modem that's already in use (see Chapter 18).

**Example:** You type this line:

```
cu somesystem
```

**Solution:** Wait until the other program finishes using the device.

# Different file system

**Meaning:** You are using the ln command to create a link to a file in a different file system (a different disk or a disk on a different computer).

**Probable cause:** If your system can't do soft links (see Chapter 26), you can't create a link from one file system to another. The file you want to link to is probably in a different file system from the directory in which you want to make the link (usually the working directory).

**Solution:** Use the df command to find out which disks your computer has and which directories are on which disk. (See Chapter 19 to figure out what file systems you are dealing with.)

If your version of UNIX can't do soft links, you are out of luck. The only solution may be to make a copy of the file rather than create a link to it.

# File exists

**Meaning:** A file already exists by that name.

**Probable cause:** When UNIX expected the name of the file you want to create, you typed the name of a file that already exists.

**Solution:** This message is rarely seen because most UNIX commands blow away an existing file when they want to create a new one by the same name (which is not always what you want).

# File table overflow

**Meaning:** The system is way too busy and can't juggle as many files simultaneously as all the users have asked it to.

**Probable cause:** The system isn't configured right or someone is doing way too much work.

**Solution:** Complain to the system administrator.

# File too large

**Meaning:** You are trying to make a file that is too big.

**Probable cause:** There is a maximum file size for each user, set by your system administrator. Maximum file sizes prevent a messed-up program from making a file that uses up the entire disk by mistake. It is unlikely that you really want to make a file this big. Usually it happens when you use >> to add a copy of a file to itself, so you end up copying the file over and over until it passes the preset size limit.

**Example:** You type this line:

```
pr myfile >> myfile
```

**Solution:** Check the command and make sure that you are saying what you mean. If you are sure that you want to make a really big file, talk your system administrator into upping your file-size limit.

# Illegal option

**Meaning:** You typed an option that doesn't work with this command. (*Options* are things that tell the command how you want it to work. They begin with a hyphen.)

**Probable cause:** You typed a hyphen in front of a filename or you typed the wrong option.

**Example:** You type this line:

```
ls -j
```

There is no -j option for the ls command, so you get an error message. Frequently, after the illegal option message, UNIX also prints a line about usage, which it its cryptic way of reminding you about which options *do* work with the command. (See also the message Usage.)

**Solution:** Check your typing. Look up the command in this book to make sure that you know which option you want. Or use the man command to display an exhaustive and exhausting list of every option the command might possibly understand.

# Insufficient arguments

**Meaning:** You left out some information.

**Probable cause:** The command you are using needs more arguments than the ones you typed. UNIX may also print a usage message in its attempt to tell you which arguments you should have typed. (See also the message Usage.)

**Example:** The cp command needs two arguments: the first one tells it what to copy from, and the second one tells it what to copy to. You can't leave out either one.

**Solution:** Check your typing. If it is a command you don't use very often, check to make sure that you have the correct arguments and options.

# I/O error

**Meaning:** *I/O* is computerese for *input* and *output*. There has been some physical problem reading or writing information on a disk, tape, screen, or wherever your information lives.

**Probable cause:** Broken disk drive.

**Solution:** Tell your system administrator; you may have big trouble ahead.

# Is a directory

**Meaning:** You typed the name of a directory when UNIX wanted a filename.

**Probable cause:** The command you typed is trying to do something to a directory rather than to a file. You can look at a directory by using a text editor, but it looks like binary junk with filenames mixed in. You can't change a directory by editing it.

Note that emacs has a special mode for "editing" directories (called dired mode). But emacs has its own special way to create, rename, and delete files.

**Solution:** Make sure that you type a filename, not the name of a directory.

# Login incorrect

**Meaning:** You are trying to log in and didn't enter a correct user name or corresponding password.

**Probable cause:** There are two possibilities: One is that you typed your password wrong, and the other is that you typed your user name wrong.

**Solution:** Type very slowly and deliberately, especially when you type your password and can't see what you are doing. If you have trouble remembering your password, use the passwd command to change it to something more memorable (see Chapter 2).

# No process can be found

See the message No such process.

# No such file or directory

**Meaning:** UNIX can't find a file or directory with the name you typed.

**Probable cause:** You spelled a filename or pathname wrong. This happens to most of us ten times a day. If you typed a path name, you may have misspelled any of the directory names it contains. You may also have capitalized something incorrectly.

**Example:** You typed this line:

```
cp june.bugdet save
```

But the file isn't called june.bugdet — it's june.budget.

**Solution:** Check your spelling and capitalization. Use the `ls` command to see how the file and directory names are spelled and whether there are any capital letters. For path names, check to see whether it should begin with a slash (which means that it is an absolute path name which describes the path from the root directory) or not (which means that it is a relative path name which describes the path from the current working directory). See Chapter 5 for more information about path names.

# No such process

**Meaning:** UNIX can't find the process you are referring to.

**Probable cause:** You have given a command that talks about processes, probably a `kill` command to stop a runaway process. (See Chapter 23 for what a process is and why you may want to kill the poor thing.)

**Solution:** The process may already have gone away, in which case there's no problem. You may have mistyped the PID that specifies which process to do in. Check your typing and use the `ps` command to check the PID.

# No more processes

**Meaning:** Your system can't create any more new processes.

**Probable cause:** This message appears when you tell UNIX to create a new process, and UNIX can't. See Chapter 23 for information about processes.

Possible reasons for this message are that the system doesn't have any more space for this kind of thing. Occasionally you get this message on very busy systems when you try to run something, or if you start dozens of background processes (see Chapter 15).

**Solution:** Wait a minute and try the command again. If you have lots of background processes, get rid of some of them. If you see this message very often, complain to your system administrator.

# No space left on device

**Meaning:** The disk is full.

**Probable cause:** Either your files take up too much space or someone else's do.

**Solution:** Delete something to make space. If you don't think you can or you don't have any large files, talk to your system administrator. She has probably already gotten the same message and is checking to see who is taking up all the space.

# Not a directory

**Meaning:** UNIX needed the name of a directory, but you typed a filename or the name of something else.

**Probable cause:** Either you spelled a directory name wrong or forgot to create a new directory.

**Example:** You type this line:

```
cd /plugh
```

But there is no directory called /plugh.

**Solution:** If you are referring to a new directory you planned to make, make it first by using the mkdir command. If you are referring to an existing directory, get the spelling right. Use the ls command to see how it is spelled.

# Not enough space

**Meaning:** The system has run out of space in memory (not on disk).

**Probable cause:** Things are much too busy in your computer system. You probably caught UNIX at a bad moment when it was in the middle of getting itself organized.

**Solution:** Wait a minute and try the command again. If you see this message very often, complain to your system administrator.

# Permission denied

**Meaning:** You don't have permission to do whatever the last command you issued tried to do.

**Probable cause:** You are trying to change, move, or delete a file you don't own.

**Example:** You type this line:

```
rm /usr/bill/resignation.letter
```

But you are not Bill. You don't have permission to delete this file, so UNIX doesn't let you.

**Solution:** Use the `ls -l` command to find out who owns the file and what its permissions are (see Chapter 28 for information about permissions). If you think that you ought to be able to mess with the file, make your own copy of it or talk to the owner of the file or your system administrator.

# RE error

**Meaning:** You are using the `grep` program and it doesn't understand what you are searching for. (*RE* stands for *regular expression.*)

**Probable cause:** You probably have to use backslashes before a character that is a wildcard in `grep`.

**Example:** You type this line:

```
grep '[x' myfile
```

**Solution:** Put a backslash before any character that has a special wildcard meaning in `grep` (grep wildcards include periods, asterisks, square brackets, dollar signs, and carets). If you are searching for text that contains special characters, put single quotation marks around the text to match.

# Read-only file system

**Meaning:** You are trying to change a file that UNIX is not allowed to change

**Probable cause:** Some disks, particularly NFS remote disks, are marked read-only so that you can't create, delete, or change files on them. It doesn't matter what the permissions are for the individual files: The entire file system can't be changed.

**Solution:** Talk to your system administrator. Or make a copy of the file you want to change and change the copy.

# Too many links

**Meaning:** You are trying to make so many links to a file that you have exceeded the maximum number of links to a file.

**Probable cause:** The maximum number of links to a file is 1,000; you must be a heck of a typist to get this message. Because the parent directory is linked to each of its subdirectories, you also get this message if you try to make more than 1,000 subdirectories in one directory.

**Solution:** Stop making links.

# Usage

**Meaning:** UNIX doesn't like the number or types of arguments you typed after the command. It is telling you (in its own cryptic way) the correct way to use the command.

**Probable cause:** UNIX usually displays this message with another, more specific message. Check out the other message to see what the real problem was. The usage message is UNIX's reminder about how to use the command. After usage you see the command, followed by the options and arguments you can use with the command. Unfortunately, there's no clue about what the options do.

**Example:** You type this line:

```
kill abc
```

UNIX responds with this:

```
usage: kill [ -signo ] pid
```

This line means that the correct way to use the `kill` command is to type `kill`, a space, (optionally) the type of signal you want to send to the process, another space, and then the process ID. Not that this is entirely clear from the message!

**Solution:** Check your typing, as always. Make sure that there are spaces between things on the line (between filenames or between a filename and an option, for example). If this is a command you don't use very often, check to make sure that you have the correct arguments (filenames and so on) and options (things that begin with a dash, like the `-l` in `ls -l`). Look up the command in this book or consult the UNIX manual page about it (see Chapter 27 for how to display manual pages).

# 444 mode? (or some other three-digit number)

**Meaning:** You don't have permission to change this file but you have told UNIX to delete it.

**Probable cause:** You are using `rm`, `mv`, or `ln` to remove or replace a read-only protected file or a file that belongs to someone else. (See Chapter 28 for information about permissions.) Rather than refuse outright to do what you asked, UNIX asks you whether you really want to do this.

**Example:** You used the `chmod` command to make a really important file read-only. Then you decide to delete it by typing this line:

```
rm important.file
```

UNIX asks whether you really want to delete it, even though the file is read-only.

**Solution:** The question mark at the end of this message indicates that UNIX is asking you a question. By divine intuition, you are supposed to guess that UNIX is asking whether you want to go ahead and do the command anyway. Press Y if you want to go ahead and do the command; press N if you want to cancel it (for this file, anyway).

If you own the file, you can change its permissions by typing this line:

```
chmod 644 filename
```

Rather than `filename`, type the real filename. This command has the result of allowing anyone to read and enabling you to write to the file.

# Part VIII

## The Part of Tens

By Rich Tennant

©RICH TENNANT

"IT'S NO USE, CAPTAIN. THE ONLY WAY WE'LL CRACK THIS CASE IS TO GET INTO PROF. TAMARAS PERSONAL COMPUTER FILE, BUT NO ONE KNOWS THE PASSWORD. KILROY'S GOT A HUNCH IT STARTS WITH AN 'S', BUT HECK, THAT COULD BE ANYTHING."

# In this part...

Τhere's a lot of stuff in UNIX — much more than we try to stuff into this book. The real, official manuals for a UNIX system take up about three feet of shelf space. (For economical reasons, all the pages in those manuals are blank because no one ever reads them, but if you don't tell, neither will we.)

In this part, we try to organize some useful facts (as useful as anything about UNIX is going to be) into neat lists of ten facts apiece so that maybe they will be easier to remember.

Astute readers might notice that none of these lists contains exactly 10 items. Well, see, we were using mixed radix arithmetic (survivors of new math may remember some of this from fourth grade), so a chapter with 8 items has 10 items counting in base 8, a chapter with 12 items has 10 items counting in base 12, a chapter — what? You say that we can't bamboozle you with nonsense like that? OK, the truth is that we can't count.

So read on — there's some good stuff in here regardless of what the numbers say.

# Chapter 25
# Ten Common Mistakes

## In This Chapter

▶ Mistyping commands

▶ Believing that it will be easy

▶ Pressing Enter or not pressing Enter

▶ Working in the wrong directory

▶ Not keeping backup copies

▶ Not keeping files organized

▶ Turning off your computer

▶ Writing your password on a note next to the computer

▶ Sending angry electronic mail (flaming)

*H*ere are ten (or so) of the most common user mistakes we have run into. Although you will probably invent some new ones yourself, at least avoid the ones on this list.

## Mistyping Commands

If you type a command the UNIX shell doesn't understand, it says that it can't find it. The reason is that it looks high and low for a file with the name you just typed, hoping to find the program you want to run. And then it says:

```
blurfle: Command not found.
```

Or perhaps it says:

```
blurfle: not found
```

The exact wording varies from shell to shell (we bet you already guessed that).

- ✔ Check your spelling (as always). You may have typed a correctly spelled English word rather than the garbled set of letters that comprise the name of the program.

- ✔ Check your capitalization. Capital and small letters count as completely different things in filenames and, therefore, in commands too. Nearly every command uses only small letters.

- ✔ Change directories (maybe). You may have given the right command, but UNIX may not know where to look for the file containing the program. If you know where the program file is, move to that directory and give the command again. If you don't know where the file is, either look for it (see Chapter 26) or give up and ask your system administrator or local wizard.

# Believing That It Will Be Easy

UNIX was designed a long, long time ago in computer time (computer years are similar to dog years, except that 50 computer years equal a human year). Software design has made a lot of progress since 1972, and UNIX has not. If you are used to a Macintosh or a PC with Windows, or even a PC with DOS, UNIX is not going to be easy to use.

On the other hand, UNIX has a certain cachet and glamor; it takes a macho person (of either gender) to face it. You should give yourself major kudos, and maybe even one or two of those cookies you made to bribe your UNIX wizard, every time you get UNIX to do something useful.

# Pressing Enter or Not Pressing Enter

Depending on which program you are using, sometimes you must press Enter (or Return) after a command, and sometimes you don't. In the UNIX shell, you *always* have to press Enter or Return before UNIX performs the command. If you don't, UNIX waits forever for you to do so.

In other programs, particularly in text editors like emacs and vi, as soon as you press the command (Ctrl-K to delete a line in emacs, for example), the program does it right away. If you press Enter or Return after the command, emacs sticks a new line in your file and vi moves down to the next line.

When you use a program you are not familiar with, hesitate a moment before pressing Enter or Return to see whether the computer might already be performing the command. If nothing is happening, press Enter or Return.

# Working in the Wrong Directory

If you use separate directories to organize your files, make sure that you are in the proper directory when you begin working. Otherwise, UNIX won't find the files you want to work on.

To find out which directory you are in, type this line:

```
pwd
```

Remember that this command stands for *print working directory*. If you are really lost, you can type this line:

```
whoami
```

or type who am i. This command tells you your user name.

To move back to your home directory, type:

```
cd
```

# Not Keeping Backup Copies

Sooner or later, it happens. You give an rm command to delete a file, and UNIX deletes the wrong file or it deletes everything in the directory. Chances are, you typed an extra space or spelled a filename wrong, but the point is — what now?

See Chapter 22 for how to proceed if you delete something important. The best approach is to keep extra copies of important files: in another directory, on a floppy disk, or on a backup tape that either you or your system administrator makes. If you haven't talked to your system administrator about backups, now is a good time to find out whether your files are backed up automatically; you can also tell him which of your directories contain files you want to have backed up.

# Not Keeping Files Organized

Unless you do all your work on one or two files, you will run into trouble if you don't do the following:

✔ Make directories for the groups of files you use (see Chapter 5 for how to do this). Directories help you separate your files into groups of files you use together.

✔ Use filenames that mean something. UNIX lets you name your files with nice long names, so take advantage of it (up to a point, anyway). Filenames should tell you what's inside the file rather than make you guess.

# Turning Off the Computer

It's better to leave the computer on all the time than to turn it off at the wrong time. Chapter 1 talks about this subject in detail. UNIX can get messed up if you turn off the computer (kick the plug out by mistake, for example) without warning it that you are going to do so.

If you use UNIX from a terminal rather than directly with a workstation, it may make sense to turn off the terminal (not the computer) at night. Check with your system administrator.

# Writing Your Password on a Note Next to the Computer

OK, maybe this doesn't apply if you work at home, live alone, and don't have any friends, cleaning people, or burglars. But, otherwise, you should keep your password to yourself. Not that anyone has malicious intent — let's not get paranoid — but people can get curious around computers. And you never know when an inquisitive 14-year-old who knows more about UNIX than you do will appear on the scene. If you can't remember your password, choose a new one that is more memorable. See Chapter 1 for hints.

# Sending Angry Electronic Mail (Flaming)

There is something insidious about electronic mail. There you sit, alone in your cubicle with your computer, and you get ticked off at something, usually some stupid message sent by a co-worker. Before you know it, you have composed and sent a tactless — not to mention downright rude — response.

It is easy in e-mail to say things you never would say in person or even write in a memo. But e-mail has an off-the-cuff, spontaneous style in most organizations, and it can get you into trouble.

Sarcasm seldom works in e-mail — instead, you just sound mean. Gentle suggestions can turn into strident demands just because they appear in ugly computer type on a computer screen. Rudely mouthing off through e-mail even has a special name: *flaming*. A message full of tactless, pointless complaints is referred to as a *flame*.

Recipients of your mail can easily forward copies of it to anyone else, so imagine that everyone in the office might read your missives. Think twice before sending e-mail that contains negative remarks!

# Chapter 26

# Ten Ways To Find Those Lost Files

. . . . . . . . . . . . . . . . . . . . . . . . . . . . . . . . . . . . . . . . . . .

## In This Chapter

▶ How to use the find program to find a file when you know the filename

▶ How to tell find where to look

▶ How to look for a file when you know only part of the filename

▶ How to look for a directory

▶ How to look for files on other computers on your network

▶ How to do something to all the files you find

▶ How to use the grep program to find a file when you know what's in it

▶ How to get something else done while the computer searches for your file

▶ How to use the ln command to make files appear in more than one directory

. . . . . . . . . . . . . . . . . . . . . . . . . . . . . . . . . . . . . . . . . . .

*I*t's great to set up lots of different directories so that you can organize your files by topic, program, date, or whatever suits you. But, after you have files in all those directories, it is also easy to lose them. Is that budget memo in your Budget directory, your Memos directory, your ToDo directory, Fred's Budget.Stuff directory, or somewhere else?

There are two programs that can help you find files: find and grep. Alternatively, you can use the ln command to create links to your files so that a file can appear in several directories at a time, and you have that many more opportunities to find it.

Here is a list of commands to try when you are looking for a file.

## When You Care Enough To Know the Filename

With luck, you know the name of the file you have lost. If so, you can use the find program to find it. When you use find, you tell it the name of the file and the place to start looking. The find program looks in the directory you indicate, and in all that directory's subdirectories.

Suppose that you are working in your home directory. You think that a file called chicken.soup is in there somewhere. Type this line:

```
find . -name chicken.soup -print
```

That is, you type these elements:

- ✔ find (just as you see it here).
- ✔ A space.
- ✔ The directory in which you want the program to begin looking. If it is the working directory, you can type just a period (which means "right here").
- ✔ Another space.
- ✔ -name to mean that you will specify a filename.
- ✔ Another space.
- ✔ The name of the file you want to find.
- ✔ Yet another space.
- ✔ -print to tell UNIX to print (on-screen) the full name, including the directory name, to let you know where UNIX finds the file. If you omit this step, and find finds the file, it doesn't tell you. (We know that this is pretty stupid, but computers are like that.) If you use UNIX SVR4 or Solaris, you will notice that they fixed up the find command so that it warns you rather than run the command pointlessly.

The find program uses a *brute-force* approach to locate your file. It checks every file in all your directories; this can take a while. When find finds the file, it prints the name and keeps going. If more than one file has the name you gave in different directories, find finds them and reports them all. After find has printed a found file, you usually will want to stop the program (unless you think that there is more than one match). You stop find by pressing Ctrl-C or Delete. If you think that it might find a lot of files, tack |more on to the end of the command.

## When You Know Where To Search

Rather than use a period to tell find to begin looking in the current working directory, you can use a path name. You can type this line, for example:

```
find /usr/margy -name chicken.soup -print
```

This command searches Margy's home directory and all its subdirectories. (Her home directory name may be something different; see Chapter 5.) To search the entire disk, use the slash (/) to represent the root of the directory tree:

```
find / -name chicken.soup -print
```

If your disk is large and full of files, a search from the root directory down can take a long time, as long as half an hour on a very large and busy system.

You can even type several directories. To search both Margy's and John's home directories for files named white.chocolate.mousse, for example, type this line:

```
find /usr/margy /usr/john1 -name white.chocolate.mousse -print
```

If you use the C Shell, rather than type the home directory name, you can type a tilde and the user name; the shell puts in the correct directory name for you:

```
find ~margy ~john1 -name white.chocolate.mousse -print
```

# When You Know Only Part of the Filename

You can use wildcard characters in the filename if you know only part of the filename. (Remember the * and ? characters that act as "jokers" in filenames?) Use ? to stand for any single character; use * to stand for any bunch of characters. There is a trick to this, however: If you use * or ? in the filename, you have to put quotation marks around the filename to keep the shell from thinking that you want it to find matching names in only the current directory.

You can search the entire disk for files that start with budget, for example, by typing this line:

```
find / -name "budget*" -print
```

If you leave out the quotation marks, the search may look like it worked, but find probably hasn't done the job right.

# When You Want To Search for a Directory

You can look for lost directories in addition to lost files. Give the find command the option -type d, like this:

```
find / -name "Budget*" -type d -print
```

This command searches the entire disk for directories with names that begin with Budget.

# When You Want To Find Files on Other Machines

If your system uses NFS (see Chapter 19), some or all of the directories and files on your machine may really be on other computers. The find command doesn't care where files are, and cheerfully searches its way into any directory it can get to. Getting to files over a network is about half as fast as getting to files stored locally, so telling find to look through a lot of files stored on a network can take a long time. Consider having a long lunch while it does its thing.

Suppose that you're looking for Tracy's famous stuffed squid recipe. The obvious way to look for it is with the following line:

```
find ~tracy -name stuffed-squid -print
```

But, if you know that Tracy's files are stored on machine xuxa, the following line can be much faster:

```
rsh xuxa "find ~tracy -name stuffed-squid -print"
```

See Chapter 20 for details about rsh.

# When You Find Them

After you find the file or files you were looking for, you can do more than just look at their names. If you want, you can tell the find command to do something with every file it finds.

Rather than end the find command with the -print option, you can use the -exec option. It tells find to execute a UNIX shell command every time it finds a file. For example:

```
find . -name "report*" -exec lpr {} ";"
```

This command tells the find command to look for files with names beginning with report. Every time it finds such a file, it runs the lpr program and substitutes the name of the file for the {}. (You type two curly braces, which was some nerd's idea of a convenient place holder.) The semicolon indicates the end of the UNIX shell command. (You have to put quotation marks around the semicolon or the shell hijacks it and thinks that you want to begin a new shell command. If that didn't make sense, take our word for it and remember to put quotation marks around the semicolon when you use find.) Every time find finds a filename beginning with report, this command prints the file it found.

You can use almost any UNIX command with the -exec option, so, after you have found your files, you can print, move, erase, or copy them as a group. A slight variation is to use -ok rather than -exec. The -ok option does the same thing except that, before it executes each command, find prints the command it's about to run, followed by a question mark, and waits for you to agree that that would be a good thing to do. Type y if you want to do it, and n if you want it to skip that particular command.

By using find and -exec rm, you can delete many unwanted files in a hurry. But, if you make the smallest mistake, you can delete many important and useful files equally as fast. We don't recommend that you use find and rm together; if you insist, however, please use -ok to limit the damage.

# When You Don't Know the Filename

"Hmm...I don't remember what the file is called, but I'm looking for a letter I wrote to Tonia, so it should contain her mailing address...that's 1471 Arcadia ...How do I find it....?"

This is a situation for grep — a great program with a terrible name. It stands for, if you can believe it, global regular expression and print, or some such thing. The grep command looks inside files and searches for a series of characters. Every time it finds a line that contains the specified characters, it displays the line on-screen. If it is looking in more than one file, grep also tells you the name of the file in which the characters occur. You control which files it looks in and which characters it looks for.

There are three grep programs: grep, egrep, and fgrep. They are very similar, so we will just talk about grep (fgrep is faster but more limited, and egrep is much faster, more powerful, and much more confusing).

To look in all the files in the working directory (but not in its subdirectories) for the characters 1471 Arcadia, type this line:

```
grep "1471 Arcadia" *
```

That is, type the following elements:

✔ grep (just as you see it here).

✔ A space.

✔ The series of characters to look for (also called the *search string*). If it consists of several words, enclose it in quotation marks so that grep doesn't get confused.

✔ A space.

✔ The names of the files to look in. If you type * here, grep looks in all the files in the current directory.

The grep program responds with a list of the lines in which it found the search string, like this:

```
ts.doc: 1471 Arcadia Lane
tonia.letter: 1471 Arcadia La.
```

The program lists the name of the file and then the entire line in which it found the search string.

You can do lots of things with grep other than look for files: In fact, we could write entire (small) books about using grep. For our purposes, however, here are some useful options you can use when you use grep to look for files.

If you want just to see the filenames and you don't want grep to show you the lines it found, use the -l (for *list*) option. (That's a small letter *l*, not a number 1.) Suppose that you type this line:

```
grep -l "1471 Arcadia" *
```

The grep program responds with just a list of filenames:

```
ts.doc
tonia.letter
```

It might be a good idea to tell grep not to worry about capital and small letters. If you use the -i (for *ignore case*) option, grep doesn't distinguish between uppercase and lowercase letters. For example:

```
grep -i DOS *
```

With this command, grep, which is extremely literal-minded, finds both references to DOS and some "false hits":

```
fruit.study: salads; in Brazil, avocados are used in desserts.
chapter.16: DOS vs. UNIX
chapter.25: Dos and Don'ts
```

Finally, if you don't know the exact characters that occur in the file, you can use grep's flexible and highly powerful (that is, cryptic and totally confusing) expression-recognition capabilities, known in nerd-speak as *regular expressions*. The grep program has its own set of wildcard characters, sort of but not very much like the ones the shell uses to let you specify all kinds of amazing search strings. If you are a programmer, this can be very useful because you frequently need to find occurrences of rather strange-looking stuff.

The reason we mention this is that grep's wildcard characters include most punctuation characters:

```
. * [ ] ^ $
```

So, if you include any of these characters in a search string, grep doesn't do what you expect. To type any of these characters in a search string, precede them with a backslash (\). To search for files containing *C.I.A.*, for example, type this line:

```
grep "C\.I\.A\." *
```

## A quick 'n' dirty database

You can use grep to treat a text file like a quick and dirty database. Using a text editor, for example, you can make a file called 411 that contains the names and phone numbers of your friends and associates, with one entry per line, like this:

```
Jordan Young, 555-4673
Meg Young, 555-5485
Lydia Spitzer, 555-8649
```

To look up someone's phone number, you just type this line:

```
grep Meg 411
```

The grep program displays the line or lines of the file containing the name or names you asked for.

The grep program is widely used by UNIX enthusiasts for searching all kinds of files for all kinds of information. As long as each item fits on one line, you can keep all sorts of data in this kind of cheap database file. One of our favorite files is called restaurants and has lines that look like this:

```
Chef Chung's Chinese Vegetarian
Cheap 555-3864
```

So, if you're in the mood for something cheap, you can say

```
grep -i cheap restaurants
```

The period (.) is grep's wildcard character, like the question mark (?) in the shell. In this example, if you hadn't preceded the periods with backslashes, grep would have matched not only *C.I.A.* but also *CHIFAS* (a Peruvian dialect word meaning *Chinese restaurants,* in case you were wondering) and lots of other things. But don't press your luck — use the backslashes with punctuation marks to be safe.

# When You Don't Want to Wait

Because the grep and find commands can take a couple minutes to do their work, you may want to run them in the background (see Chapter 15). To do this, redirect their output to a file so that you can review the results of the search at your leisure; end the command with an ampersand (&), which tells UNIX to run the command in the background. You can type these two commands, for example:

```
find / -name "budget*" -print > budget.files &
grep "chocolate mousse" * > mousse.recipe.files &
```

When the jobs end, you can type the following to see what they found:

```
cat budget.files
cat mousse.recipe.files
```

# When You Want To Share a File

Sometimes it's nice for a file to be in more than one place (that budget file we keep mentioning, for example). If you were working on it with someone else, it would be nice if it could be in both your home directory and your co-worker's home directory so that neither of you would have to use the cd command to get to it.

A nice feature of UNIX (and you thought there weren't any!) is that this is possible — even easy. A single file can have more than one name, and the names can be in different directories.

Take, for example, two authors working on a book together (a totally hypothetical example). The chapters of the book are in John's directory: /usr/johnl/book. But what about Margy? It's annoying to have to type this line every time work on the book begins:

```
cd /usr/johnl/book
```

Instead, it would be nice if the files could also be in /usr/margy/book.

# How can you be in two places at a time when you're not anywhere at all?

The way to do this is with the `ln` (for *link*) command. You tell `ln` two things:

- ✔ The current name of the file or files you want to create links to
- ✔ The new name

Let's start with just one file. Margy wants to make a link to the file named `chapterlog` (it contains the list of chapters). The file is in `/usr/johnl/book`. In her `book` directory, Margy types this line:

```
ln /usr/johnl/book/chapterlog booklog
```

UNIX says absolutely nothing; it just displays another prompt. (No news is good news.) But it just created a *link*, or new name, to the existing `chapterlog` file. The file now appears also in `/usr/margy/book` as `booklog`.

## How to play the links

After you create a link by using `ln`, the file has two names in two directories. The names are equally valid. It isn't as though `/usr/johnl/book/chapterlog` is the "real" name and `/usr/margy/book/booklog` is an alias. UNIX considers both names to be equally important links to the file.

## How to delete links

To delete a link, you use the same `rm` command you use to delete a file. In fact, `rm` always just deletes a link. It just so happens that, when there are no links to a file, the file dries up and blows away. So when you `rm` a file that has just one name (link), the file gets deleted. When you `rm` a file that has more than one name (link), the command deletes the specified link (name), but the file remains unchanged, along with any other links it may have had.

## How to call a link a lunk

You can use the old `mv` command to rename a link too. If Margy decides that it would be less confusing for the book-status file to have the same name in both places (as it stands now, it's `chapterlog` to John and `booklog` to Margy), she can type this line:

```
mv booklog chapterlog
```

You can even use the `mv` command to move the file to another directory.

## *How to link a bunch of files*

You can also use ln to link a bunch of files at the same time. In this case, you tell ln two things:

- ✔ The bunch of files you want to link, probably using a wildcard character like chapter*. You can also type a series of filenames or a combination of names and patterns. (UNIX may be obscure, but it's flexible.)

- ✔ The name of the directory in which you want to put all the new links.

The ln command uses the same names the files currently have when it makes the new links. It just puts them in a different directory.

The chapterlog business in the preceding example, for example, works so well that Margy decides to link to all the files in /usr/john1/book. To make links in /usr/margy/book, she types this line:

```
ln /usr/john1/book/* /usr/margy/book
```

This command tells UNIX to create links for all the files in /usr/john1/book and to put the new links in /usr/margy/book. Now every file that exists in /usr/john1/book also exists in /usr/margy/book. Margy uses the ls command to look at a file listing for her new book directory. It contains all the book files. This arrangement makes working on the files much more convenient.

## Linking once and linking twice

Here's one caveat, though. The ln command in the previous example links all the files that exist at the time the command was given. If you add new files to either /usr/margy/book or /usr/john1/book, the new files are not automatically linked to the other directory. To fix this, you can type the same ln command every few days (or whatever frequency makes sense). The command tells you that lots of files are already identical in the two directories and makes links for the new files.

If you create links to someone else's files that you don't have permission to write to, the new links don't change your permissions. Although you still can't write to the files, you can fool around with

links to them. If you use the ln command to update the links, UNIX notices that you didn't have permission to write the old version. Maybe it was an important file that you shouldn't replace, so it displays a warning message, something like this:

ln: chapter13: 644 mode?

See Chapter 24 for the exact meaning of this uniquely obscure message. Type y if you want to replace the link, which you probably do in this case, or n if you don't.

You might think that having made the link, you now can't change the link either. You *can* change the link, you just can't change the file.

# How to link across the great computer divide

All this talk about links assumes that the files you are linking to are on the same file system (that's UNIX-speak for *disk* or *disk partition*). If your computer has several hard disks, or if you are on a network and use files on other computers (through NFS or some other system, as explained in Chapter 19), some of the files you work with may be on different file systems.

Here's the bad news: The `ln` command can't create links to files on other file systems. Bummer. But there's good news for some readers: UNIX BSD and SVR4 systems have things called soft links that are almost as good.

*Soft links* or *symbolic links* (*symlinks* for short) let you use two or more different names for the same file. But, unlike regular links (or *hard links*), soft links are just imitation links. UNIX doesn't consider them to be the file's real name.

### Making soft links (for users of UNIX BSD and SVR4 only)

To make a soft link, add the `-s` option to the `ln` command.

Suppose that you want a link in your home directory to the `recipe.list` file in `/usr/gita`. In your home directory, you type this line:

```
ln /usr/gita/recipe.list gitas.recipes
```

Rather than respond with serene silence, UNIX responds with this line:

```
ln: different file system
```

Drat! Gita's home directory is on a different file system from yours, perhaps even on a file system that resides on a different computer. So you make a soft link by sticking a `-s` in the command:

```
ln -s /usr/gita/recipe.list gitas.recipes
```

As usual, no news is good news; `ln` says nothing if it worked. Now there appears to be a file in your home directory called `gitas.recipes`. All through the magic of soft links.

### Using soft links

You can look at, copy, print, and rename a soft-linked file as usual. If you have the proper permissions, you can edit it. But, if Gita deletes her file, the file vanishes. Your soft link now links to an empty hole rather than to a file, and you get an error message if you try to use the file. UNIX knows that the soft link isn't the file's "real" name. When you see a soft link in a long ls listing, UNIX gives the name of the soft link and also the name of the file it refers to.

If you try to use a file and UNIX says that it isn't there, check to see whether it's a dangling soft link. Type ls -l to see whether the file is a soft link. If it is, use another ls -l on the real filename to make sure that the file really exists.

To get rid of a dangling soft link (a link to a non-existent file), use the rm command to delete it.

# Chapter 27

# Ten Times More Information Than You Want about UNIX

*Y*ou thought that UNIX was completely unhelpful. For the most part, you are absolutely right. But a standard UNIX command called man (for *man*ual) can give you on-line help.

Sound good? Well, yes and no. The information is there, all right, but it is written in a rather nerdy style and can be difficult to decipher; of course, each part of the on-line manual is written on the assumption that you have read all the other parts and know what all the commands are called.

It's definitely worth knowing about, though, when you just can't remember the options for a command or what to type where on the command line after the command name.

## Let's Hear It from the man

The man's on-line manual contains *manual pages* for every UNIX command, and other pages about internal functions that programmers use, formats for various system file types, descriptions of some of the hardware that can be attached to your UNIX system, and other odds and ends. When you type the man command, you indicate which page or pages you want.

All manual pages have a standard format. Figure 27-1 shows part of the manual page for dcheck, a program a system administrator might use to deal with people whose files take up too much space on the disk.

```
DCHECK(1)        Diskhog          DCHECK(1)
NAME
  dcheck - send mail to potential disk hogs
SYNOPSIS
  dcheck
DESCRIPTION
  dcheck is normally run from the cron procedure to check
  if users are taking up too much space. It creates a tag
  file for such users, will send them warning mail, and
  also sends mail to the system administrator about what
  it's done.
SEE ALSO
  diskhog(1).
FILES
  $DQUOTAS/hogs/$LOGNAME -  tag file indicating that
                           diskhog should be run
WARNINGS
  Should know about multiple file systems.
BUGS
  None.
```

**Figure 27-1:** Part of the manual page for dcheck.

The parts of the manual page include the following:

✔ The title of the manual page is the first line. It includes the name and page number of the manual page at the left and right ends of the line. Centered on the line may be the name of the system of which the command is a part. In this example, the dcheck command is part of the diskhog system.

✔ NAME: The one-line name of the manual page. The name is usually the command or commands the page is about, as well as a brief description.

✔ SYNOPSIS: What you type when you give the command, with a terse and cryptic example of every option available. This often makes no sense until you read the description that follows. Sometimes it still makes no sense.

✔ DESCRIPTION: A few paragraphs about the command. For commands with a lot of options, the description can run for a few pages. There is usually a list of the options with an explanation of every one. Sometimes there are examples, although not often enough.

✔ SEE ALSO: This section lists names of related manual pages, if any.

✔ WARNINGS and BUGS: If the command has known bugs or common problems, they may be listed here. Then again, they may not be.

✔ FILES: A list of the files this command uses. The elm and mail commands, for example, use your Mail directory, the central list of mailboxes, and other files. (These files usually are set up by your system administrator and rarely are things you want to fool with yourself.) The manual pages for elm and mail mention these files.

## Reading manual pages

To see a manual page, type this line:

```
man unixcommand
```

Except, of course, you substitute for *unixcommand* the name of the UNIX command you are interested in. Some versions of man present the manual page a screen at a time. Other versions just whip the page by at maximum speed and assume that you can read 150,000 words per minute. If that happens (and you can't read that fast), you can use the usual more command to show you the manual page a screen at a time:

```
man unixcommand | more
```

On the other hand, if you're on a system that normally presents a the manual a screen at a time and you want it to whip by at full speed because you're an Evelyn Wood graduate (or, more likely, because your terminal is really a PC and you've turned on screen capture mode), type this line:

```
man - unixcommand
```

## Printing manual pages

You can also print the manual pages for later perusal. To print the manual pages, type this line:

```
man unixcommand | lpr
```

Remember to use lp, if that is the command you use to print. It might be better to put the manual pages in a file first, remove the information you don't want, and print the result. You could type this line, for example (remember to substitute for filename the name of the file you want the information in):

```
man unixcommand > filename
```

Then edit the file with a text editor (see Chapter 12) and print it (see Chapter 9). Before you print the file, however, keep in mind that the on-line manual pages are generally identical to the printed manual pages in the dusty UNIX manuals on the shelf, except that the printed manual pages are typeset so that they're easier to read. Rather than print the on-line page, it's often better to look it up in the paper manual. (Bet you didn't think we would *ever* tell you to do that!)

## Finding the manual page you want

If you use the man command, there is no good way to find out which manual pages are available. Sometimes it can be difficult to find the one you want. Suppose that you type this line:

```
man ln | more
```

UNIX shows you this message:

```
man: ln not found
```

There is no separate manual page for the ln command. Instead, it shares a set of pages with cp and mv. You get information about ln by typing this line:

```
man cp | more
```

(Typical UNIX ease of use!) If man doesn't display anything about the command you want, try some similar commands. BSD UNIX systems have an apropos command that suggests manual pages relevant to a particular topic, so you can type apropos ln to see what it has to say.

In addition to manual pages about commands, there are lots of pages about other topics. You can type this line, for example:

```
man ascii
```

If necessary, you can type this line:

```
man ascii | more
```

This command shows you a table of the ASCII-character codes for all the characters text files can contain. You probably aren't interested in them, but it does look impressively technoid.

## It's a bird, it's a plane, it's xman!

If you use X Windows (or OPEN LOOK or Motif), you can use the xman command to look at manual pages. The nice thing about xman is that it displays a list of the available manual pages. When you run xman, it pops up a little box with three buttons, one of which is labeled Manual Page. If you click on it, a larger window then displays a manual page describing xman. Select Display Directory from the Options menu on that page, or press Ctrl-D as a shortcut, to see a screen of all of the manual pages it has, probably more than 100 of them. Click on the one you want to see, and xman switches to that page. Press Ctrl-D again to return to the directory of manual pages. Read the initial description of xman for other tricks you can get xman to do, like show you two or three different pages at a time, or search for keywords in manual-page titles.

# Other Sources of Information

Your system administrator or nearby UNIX users probably have copies of UNIX manuals lying around. The pages of some of these manuals usually look very much like the manual pages you get with man.

The advantage of the printed manual is that an index is in the front (or the back). It is usually a permuted or KWIC index (an overly clever abbreviation for *key word in context*), which means that you can find an entry by looking under any of the words in the title except for boring ones like *the*. To find the page for the cp command (the title of the manual page is *cp, ln, mv - copy, link, or move files*), for example, you can look in the permuted index under *cp, ln, mv, copy, link, move,* or *files.*

Then again, it's not a bad idea to try typing this line, just to see what happens:

```
help
```

Someone may have installed some kind of help system — you never know.

UNIX is used widely enough that a growing industry of UNIX books, magazines, user groups, and conferences has sprung up. Any of them can provide additional help and information.

## Read a magazine or a book

Four or five weekly or monthly magazines cover UNIX. Most of them include in their titles either the name UNIX or the code phrase Open Systems (for systems that act like UNIX but haven't licensed official UNIX-brand UNIX). You probably have already thrown away mail inviting you to subscribe to most of them, so we won't belabor the point. The major brands of workstations (Sun, Hewlett-Packard, and IBM) also have magazines that specifically cover those product lines.

These magazines tend to be awfully technical, but they can be interesting for product reviews and announcements about new UNIX hardware and software packages.

Many books about UNIX are available. You probably saw a shelf full of them when you picked out this one. We like *UNIX in a Nutshell,* by Daniel Gilly (O'Reilly, 1992). It has, in one place, nearly all the useful parts of the UNIX manual without all the extra verbiage.

## Join a user group

There are two major UNIX user groups. The older one is called *Usenix*, which dates back to about 1976; it is traditionally for technical users. The other is *Uniforum*, formerly */usr/group*, which is more for business users. Both sponsor annual conferences and publish a newsletter. There are also local and regional UNIX user groups; you tend to find out about these groups from notes posted on physical or electronic bulletin boards. User groups can be great sources of help because chances are pretty good that someone out there has already run into many of the same problems you have and has some ideas that might help.

# Chapter 28

# Ten Totally Unrelated Topics You Don't Want To Know About

This chapter covers some odds and ends that are useful but more technoid than the stuff in the rest of the book. You can get along perfectly well without them, but, if you're feeling brave, they can come in handy.

## Mother, May I?

Because UNIX was designed from the beginning to be used by more than one person, UNIX systems have something called permissions. *Permissions* determine who can use which file or directory and how they can use it.

There are three types of permissions:

✔ **Read permission** lets you look at a file or directory. You can use `cat` or a text editor to see what's in a file that has read permission; you can also copy this type of a file. Read permission for a directory lets you list the directory's contents.

✔ **Write permission** lets you make changes to a file. Even if you can write (change) a file, you can't necessarily delete it or rename it; for those actions, you must be able to write in the directory in which the file resides. If you have write permission in a directory, you can create new files in the directory and delete files from it.

✔ **Execute permission** lets you run the program contained in the file. The program can be a real program or a shell script. If the file doesn't contain a program, execute permission doesn't do you much good and can provoke the shell to complain bitterly as it tries (from its rather dim point of view) to make sense of your file. For a directory, execute permission lets you open files in the directory and use cd to get to the directory to make it your working directory.

## That's mine!

Every file and directory has an owner. The owner is usually the person who made the file or directory. In UNIX System V, you can change who owns a file with the chown command (described later in this chapter).

## Groups

Every UNIX user is a member of a *group*. When the system administrator created your user name, she assigned you to a group. To see which group you are in, type this line:

```
id
```

Groups usually indicate the kind of work you do. UNIX uses groups to give a bunch of people the same permissions to use a set of files. All the people who work on a particular project are usually in the same group so that they can look at and perhaps change each others' files.

If you are part of the accounting department, for example (it's a dirty job, but someone has to do it), you and the other accounting staff members might need read, write, and execute access to more or less the same files. People in other departments should not have the same access to accounting programs and data. The system administrator probably made a group called something like acctg and put all you accounting guys and gals in it.

In BSD and SVR4 UNIX, you can be in several groups at a time, which is handy if you're working on several projects.

# *Who can do what?*

To see who can do what to a file, use the `ls` command with the `-l` option. Type this line:

```
ls -l myfile
```

You see something like this:

```
-rw-r--r--  1 johnl  staff   335 Jan 22 13:23 myfile
```

If you don't specify a filename, UNIX lists all the files in the directory, which is often more useful. For every file, this listing shows all this information:

✔ Whether it is a file, symbolic link, or directory. The first character in the line is a hyphen (-) if it is a file, an *l* if it is a symbolic link, and a *d* if it is a directory. In the preceeding example, the hyphen shows that it's a file.

✔ Whether the owner can read, write, or execute it (as shown by the next three characters, 2 through 4, on the line). The first character is an *r* if the owner has read permission, and a hyphen (-) if not. The second character is a *w* if the owner has write permission, and a hyphen (-) if not. The third character is an *x* (or sometimes an *s*) if the owner has execute permission, and a hyphen (-) if not. In this example, `rw-` means that the owner can read or write it.

✔ Whether the members of the group can read, write, or execute the file or directory (as indicated by the next three characters, 5 through 7). An *r*, *w*, or *x* appears if that permission is granted; a hyphen (-) appears if that permission is not granted. In this example, group members can only read the file (`r--`).

✔ Whether everyone else can read, write, or execute the file or directory (as indicated by the next three characters, 8 through 10). An *r*, *w*, or *x* appears if that permission is granted; a hyphen (-) appears if that permission is not granted. In this example, everyone else can only read it (`r--`).

✔ The link count, that is, how many links (names) this file has. For directories, this number is the number of subdirectories the directory contains plus 2 (don't ask). For most files, this shows 1 (as in the preceeding example).

✔ The owner of the file or directory (`johnl`, in this example).

✔ The group to which the file or directory belongs (`staff`, in this example).

✔ The size of the file in bytes (characters).

✔ The date and time the file was last modified.

✔ The filename (at last!).

| Table 28-1: | Absolute Permissions Decoded |
|---|---|
| *Digit* | *Permissions* |
| 0 | None |
| 1 | Execute only |
| 2 | Write only |
| 3 | Write and execute |
| 4 | Read only |
| 5 | Read and execute |
| 6 | Read and write |
| 7 | Read, write, and execute |

## *Permissions by number*

It is not too difficult to figure out which permissions a file has by looking at the collection of *r*s, *w*s, and *x*s in the file listing. Sometimes permissions are written another way, however: with numbers. Only UNIX programmers could have thought of this. (This is an example of lazy typists at their finest.) Numbered permissions are sometimes called *absolute permissions* (perhaps because they are absolutely impossible to remember).

When permissions are expressed as a number, it is a 3-digit number. The first digit is the owner's permissions, the second digit is the group's permissions, and the third digit is everyone else's permissions. Every digit is a number from 0 to 7. Table 28-1 lists what the digits mean.

---

### Why those numbers?

You may well ask why those particular numbers were assigned to permissions. They weren't assigned at random. For those of you who remember New Math from fourth grade, all this makes sense if you think in octal.

Think of every permission digit as a 3-digit binary number, like 010 (that's binary for 2). The first digit is 1 if you have read permission, and 0 if you don't.

The second digit is 1 if you have write permission, and 0 if you don't. The third digit is 1 if you have read permission, and 0 if you don't.

So, the permission digit 6, which is 110 in binary, means that you can read and write, but not execute. If this still doesn't make sense, find a fourth-grader to work it out for you.

## *If Mom says no, ask Dad*

If you own a file or directory, you can change its permissions. You use the chmod (for *change mode*) command to do it. You tell chmod the name of the file or directory to change and the new permissions you want the file to have for yourself (the owner), your group, and everyone else. You can either type the numerical absolute permissions (like 440) or use letters.

To use letters to type the new permissions, you use a cryptic collection of letters and symbols that consists of the following:

- Whose permissions you are changing: u for user (the file's owner), g for the group, and o for other (everyone else).
- If the permission should be + (on, yes, OK) or - (off, no, don't let them).
- The type of permission you're dealing with: r for read, w for write, and x for execute.

Type the following line, for example, to allow everyone to read a file called announcements:

```
chmod ugo+r announcements
```

This line says that the user/owner, group, and everyone else can read the file. To prevent anyone except the user/owner from changing the file, type this line:

```
chmod go-w announcements
```

You can also use numeric (absolute) permissions with chmod. To let the owner and associated group read or change the file, type the following:

```
chmod 660 announcements
```

This line sets the owner permission to 6 (read and write), the group permission to 6 too, and everyone else's permission to 0 (can't do anything).

You can change the permissions for a directory in exactly the same way as you do for a file. Keep in mind that read, write, and execute mean somewhat different things for a directory.

You can also use wildcards and give several names on the command line. For example:

```
chmod go-w *
```

This line says to turn off write permission for everyone but you for all the files in the directory. The following command does the same thing to the book directory:

```
chmod go-w /usr/margy/book
```

## Finding a new owner

When someone gives you a file, he usually copies it to your home directory. But, as far as UNIX is concerned, the person who copied the file is still the file's owner. In System V, you can change the ownership of a file you own by using the chown command. In BSD, only the superuser can change the owner of files, so BSD users might as well skip to the next section.

You tell chown the new owner for the file and the filename or filenames whose ownership you are changing. For example:

```
chown john chapter6
```

This command changes the ownership of the file named chapter6 to john. Keep in mind that only you can give away files you own; if you put a file in someone else's directory, it's polite to chown the file to that user.

Another way to change the owner of a file is to make a copy of the file. Suppose that Fred puts a file in your home directory and he still owns it. You can't use chown to change the ownership because only the owner can do that (we have a chicken-before-the-egg problem here). You can get ownership of a file if you copy the file. When you copy a file, you own the new copy. Then delete the original.

## File seeks new group; can sing, dance, and do tricks

If you own a file or directory, you can change the group that can access it. The chgrp command lets you change the group associated with the file. For example:

```
chgrp acctg billing.list
```

This command changes the group associated with the file billing.list to the group called acctg.

# *Do I Have To Type the Same Things Every Time I Log In?*

Most users find that, every time they log in, they type the same commands to set up the computer the way they like it. You may typically change to your favorite directory, for example, change the terminal settings (see the next section), check your mail, or any of a dozen other things.

The Bourne or Korn Shells look for a file called .profile in your home directory when you log in; if the file exists, the shell executes the commands in that file. The C Shell has two corresponding files: .login (which it runs when you log in) and .cshrc (which it runs every time you start a new C Shell, either at login time or when you type csh).

Your system administrator probably gave you a standard .profile or .login file when your account first was set up; it is definitely not a good idea to mess with stuff that's already there. You might end up unable to log in and have to crawl to your system administrator and beg for help. So, don't say we didn't warn you.

The standard .profile, .login, and .cshrc files vary considerably (why do we even finish this sentence? — you know what we're going to say) from one system to another depending on the tastes of the system administrator. These files usually perform the following tasks:

✔ Set up the search path the shell uses to look for commands

✔ Arrange to notify you when you have new mail

✔ (Sometimes) change the shell prompt from the usual $ or % to something more informative

If you always type the same commands when you log in, it is relatively safe to add new commands at the end of .profile or .login. If you do most of your work in the directory bigproject, for example, you might add the following three lines to the end of the file your shell uses to start up your UNIX session:

```
# change to bigproject, added 3/94
cd bigproject
echo Now in directory bigproject.
```

The first line is a comment the computer ignores but is useful for humans trying to figure out who changed what. Any line that starts with a pound sign (#) is a comment. The second line is a regular cd command. (For those of you who haven't read Chapter 23, the cd command works because the .profile or .login script is read by the shell, not by a subprocess.) The third line is an echo command that displays a note on-screen to remind you of the directory you're in.

If you use the C Shell, a frequently useful command to put in `.login` is this one:

```
set ignoreeof
```

Normally, if you press Ctrl-D in the shell, the shell assumes that you're finished for the day and logs you out — in keeping with the traditional UNIX "you asked for it, you got it" philosophy. Many people think that you should be more explicit about your intention to log out and use `ignoreeof` to tell the shell to ignore a Ctrl-D (refer to the following section to see what `eof` has to do with Ctrl-D) and log out only when you type `exit` or `logout`.

# Setting Up the Terminal the Way You Like It

There are about 14 zillion different settings associated with each terminal or pseudo-terminal attached to a UNIX system, any of which you can change with the `stty` command. About 13.999 zillion of the 14 zillion shouldn't be messed with or your terminal will vanish in a puff of smoke (as far as UNIX is concerned) and you will have to log in all over again or even get your system administrator to undo the damage. You can, however, safely change a few things.

All the special characters that control the terminal, such as Backspace and Ctrl-Z, are changeable. People often find that they prefer characters other than the defaults, because they got used to something else on another system, because the placement of the keys on the keyboard makes some choices more natural than others, or because their terminal emulator is dumb about switching Backspace and Delete. The special characters that control the keyboard are listed and described in Table 28-2.

To tell `stty` to change any of these control characters, you give it the name of the special character to change and the character you want to use. If, as is common, you want to use a control character (a combination of the Ctrl or Control key and another key), you can type a caret (^ — the thing above the 6 on the key) followed by the plain character, both enclosed in quotation marks. As a special case, `^?` represents the Del or Delete key. The Tab key is represented as `^I`; the Backspace key is usually `^H`. To make the Delete key the `erase` character and Ctrl-X the `kill` character, for example, type this line:

```
stty erase '^?' kill '^X'
```

| **Table 28-2:** | | **Terminal-Control Characters** |
| --- | --- | --- |
| **Name** | **Typical character** | **Meaning** |
| erase | Ctrl-H | Erases (backspaces over) the previous character |
| kill | Ctrl-U | Discards the line typed so far |
| eof | Ctrl-D | Marks the end of input to a program |
| swtch | Ctrl-Z | Pauses the current program (Chapter 15) |
| intr | Ctrl-C | Interrupts or kills whichever program is running |
| quit | Ctrl-\ | Kills the program and writes a core file (see Chapter 23) |

If you're feeling perverse, you can set the various control characters to whatever you want. You can make the erase character q and the intr character 3, although doing so makes it difficult to get any work done because you couldn't use *q* or *3* in anything you type.

The other thing you can change is the *terminal output stop mode,* which controls whether background jobs can display messages on your terminal. (Chapter 15 explains what this means.) To allow output from background jobs to display on your terminal, turn off output stop mode by typing the following:

```
stty -tostop
```

To prevent output from background jobs, or, more exactly, to make background jobs stop and wait when they want to display something, turn on output stop mode by typing this line:

```
stty tostop
```

All these stty commands usually go in the .login or .profile file so that the terminal is set up the way you want every time you log in.

# A Really Gross Old Network

About 15 years ago, before many UNIX systems were attached to real networks, a guy named Greg whipped up a little program (for temporary use) to use regular modems over regular phone lines to transfer files between two UNIX systems. He called it UNIX to UNIX Copy, or uucp. It's sort of like the Kermit or ZMODEM software that PC users may be familiar with.

Well, 15 years later, we're still using uucp. Its disadvantages are that it's slow (limited by the phone) and a pain to use. Its advantages are that it comes free with every version of UNIX; all you need to use it is a $75 modem plugged into the phone line. The uucp program can do basically one thing: copy files between computers. But it also has a "remote execution" facility (sounds painful, doesn't it?) that lets you execute a small set of commands on other computers. In practice, 95 percent of what uucp does is to carry electronic mail and news between UNIX computers.

## Do you copy, UNIX?

In its simplest form, you use uucp to copy a file from your computer to another, or vice versa:

```
uucp myfile fluffy!hisfile
```

This command says to take the local file called myfile and make a copy called hisfile on the machine called fluffy. (If you use the C Shell, you have to type \! rather than ! because exclamation points are special characters to the C Shell.) Unless the fluffy machine has its disks logically set up exactly the way your machine's are set up (with the same names for home directories), you also need to specify in whose directory you want to put the copy:

```
uucp myfile fluffy!~elvis/hisfile
```

This command tells uucp to put the copy in Elvis' directory. Every machine's uucp command is set up with controls that specify which remote machines are allowed to read and write using uucp. Invariably, the controls permit limited reading and almost no writing. Usually the only place you're allowed to put an incoming file is in uucp's own directory, written this way:

```
uucp myfile fluffy!~/hisfile
```

Unlike most other modem programs, the copy doesn't happen as you wait. A background daemon makes the phone call and does the copying, and tries as many times as necessary if the phone is busy. If the copy fails, either because the file isn't there (more likely when you told it to copy from a remote machine to your own) or because you're not allowed access to the files, uucp sends you electronic mail telling you about the problem.

The uucp program doesn't need a modem: Two machines in the same building can talk uucp over a simple terminal-type cable. If you have a few machines and no networking budget, this is an easy way for a system administrator to get at least a little networking going to avoid carrying around disks or tapes.

## *UNIX mail without the stamp*

People use `uucp` mostly to send mail and `netnews` (described in the following section), particularly if they don't have a direct Internet connection. Mail addresses for `uucp` are also written with exclamation points (see Chapter 18 to learn how to send e-mail). To send `uucp` mail to Tracy on machine `fluffy`, you type the following:

```
mail fluffy!tracy
```

Alternatively, you can use `elm` or some other, better mail program. If you use the C shell, type `\!` for `!`. You can forward `uucp` mail from one machine to another: If you want to send a message to Tracy on machine `fluffy` but your machine doesn't talk directly to `fluffy` and does talk to `itchy`, which in turn talks to `fluffy`, you can type this line:

```
mail itchy!fluffy!tracy
```

This electronic whisper-down-the-lane method often goes to extremes, and mail sometimes has to take six or seven hops to get where it's going. If your system handles a lot of mail, your system administrator probably has installed automatic routing software that figures out which route to use to get to which machines, based on `uucp` maps distributed on `usenet` (see the following section). If this is the case, you merely type the destination-machine name and the user name, and UNIX figures out how to get it there. A lot of `uucp` systems are out there; the `uucp` routing list on our system lists more than 20,000 other machines to which it has `uucp` paths!

If your system administrator is really on the ball, your mail system is set up so that it can automatically figure out which kind of network to use for each mail message. You can mail to `tracy@fluffy` and the computer takes care of passing it to `uucp` or whatever other network is appropriate.

# *How to Read So Much Electronic Gossip That You Have No Time Left To Work*

Not long after `uucp` and `uucp` mail arrived, some people in North Carolina thought that it would be neat to have a distributed bulletin-board system. People could send in messages from their local machine, the messages would be distributed to a couple of other machines, and users on all the machines could see all the messages. They figured that it would be pretty popular and there could be dozens of messages per day.

Well, they were right: It's pretty popular. There are now more like 100,000 machines hooked up, with sites on every continent. (We hear that there's even a machine on the net at one of the research stations in Antarctica.) There are about 20,000 messages totaling more than 50 megabytes (that's 50 million keystrokes) of text handled every day. This monster is known as `usenet`, or sometimes `netnews`.

Messages are filed in topic categories called *newsgroups,* of which there are about 1,500. Newsgroup topics range from technical discussions of computer architecture to gossip about old trains, nudism, and interminable political arguments. Reading all this stuff could take a large chunk of your workday (about 10 hours daily). Fortunately, the standard news-reading programs let you specify which groups you want to see and which ones you don't; you can identify, within groups, the topics and authors in which you are or are not interested.

There are quite a few news-reading programs, with names like `readnews` (the original, now considered old and klunky), `rn`, `trn`, `tin`, and `nn`, all of which do basically the same thing but have different ways to navigate around the enormous mass of messages. If your site gets news, have an experienced user show you how to use the local news-reading program.

If you get `usenet`, you can probably send out your own `usenet` messages. Please resist the urge to do so until you have been reading news for a few weeks so that you have an idea of what's appropriate to send and what isn't. Also read the newsgroup called `news.announce.newusers`; it contains helpful advice for new `usenet` users.

The most amazing thing about `usenet` is who's in charge of it: no one. It's just a big, informal, cooperative setup. The programs most commonly used to file and transfer news were written by two guys in the zoology department at the University of Toronto who probably should have been working on their regular jobs instead. The various news-reading programs come from educational and commercial sites all over the world. The money to pay for the network time is, by and large, hidden in corporate telephone budgets. It's the definitive example of pioneer networking.

# Running DOS Under UNIX

UNIX bigots tend to sneer at DOS machines and DOS users. There's no doubt that DOS is a pretty bad system, but there's no doubt that it also supports some pretty good software.

DOS users who switch to UNIX don't have to leave DOS behind. PC and workstation versions of UNIX have DOS-under-UNIX packages that let you run DOS in a UNIX process. If you're running an Intel 386 or 486 PC, the CPU chip has a special hardware feature called *V86 mode* that makes it possible to create a faithful emulation of a bare PC inside a UNIX process so that a regular version of DOS runs on that emulated PC.

Two competing V86 DOS emulators called vp/ix and DOS Merge both work quite well. While writing this book, we used vp/ix to run the regular DOS version of Microsoft Word to do some text editing and to read and write DOS floppy disks. The emulated DOS runs nearly as fast as a separate DOS machine and has the advantage that the computer can simultaneously continue to do all the other UNIX stuff and give DOS access to all your UNIX files.

If you have a non-Intel workstation, a package called SoftPC translates 386 code on the fly to the native code used by the workstation's CPU in a UNIX process. Again, this provides an environment in which regular DOS can run. Although the translation involves considerable overhead, workstations have become so fast that, even with the overhead, the emulated DOS machine can be faster than a real PC.

One problem with existing DOS-under-UNIX systems is that they don't emulate the protected-mode features that Windows needs in order to run; you can run only older, pre-3.1 versions of Windows, and Windows can't share the screen with X or OPEN LOOK or Motif. By the time this book is in your hands, however, Windows-under-X emulators should be available on 386 and 486 UNIX systems so that you can run Windows applications under X (as well as under OPEN LOOK and Motif because they're based on X). Windows windows will be able to share the screen with native X, Motif, and OPEN LOOK applications, all running at full speed. Way cool.

# Chapter 29

# The Top Ten (or so) UNIX Commands

• • • • • • • • • • • • • • • • • • • • • • • • • • • • • • • • • • • • • • • • • • • • •

## In This Chapter

▶ cat

▶ cd

▶ cp

▶ find

▶ grep

▶ ln

▶ lp (UNIX System V only)

▶ lpq (BSD UNIX only)

▶ lpr (BSD UNIX only)

▶ lpstat (UNIX System V only)

▶ ls

▶ mkdir

▶ more

▶ mv

▶ pwd

▶ rm

▶ rmdir

• • • • • • • • • • • • • • • • • • • • • • • • • • • • • • • • • • • • • • • • • • • • •

*T*hese are the UNIX commands you use every day (or once a month, any-way). The rest of the UNIX commands are listed in Chapter 30; although you may need the other commands occasionally, here are the biggies.

# The cat *Command*

**Purpose:** To display a file on-screen so that you can read it

**Sample:** `cat letter.to.santa`

**Comments:** The `cat` command displays any file you tell it to, but, if the file contains anything other than plain ASCII text, the display looks like Greek, or worse. The `cat` command works for any file that looks OK in a text editor. It doesn't work as well for data files, word processing files, and other files that contain binary data, formatting codes, and that kind of thing.

**Where to look:** The Chapter 4 section "Looking at the Guts of a File." Also check out the `more` command.

# The cd *Command*

**Purpose:** To change to another directory

**Sample:** `cd /usr/santa/presents`

**Comments:** The `cd` command is followed by the name of the directory you want to work in. If the path name starts with a slash (/), the path is the path from the root of the disk to the specified directory. If the path name doesn't start with a slash, the path is the path from the current working directory to the specified directory.

**Where to look:** The Chapter 5 sections "Paths to power" and "Moving around: the working directory"; look in Chapter 19 for information about changing directories that are mounted using NFS; see Chapter 26 for finding lost files.

# The cp *Command*

**Purpose:** To copy a file

**Sample:** `cp important.file important.file.backup`

**Comments:** This command creates a duplicate copy of the first file you name. The duplicate copy has the second name you enter.

**Where to look:** The Chapter 4 section "Copying Files"

# *The* `find` *Command*

**Purpose:** To find one or more files (assuming that you know at least their approximate filenames) and to do something to them

**Sample:** `find . -name chicken.soup -print`

**Comments:** You use this command when you can't figure out the directory in which you put one or more files but you know the filename or filenames. When you use the `find` command, you tell it where to start looking, usually either `.` (which means "right here") or `/` (which means "search the entire disk"). Then you give the name of the file (you type `-name`, a space, and the filename, possibly using wildcard characters), and then you tell `find` what to do when it finds the files, usually `-print` (to mean "display the full filenames, including the names of the directories they are in").

**Where to look:** "When you care enough to know the filename" in Chapter 26.

# *The* `grep` *Command*

**Purpose:** To find one or more files (assuming that you know something they contain)

**Sample:** `grep "chocolate mousse" *`

**Comments:** You use this command when you don't know which file contains the information you want. If you know a word or phrase that identifies the information, `grep` finds it. To use `grep`, you tell it the text to look for (surrounded by quotation marks if it is more than one word) and the files to check, often `*` (to mean "all the files in this directory"). There are two similar commands, `fgrep` and `egrep`, which you probably will never use.

**Where to look:** The Chapter 26 section "When you don't know the filename"

# The ln *Command*

**Purpose:** To create a link to a file so that the file lives in more than one directory at the same time

**Sample:** `ln /usr/celeste/dept.budget celestes.fantasy.budget`

**Comments:** If you use a file all the time and are tired of moving to the directory where it lives, link it to your home directory or to another convenient place. When you use ln, you tell it the current path name of the file and the new name you want it to have in the current working directory.

**Other Purpose:** To link all the files in a directory to a new directory

**Other Sample:** `ln /usr/celeste/Budget/ Budget.files`

**Other Comments:** You can link an entire directory full of files with one ln command. To do this, tell the ln command the names of the group of files, usually ending with * to identify an entire group at a time, and the name of the new directory to link them to. The links in the new directory use the same filenames as the existing files.

**Where to look:** The Chapter 26 section "Making Links"

# The lp *Command (UNIX System V Only)*

**Purpose:** To print a file

**Sample:** `lp letter.to.santa`

**Comments:** The lp command puts your file in line to get printed.

**Where to look:** The Chapter 9 section "Printing on UNIX System V" (for the lp command); flip through the rest of the chapter for general information about printing.

# The lpq *Command (BSD UNIX Only)*

**Purpose:** To list the status of all available printers

**Sample:** `lpq -a`

**Comments:** This command tells you which printers are out there and what they are printing.

**Where to look:** The Chapter 9 section "Which printers are available?"

# The lpr *Command (BSD UNIX Only)*

**Purpose:** To print a file

**Sample:** lpr letter.to.santa

**Comments:** The lpr command puts your file in line to be printed.

**Where to look:** The Chapter 9 section "Printing on BSD UNIX"; flip though the rest of the chapter for general information about printing.

# The lpstat *Command (UNIX System V Only)*

**Purpose:** To list the status of all available printers

**Sample:** lpstat -a all

**Comments:** This command tells you which printers are out there and what they are printing.

**Where to look:** The Chapter 9 section "Which printers are available?"

# The ls *Command*

**Purpose:** To list the files in a directory

**Samples:** ls

```
ls /usr/harold/crayons/*
```

**Comments:** If you don't tell it otherwise, the ls command lists all the files in the working directory. You can tell it the name of another directory to list, and you can specify the files you want listed by using a filename (which can include wildcards).

**Other Purpose:** To list files with their sizes, dates, and other information

**Other Sample:** ls -l

**Where to look:** The Chapter 4 section "Which Files Do You Have?" Also, see "Who can do what?" in Chapter 28 to learn how to interpret the information displayed by ls -l.

# The mkdir Command

**Purpose:** To create a new directory

**Sample:** mkdir Games

**Comments:** You tell the mkdir command the name of the directory to create. If the name starts with a slash (/), it is the pathname from the root directory to the new directory. If the name does not start with a slash, mkdir creates the directory as a subdirectory of the working directory.

**Where to look:** The Chapter 5 section "Making directories"

# The more Command

**Purpose:** To display information one screen at a time so that you have time to read it

**Samples:**

```
more long.report
ls | more
```

**Comments:** When you use the more command by itself, you tell it the name of the file you want displayed one screen at a time. When you use it after a pipe (|), it displays the output of the preceding command. When the screen is full, more pauses. To tell it to show you more, press the spacebar. To make more stop, press q.

**Where to look:** The Chapter 6 sections "Displaying file listings one screen at a time" and "Listing long files on-screen"

# The mv *Command*

**Purpose:** To rename a file

**Sample:** `mv stupid.file.name crucial.report`

**Comments:** To rename a file using the `mv` command, tell it the current name of the file and then the name to change it to.

**Other Purpose:** To move a file to another directory

**Other Sample:** `mv crucial.report /usr/boss/Reports`

**Other Comments:** To move a file, tell the `mv` command the current name of the file (or its pathname if it is not in the working directory) and the directory you want it moved to.

**Where to look:** The Chapter 4 section "What's in a name?"

# The pwd *Command*

**Purpose:** To tell you the name of the current working directory

**Sample:** `pwd`

**Comments:** This command tells you where you are.

**Where to look:** The Chapter 5 section "Moving around: The working directory"

# The rm *Command*

**Purpose:** To delete a file permanently

**Sample:** `rm junk.file`

**Comments:** If there are other links to the file, the file continues to exist. The `rm` command just deletes one name (link) to the file.

**Where to look:** The Chapter 4 section "Erasing Files." For information about deleting links to a file, see "Deleting links" in Chapter 26. For information about what to do if you delete a file by mistake, see Chapter 22.

# *The* rmdir *Command*

**Purpose:** To delete a directory

**Sample:** rmdir Budget

**Comments:** Before you can delete a directory, delete the files and subdirectories it contains. The rm -r command does all this for you at one time, but make sure that this is what you really want to do.

**Where to look:** The Chapter 5 section "Erasing a directory"

# Chapter 30

# The Bottom Ten UNIX Commands

● ● ● ● ● ● ● ● ● ● ● ● ● ● ● ● ● ● ● ● ● ● ● ● ● ● ● ● ● ● ● ● ● ● ● ● ● ● ● ● ● ● ● ● ● ●

*T*his chapter lists many UNIX commands you may want to use, commands you may occasionally hear about, commands you definitely should not use, and commands you may see wizards and system administrators use if you look over their shoulders. Some of these commands have been mentioned elsewhere in this book (we tell you where). Others deserve just a little attention (or derision), and this seems like the best place to do it.

# *Commands You May Use Frequently*

bg          Runs a stopped job in the background (see the section "The Magic of Job Control" in Chapter 15).

clear       Clears the screen. This command has no effect on files or anything else — just what appears on-screen.

dircmp      Compares two directories and tells you which files are in both, which are in just one, and which are in just the other. For files in both directories, the dircmp command tells you whether the contents of the files are the same. This command is great if you and someone else keep directories of more or less the same files.

emacs       A powerful text editor that is not difficult to use (see "Using emacs" in Chapter 12).

exit        Logs you out (see Chapter 1). You may also be able to press Ctrl-D to log out.

fg          Continues a stopped job in the foreground (see "The Magic of Job Control" in Chapter 15).

kill        Cancels a process you don't want to continue. The process has to belong to you and not to any other user (see Chapter 23).

man        Displays a manual page about a UNIX command (see Chapter 27).

passwd        Changes your password. You have to know your current password to change it to a new one (see "Changing your password" in Chapter 2). But then, you must have known your password to log in.

pr        Prints a text file with page numbers, line numbers, or other options (see "Prettying Up Your Printouts" in Chapter 9).

ps        Lists information about your process or processes. This information is important when a process runs amok and you have to kill it (see Chapter 23).

# Commands You May Occasionally Use

cancel        *(UNIX System V only.)* Cancels a print job (see "Stopping the printer on UNIX System V" in Chapter 9).

chmod        Changes the permissions for a file (see "Changing permissions" in Chapter 28).

cmp        Compares two files and tells you the line numbers where they differ. As alternative commands, you can use comm, diff, or sdiff (see "Comparing Apples and Oranges" in Chapter 13).

compress        Makes a freeze-dried copy of a file so that it occupies less space on the disk (see "Squashing Your Files" in Chapter 13). Other similar commands are uncompress, pack, unpack, pcat, and zcat.

csh        Runs the C Shell (see "She sells C shells" in Chapter 2).

df        Tells you how much space is free on your disk (see "The df command" in Chapter 19).

diff        Compares two files and prints the lines in which the files differ (see "Comparing Files" in Chapter 13). If the file is too large for diff to handle, use bdiff (for *big diff*erence). To compare the two files side-by-side, use sdiff.

du        Tells you how much space your files take up on the disk (see "CHKDSK" in Chapter 16).

echo    Echoes back whatever you type on the command line after
        echo, expanding any wildcards using *, ? or [ ]. In shell scripts,
        this command is a way to put messages and prompts on-
        screen.

help    If your UNIX system has an on-line help system, this command
        displays somewhat technoid information that may be useful
        after you have read parts of this book (now that you are more
        used to UNIX's little peculiarities). Try typing help to see what
        happens.

glossary If your UNIX system has an on-line help system, this command
        lets you see somewhat nerdy definitions of some UNIX terms.
        Try typing glossary to see what happens.

id      Tells you which group you are in (see "Groups" in Chapter 28).

jobs    Lists the jobs (foreground and background commands) you are
        running (see "Take this job and..." in Chapter 15).

mesg    Lets you control whether other people can use the write com-
        mand to interrupt you with messages. Type mesg n to turn off
        messaging to your terminal so that you aren't interrupted.
        Type mesg y to turn messaging back on so that you can be
        more sociable (otherwise, you might miss the announcement
        about the pizza in the conference room).

sort    Sorts the lines in a text file (see "Sorting, sort of" in Chapter 6).

stty    Sets the options for your terminal. See "Taming background
        terminal output" in Chapter 15 for information about how to
        use stty to turn on and off terminal output stop mode (that
        chapter even explains what the heck that mode is). See "Setting
        Up the Terminal the Way You Like It" in Chapter 28 for informa-
        tion about how to set other stty options. The stty commands
        should be put in your .profile, .login, or .cshrc file (see
        Chapter 28).

tty     Tells you the terminal ID of your terminal. The terminal ID usu-
        ally looks like the pathname of a subdirectory of the /dev
        directory. Actually, /dev is a directory (dev stands for *device*)
        that contains special files which are really connections to de-
        vices like your terminal.

uniq    Removes repeated, identical lines from a file. If a file contains
        several adjacent lines that are the same, the uniq command
        deletes all but one of them. You can also use it to count the
        number of times each line appears in a file. This command is
        often used after sort puts common lines together.

# *Commands That Are Kind of Cute*

at
: Schedules a command to be run at a particular time. This command is useful for running time-consuming commands in the middle of the night. (See "Time Is Money — Steal Some Today" in Chapter 13.

bc
: A calculator (see "A Desk Calculator" in Chapter 13). UNIX has another calculator, called dc, that uses reverse Polish notation (you type the numbers and *then* tell it what to do with them).

cal
: Prints a calendar for a month or year (see "Time Is Money — Steal Some Today!" in Chapter 13).

date
: Tells you the current date and time and takes into account your time zone (see "Time Is Money — Steal Some Today!" in Chapter 13).

diff3
: Compares three files with each other. Tricky, but cute.

finger
: Lists the people using your computer — with their real names and not just their UNIX user names (see "Finding Out Who's On Your Computer" in Chapter 17).

head
: Lists just the first few lines of a text file. This command is similar to the cat command, but it stops after a few lines.

history
: *(C shell only.)* Lists the last 20 or so commands you typed.

news
: Lets you read news items the system administrator has posted.

script
: *(BSD and SVR4 only.)* Saves in a text file the conversation you are having with UNIX. That is, it stores everything you type and everything UNIX types back at you. If you are having trouble getting something to work, this can be a useful way to show a wizard what you did and what UNIX did to you.

sdiff
: Compares two files by listing them side by side. If the lines in the two files differ, UNIX puts a symbol in the column between the two files. Be sure to use the -w option to tell UNIX the number of characters across your screen (probably 80); otherwise, sdiff assumes that it can display 130 characters across and the display is a mess.

spell
: Looks through a text file and reports which words are not in the UNIX dictionary. Of course, what UNIX considers misspellings includes your name and lots of other perfectly good words.

sum

Calculates the checksum for a file. This is a good way to make sure that a file was not fouled up after being transmitted from one system to another, especially over a phone line. When you type this line:

```
sum filename
```

UNIX tells you the checksum (a number), another number indicating the amount of disk space the file occupies, and the filename (in case you forgot). Do a checksum before and after transmitting a file and compare the numbers. If they are the same, the file probably hasn't changed.

*Note to System V users:* For reasons no one remembers, the BSD and System V versions of sum produce different answers. On System V, use sum -r to get the answers the BSD version produces.

tail

Displays the last few lines of a file.

talk

Lets you talk to another computer user by typing messages to each other on-screen. See "Chatting with Other People on Your Computer" in Chapter 17.

tee

Copies information from the standard input (the keyboard, unless you redirect input from somewhere else), stores in it a file, and displays it on-screen. Useful in pipelines to see the output of a command and store it in a file at the same time.

time

Tells you how long a command took to run (from the time you pressed Enter or Return to the time you see the next shell prompt).

uname

Tells you the name of the UNIX system you are using. This command may also display other information about the system.

wc

Tells you the number of words (wc -w), lines (wc -l), or characters (wc -c) in a file.

who

Tells you who else is using this computer (see "Finding Out Who's On Your Computer" in Chapter 17).

who am i

Lists your own user name and user information (see "Finding Out Who's on Your Computer" in Chapter 17). Some versions of UNIX also have a whoami command that reports your user name.

# Commands You Won't Have Much Use For

ed
: A yucky line editor (see "Using ed" in Chapter 12).

red
: A restricted version of the ed text editor that makes red an even dumber thing to run than ed.

vi
: A yucky screen editor (see "Using vi" in Chapter 12).

ex
: An extended (but still pretty yucky) version of ed. It's actually vi slumming as a line editor; see Chapter 12.

# Commands You May See Others Use

ar
: Creates an *archive* — a bunch of files glommed together in one file. Programmers like this command.

batch
: Lets you enter a bunch of commands to run when the computer isn't busy.

awk
: A strange little programming language.

chgrp
: Changes the group that has access to a file or directory. You have to own the file or directory in order to use this command (see "File seeks new group; can sing, dance, and do tricks" in Chapter 28).

chown
: *(UNIX System V only.)* Changes the ownership of a file. You have to own the file in order to make this change (see "Finding a new owner" in Chapter 28).

cpio
: Copies files to and from things other than hard disks. This command is useful for making backup copies of files and copying files from backups (see Chapter 22).

crontab
: Makes a list of programs you want to run every day at the same time. System administrators love crontab because they can use it to do backups and clean-up operations in the middle of the night. You can use crontab only if your system administrator sets it up for you.

| | |
|---|---|
| cut | Lets you extract just the columns you want from a text file that contains information in columns. If characters 1 through 30 on each line are names, for example, and characters 31 through 50 are the corresponding phone numbers, the cut command lets you isolate just the phone numbers or just the names. The paste and join commands can put the columns back together. |
| env | Shows you information about your UNIX user environment variables. Sometimes called printenv. |
| file | Tells you if something is a file, a directory, or something else entirely. If the thing is a text file, the file command tries to guess what's in it. |
| ksh | Runs the Korn Shell (which is a souped-up version of the Bourne Shell — see Chapter 2). |
| login | Logs you in as someone else. |
| nice | Runs a command with lower priority. This is a good thing to do if you have a program that consumes a lot of computing power and that slows down the computer while it runs (see Chapter 15). |
| nohup | Continues to run a command in the background even if you log out (see Chapter 15). |
| od | Displays the contents of a file (as does the cat command), but in a super-nerdy format called octal ASCII codes. Wizards can use this to see what's really in a file. |
| rlogin | Logs in to a remote computer (see "Logging In and Out" in Chapter 20). |
| rn | Reads the news in usenet news groups (see Chapter 28). This is a way to get all kinds of valuable information and to waste infinite amounts of time. Other commands for reading usenet news are readnews, trn, nn, and vnews. |
| rsh | Runs a command on another machine (see "One Command at a Time" in Chapter 20). |
| sed | Lets you use prerecorded commands to make changes to a text file. It's similar to using ed, but with all the commands you plan to use prewritten (that's why sed means *stream editor*). The sed editor understands almost exactly the same commands you use in ed or ex. |

| | |
|---|---|
| set | Shows you which shell variables are defined. One of the variables is usually `path` or `PATH`, which tells you where UNIX looks for programs. |
| setenv | *(C shell only.)* Sets the value of an environment variable. |
| sh | Runs the Bourne Shell (see "Cracking the Shell" in Chapter 2). |
| tar | Copies files to or from a backup tape (see "Call in the backup squad tapes" in Chapter 22). A related command is `bar`. |
| telnet | Lets you log in to a remote computer (see "Logging In and Out" in Chapter 20). |
| touch | Changes the date and time a file was last modified to right now. This command doesn't change the contents of the file. |
| tr | Replaces all occurrences of one character in a file with another character. You can replace all the tab characters in a file with commas, for example. Whoopee. |
| troff | A baroque old text formatter (see "Text formatters" in Chapter 12). |
| umask | Tells UNIX which permissions to give to files you create. |
| unset | Removes an environment variable. |
| uucp | Makes a UNIX-to-UNIX copy (see "A Really Gross Old Network" in Chapter 28). |
| xargs | Creates a list of *arguments* (a list of filenames) and executes a command with that list. This command is great for doing something to every file in a directory. |

# Commands That Are Useful Only in Shell Scripts

| | |
|---|---|
| basename | Grabs just the last part of a pathname — the part after the last slash. The result is either a filename or a directory name. |
| dirname | Displays the name of the directory that contains a particular file or subdirectory. |

export          *(Bourne and Korn Shells only.)* If the shell script makes changes to shell environment variables, this command passes the changes to commands and subshells run from the script.

read            *(Bourne and Korn Shells only.)* Accepts a line of characters (whatever you type until you press Enter or Return) and lets you do something with it in a shell script. This command lets a shell script ask the user for some information like a filename or directory name.

sleep           Waits a little while, which is measured in seconds (see "Time Is Money — Steal Some Today!" in Chapter 13).

test            Tests to see whether something is true or false. This command is useful in a shell script so that you can do different things depending on circumstances (if the file doesn't exist, create it, for example; otherwise, do something to it).

# *Some Hard-Core Nerd Commands*

alias           *(C and Korn Shells only.)* Creates an alias for a command or shows which aliases exist.

fmt             An extremely stupid text formatter that makes all the lines approximately the same length.

pg              Similar to more but with fewer features.

unalias         *(C and Korn Shells only.)* Removes an alias name.

# Glossary

• • • • • • • • • • • • • • • • • • • • • • • • • • • • • • • • • • • • • • • • • • • • • • • • • • • • • • • • •

**absolute pathname.** A pathname that tells you how to find a file by starting at the root directory and working down the directory tree.

**address.** The name you use to say who is supposed to receive an electronic-mail message. An electronic-mail address consists of the person's user name and, if the person is on a different computer than you are, the name of the computer (see Chapter 18).

**AIX.** IBM's version of UNIX.

**Alt key.** If your keyboard has an Alt key, it is used as a Shift key; it does nothing on its own. To use it, hold it down, press another key, and release it. To press Alt-A, for example, hold the Alt key, press and release the A key, and release the Alt key. Simple.

**anonymous ftp.** Uses the `ftp` file transfer program and the Internet to copy files from other computers to your own. It is *anonymous* because many computer systems allow anyone to log in and transfer files without having accounts (user names) on the computer. You type `anonymous` as the user name and your electronic-mail address as the password. See Chapter 20.

**application.** A program that really gets some work done. Some programs just organize the computer, get its parts talking to each other, and do other housekeeping chores. Application programs do real-world work, like word processing or accounting.

**argument.** Something that appears on a command line after the command. Suppose that you type this line:

```
cp old.file new.file
```

In this command, `cp` is the name of the command or program, `old.file` is the first argument, and `new.file` is the second argument. See Chapter 14 for how to use arguments with shell scripts.

**ASCII.** American Standard Code for Information Interchange. ASCII defines the codes the computer uses internally to store letters, numbers, punctuation, and some control codes. Almost all UNIX computers use ASCII (except for some mainframes).

**background.** UNIX can run many programs at the same time. If a program runs behind the scenes, with no interaction with you, it runs in the background (see Chapter 15).

**backslash (\).** UNIX uses a backslash to set off otherwise special characters. In the UNIX shell, for example, \* is a literal asterisk (a plain * matches every file in the current directory); \\ is an actual backslash, if you want one for some reason. DOS users tend to type backslashes by mistake when UNIX would rather see a regular slash (/).

**backup.** A spare copy of your data to keep on the shelf just in case. If you (or a co-worker) delete a file by mistake or if parts of your computer break, you will be inexpressibly happy and smug if you have recently made a backup copy of your important files.

Copying files back from your backups is called *restoring*.

**bang (!).** In UNIX-ese, an exclamation point. The C Shell command `!!`, which repeats the last command, for example, is pronounced "Bang! Bang!" Try this with your small children — they will love it.

`bin`. A directory that contains programs. Your home directory probably has a subdirectory named `bin`. The system has directories called `/bin` and `/usr/bin` (see Chapter 14).

**bit.** A tiny piece of information that can be either a 1 or a 0. Bits tend to get lumped into groups of eight bits, called *bytes.*

**Bourne Shell.** The Bourne Shell is the most widely used UNIX shell. It prompts you with $. Its program name is `sh`.

**Break key.** The Break key is used before you log in when you are dialing on a modem to tell UNIX that it has guessed wrong about which kind of modem you're using. You may have to press Break two or three times until you get a proper `login:` message. Some keyboards have a key labeled Break. If yours doesn't and you're using a PC with a modem program, try Alt-B or check your modem program's help screen.

**BSD UNIX.** A version of UNIX developed and distributed by the University of California at Berkeley. BSD stands for Berkeley Software Distribution.

**buffer.** A small storage area in which information is stored temporarily until it is needed. Lots of things have buffers: printers frequently have buffers to store the next few lines or pages to print; `emacs` (a text editor) refers to its copies of the files you are editing as buffers.

**byte.** Eight bits in a row. That is, a series of eight pieces of information, each of which can be either 1 or 0. A little higher math tells you that there are 256 different combinations of eight 1s and 0s. (256 is 2 to the 8th power.) There are therefore 256 different values for a byte of information. Most computers use a system of codes called *ASCII* to determine what each pattern means. The combination 01000001 means *A,* 01000010 means *B,* and 00001010 means "end of the line, start a new one."

**C.** A programming language invented at the same time as UNIX, and in which nearly all UNIX programs are written. C is a great programming language for lots of reasons. C programs look a lot like random punctuation strewn across the page. Luckily, you do *not* have to know or use C to use UNIX, so we don't talk about it anywhere else in this book.

**C Shell.** The C Shell is a UNIX shell written to look like the C programming language, sort of. It prompts you with %. Its program name is `csh`.

**CD-ROM.** A computer disk that looks just like a music CD but contains data rather than music.

**central processing unit.** The heart of the computer, the part that does the thinking (such as it is). These days, in all but the largest computers, the CPU is contained entirely on a little, black chip the size of your thumb and that costs maybe $200. CPU chips are named by using numbers, like 68040 and 80486, by using acronyms, like SPARC, or made-up names, like Pentium.

**checksum.** A number computed by glomming together all the characters from an entire file in a special mathematical way. If you are afraid that a file is going to change, perhaps getting messed up by being transmitted across noisy phone lines, you can calculate a checksum before and after transmitting it. If you get the same checksum, the file probably didn't change.

**CISC.** Complex Instruction Set Computer. A type of CPU (central processing unit) chip. Pronounced "kisk." The other kind of CPU is a RISC. You don't care.

**click-to-type.** A system GUIs use to control which window you are working in. When you want to move to a different window, move the mouse and click in the new window to tell the GUI you want to use that window. It's a pain in the neck, actually. See Chapters 10 and 11.

**clicking.** "Clicking with a mouse" means moving the mouse until the cursor is on the thing you want to select and then pressing and releasing the mouse button. If your mouse has several buttons, use the leftmost button unless instructed otherwise (see Chapter 10).

**client.** In the X Window System and its relatives, Motif and OPEN LOOK, a program that does real work, as opposed to a program that displays the results on-screen (see Chapter 11).

**client-server architecture.** A system (used by the X Window System) that enables a program (the client) to run on one machine while the program that displays its results (the server) runs on another machine (see Chapter 10).

**command.** A word you type to get UNIX to do something. Actually, the *UNIX shell* listens to the commands you type and tries to execute them. Some commands are things the shell knows how to do. Other commands are separate programs, stored in files

on the disk. When you type a command, press Enter or Return at the end of the line.

**command mode.** When you use the `ed` or `vi` text editors, you are in either command mode or input mode. In command mode, whatever you type is interpreted as a command. See Chapter 12 for how to use `ed` and `vi`.

**compression.** A way to shrink files so that they don't take up so much space. File-compression programs that do this include `compress` and `pack`. To uncompress a compressed file, use `uncompress`, `unpack`, `pcat`, or `zcat` (see Chapter 13).

**computer.** You mean that you've gotten this far and you still don't know what a computer is? True, sometimes it can be hard to tell. A computer is the part of the system that contains a processing unit that does the thinking. Sometimes people refer to the computer as the entire package: the processing unit, keyboard, screen, disk drives — the works.

You may need to know if you have a computer on your desk or if you have a terminal connected to a computer somewhere else. If you are using a PC with a program such as Kermit or Procomm as a terminal to communicate with a computer running UNIX, when we talk about the "computer," we mean the UNIX machine (see Chapter 1).

**Control key.** The key on the keyboard labeled Control or Ctrl. It is used as a Shift key: It does nothing on its own. To use it, hold it down, press another key, and release it. To press Ctrl-D, for example, hold the Ctrl key, press and release the D key, and release the Ctrl key.

**core.** An old-fashioned term for "memory." A long time ago (in the '60s and '70s), most memory consisted of thousands of tiny, metal donuts, called *cores,* strung on arrays of teeny-tiny wires. Some UNIX enthusiasts still refer to memory as "core."

**CPU.** See *central processing unit.*

**Ctrl key.** See *Control key.*

**current directory.** See *working directory.*

**current job.** The job most recently started or stopped. When you use the jobs command to list jobs, the current job is marked with a plus sign (+). See Chapter 15.

**cursor.** The little indicator on your screen that shows where you are working. Its shape depends on the program you are using. It may be a blinking underscore, a box, an arrow, a little hourglass, a little pencil — you name it.

**daemon. (Pronounced "demon")** A process that runs around on its own to see to some housekeeping task. Your computer, or some computer on your network, has a printer daemon whose job is to print things waiting in the print queue.

**data.** Information, in computer-speak.

**desktop publishing.** A fancy type of word processing. A desktop publishing program lets you do typesetting and is useful for preparing books, newsletters, and the like. The most common UNIX desktop publishing programs are Interleaf and FrameMaker (see Chapter 12).

**directory.** A collection of files with a name. A directory can be compared to a file folder that contains one or more files. Directories can also contain other directories. You can think of a directory as a work area because one directory is always the current *working directory.* Directories, particularly directories contained in your home directory,

sometimes are called subdirectories, for no good reason. See Chapter 5.

**disk.** Also known as DASD (only to IBM types, who pronounce this "daz-dee"), it is a round, flat thing on which information is recorded in much the same way as you record stuff on a cassette tape. See Chapter 7 for descriptions of the various kinds of disks.

**diskette.** A removable disk, also called a floppy disk. See Chapter 7 for descriptions of the two sizes of diskettes.

**display.** See *screen.*

**display adapter.** The thing inside your computer that lets it talk to the screen (see Chapter 8).

**DOS.** An operating system patterned in some ways after UNIX. DOS runs on PCs. See Chapter 16 for a comparison of DOS and UNIX commands.

**dot-matrix printers.** Printers that work by hitting a ribbon against the paper using a grid (or a matrix) of little pins, each of which makes a tiny dot on the page (see Chapter 9).

**double-clicking.** "Double-clicking with a mouse" means moving the mouse until the cursor is on the thing you want to use and then quickly pressing and releasing the mouse button twice. It takes some practice to get the two clicks fast enough but not too fast. If your mouse has several buttons, use the leftmost button unless you are instructed otherwise (see Chapter 10).

**dragging.** "Dragging with a mouse" means moving the mouse until the cursor is on the thing you want to drag, pressing and holding the mouse button, moving the mouse until the thing is where you want to drag it to (with the button still down), and then releasing the mouse button. If your mouse has several buttons, use the leftmost button unless you are instructed otherwise (see Chapter 10).

**dumb terminal.** A terminal that has no processing power of its own. It usually doesn't have any nice options either, like mice or screens that can do graphics. See Chapter 1 for information about how to use a dumb terminal.

**editor.** See *text editor*.

**electronic mail (or e-mail or email).** Typed messages sent on a computer network rather than on paper (see Chapter 18).

**end of input.** Usually the Ctrl-D character.

**Enter key.** In a UNIX shell, pressing Enter means that you have just typed a command and you want UNIX to do it. In a text editor, pressing Enter means that you want to begin a new line. The Enter key and the Return key usually do the same thing (your keyboard may have one, the other, or both).

**Escape key.** The key labeled Escape or Esc. What this key does depends on the program you are using. The vi editor uses it to switch from input mode to command mode.

**executable file.** A file that UNIX can run like a program. An executable file can contain binary machine instructions the computer knows how to execute, or it can contain a *shell script* (a list of UNIX shell commands) that UNIX knows how to execute (see Chapter 14).

**external command.** A command the shell doesn't actually know how to do. Instead, a program is stored in a file with the same name as the command. If you type the ed command (to run the dreadful ed editor),

for example, UNIX runs the program contained by a file named ed.

**file.** A bunch of information stored together with a name. A file can contain text, programs, or data in any format.

**file system.** A set of files stored on a disk or on one partition of a disk. A file system has one root directory that contains files and subdirectories. These subdirectories can in turn contain files and other directories (see Chapter 5).

**file transfer.** Copying files from one computer to another (see Chapter 20).

**filter.** A small UNIX program used with input or output redirection. The most commonly used filters are the more and sort commands. See Chapter 6.

**fixed disk.** A disk that used to be broken but that now works. No, sorry! See *disk*.

**flag.** See *option*.

**floppy disk.** A removable disk, also called a *diskette*. See Chapter 7 for descriptions of the two sizes of floppy disks.

**folder.** A file that contains electronic-mail messages you have decided to save (see Chapter 18).

**foreground.** A program currently able to talk to your terminal. See Chapter 15 for information about how to run programs in the foreground or background.

**fork.** When UNIX starts a new process, it does so by cloning an existing process. The cloning process is known in UNIX-ese as *forking*. Pronounce it carefully to avoid embarrassment.

**FTP.** A file-transfer program that enables you to log in to another computer and transfer files to or from your computer. See "The he-man's file-transfer program" in Chapter 20.

**gateway.** A connection between one network and another, usually networks of different types (see Chapter 17).

**GUI.** A *graphical user interface*. GUIs let you use the computer by pointing at things with a mouse rather than typing commands. The most common UNIX GUIs are Motif, OPEN LOOK, and the X Window System. GUIs sometimes are called *windowing systems* (see Chapter 10).

**hardware.** The physical components of your computer system, that is, the boxes. Your computer hardware may include the computer, terminal, keyboard, screen, modem, printer, mouse, trackball, disk drive, and even a scanner. See Chapter 7.

**header.** The first part of an electronic-mail message that contains the address of the sender and recipient, the subject, and lots of other stuff that is less interesting (see Chapter 18).

**hidden file.** A file with a filename that begins with a period. These files do not appear on regular `ls` directory listings. Use `ls -a` to include hidden files in a directory listing.

**home directory.** The directory you start in when you log in, usually a subdirectory of `/usr`. You should keep your files in your home directory, or in subdirectories of your home directory.

**Huffman coding.** A terribly clever method of compressing information (like the stuff in your files) so that it takes up less space (see Chapter 13).

**icon.** A cute, little picture used in conjunction with a GUI. A well-designed icon is supposed to be an obvious, unmistakable symbol of whatever it stands for, occupy much less space than do the equivalent words, and be cute. In practice, many icons are peculiar little pictures with no obvious meaning (see Chapter 11).

**impact printers.** Printers that work by hitting a ribbon against the paper. They're old-fashioned, but they still work (see Chapter 9).

**inbox.** See *mailbox.*

**incremental backup.** A backup copy of only the files that have changed since the last full backup. See the sidebar "Backup strategies" in Chapter 22.

**inkjet printers.** Printers that work by spitting tiny drops of ink at the page. They are quiet and relatively fast (see Chapter 9).

**Internet.** A large and growing set of interconnected computer networks to which many UNIX systems are directly or indirectly connected.

**input mode.** When you use the `ed` or `vi` text editors, you are in either command mode or input mode. In input mode, whatever you type is entered into the file. See Chapter 12 for information about how to use `ed` and `vi`.

**I/O.** Input and output, that is, information going into or coming out of a program, computer, or other computer-type device.

**I/O redirection.** See *redirection.*

**job.** A program you started from the shell that can start, stop, and move between the foreground and background (see Chapter 15).

**K (also KB or kilobyte).** A measure of memory or disk size which is 1,024 bytes of information. This number happens to be 2 multiplied by itself 10 times, which is a nice, round number for computers.

**keyboard.** The thing you type on to tell your computer what to do. There are many different keyboards, with a wide variety of keys on them.

**kill.** To stop a process from running (see Chapter 23).

**kludge.** A program or feature that works but that the author is embarrassed about. Rhymes with "huge," not with "fudge." Sometimes misspelled as kluge.

**Korn Shell.** An enhanced version of the Bourne Shell, written by a guy named Korn. For your purposes, it's mostly like the Bourne Shell, and prompts you with a $. Its program name is ksh.

**laser printer.** A printer that works like a photocopying machine, except that, rather than a paper original, the information to copy is drawn on the drum by a laser. Pretty cool. (See Chapter 9.)

**line editor.** A text editor that deals with text one line at a time. Most modern text editors let you see and work with the file an entire screen at a time. The ed program is a line editor; we recommend that you use something better. See Chapter 12.

**link.** An additional name for a file. When you create a file, you create its contents, which are stored on the disk somewhere, and you give it a name, which is stored in a directory. There is a connection between the filename and its contents. You can create additional filenames and connect them to the same contents by using the ln command. See the section "When You Want To Share a File" in Chapter 26.

**local mount.** To logically connect several disk drives on the same machine so that they appear as one file system. See Chapter 19.

**log in.** To identify yourself to the UNIX system and provide your password so that UNIX believes that it's really you and lets you use the computer. You have a login ID, or user ID, or user name, that is the name by which UNIX knows you. When you finish working, you log out. See Chapter 1.

**.login.** A hidden file containing a shell script. If you use the C Shell, this script runs automatically every time you log in. See Chapter 14.

**login directory.** See *home directory*.

**mailbox.** The file in which the electronic-mail system puts your incoming mail. See Chapter 18.

**man page.** A short file of information about a UNIX command. The man command displays manual pages about all UNIX commands and a few other topics, although they usually are written in a hopelessly technoid style. See Chapter 27.

**M, MB, or Megabyte.** A measure of memory and disk size that is 1,048,576 bytes, or 1K times 1K, or 2 multiplied by itself 20 times.

**memory.** The storage area where the computer puts information it is working on right now. This is useful for only short-term storage (like until tomorrow). For long-term storage, computers put information on disks. Also known as *main memory* or *RAM*.

**menu.** A list of choices, usually commands, from which you can choose.

**Meta key.** If your keyboard has an Alt key, it is also the Meta key. If not, press the Esc key to achieve the same effect. The effect depends on the program you are running. emacs uses the Meta key for many commands (see Chapter 12).

**modem.** A box that connects your computer or terminal to a phone line. It converts information from your computer to little whistling or hissing noises on the phone line and back again.

**monitor.** See *screen.*

**Motif.** A GUI based on the X Window System and distributed by the Open Software Foundation (see Chapter 10).

**mounting directories.** Logically attaching the root directory of one file system to some other directory so that you can treat all the files in the file system as though they were subdirectories. Mounts can be *local* (on the same machine) or *remote* (on a different machine). See Chapter 19.

**mouse.** A pointing device that lets you move the cursor on-screen. Mice (not "mouses") are used in conjunction with GUIs (see Chapter 10).

**nerd.** A person who spends too much time at the computer. A person, for example, who wanders away from dinner parties to check the computer to see whether any good electronic mail has arrived.

**netiquette.** Rules of polite behavior for sending electronic mail. See Chapter 18.

**network.** A bunch of computers connected by some combination of cables, phone lines, satellites, or whatever. A network enables computers (and their users) to share information and peripherals. They are especially good for sharing printers (so that you can

all share one good but expensive laser printer) and for passing around electronic mail.

**NeXTstep.** An extremely cool GUI that runs on NeXT machines (see Chapter 10).

**NFS.** Network File System. A network system that lets you treat files on another computer in more or less the same way you treat files on your own computer (see Chapter 19).

**NIS.** Network Information System. A database containing the user names, machine names, and directory names NFS use to give consistent names on all machines on a network (see Chapter 19).

**Novell NetWare.** A network system that works on PCs, Macs, and UNIX (see Chapter 19).

**on-line service.** A computer you can call, log in to, and use, usually for a fee per hour. Some services provide a specific set of information: Lexis, for example, provides legal information, and Nexis provides news. Others provide general information: CompuServe, Delphi, and Prodigy, for example, provide a wide range of information, including weather, airline flights, and support for many software programs. Others, like MCI Mail, provide electronic mail. (See Chapter 18.)

**OPEN LOOK.** A GUI based on the X Windows System and developed by USL (see Chapter 10).

**Open Software Foundation (OSF).** A source of UNIX-like and related software. Its best-known products are OSF/1 and Motif.

**operating system.** A special program that controls the way the computer, keyboard, screen, and disks work together. UNIX is an operating system, as is DOS.

**option.** Known also as a *flag* or *switch*. An option is something that tells UNIX how to do a command. You type an option on the command line after the name of the command, separated from the command by a space. All options begin with a dash (-). The ls command used with the -1 option, for example, produces a file listing with more information about each file.

**OSF/1.** A version of UNIX from the Open Software Foundation.

**parent directory.** The directory that contains the current working directory. That is, the current working directory is a subdirectory of the parent directory.

**password.** A secret blend of herbs and spices...no! A secret series of characters known only to you. You type your password when you log in. See Chapter 1 for advice about choosing a password.

**pathname.** Instructions for how to get to a file. An *absolute pathname* tells you how to find a file beginning at the root directory and working down the directory tree. A *relative pathname* tells you how to find the file starting where you are now.

**PC.** A personal computer, usually one running DOS. As a UNIX user, you now can sneer at PCs as "just toys." Now you have a "real computer." Ha! A PC can be used also to act as a terminal so that you can use a computer running UNIX. (One of the authors is doing that at this very moment.) A big-enough PC can run UNIX on its own (that's what the other author is using.) See Chapter 1.

**PCL.** *P*rinter *c*ontrol *l*anguage, understood by a variety of printers made by Hewlett-Packard (see Chapter 9).

**peripheral.** Something that lets the computer communicate with the outside world — mainly with you. The keyboard, screen, mouse, printer, and modem all are peripherals.

**permissions.** Whoever has permission to look at, change, and execute stuff in a file or directory. See the section "Mother, May I?" in Chapter 28.

**pipe.** The | character used to redirect the output of one command so that it becomes the input of another command (see Chapter 6).

**policy independence.** A characteristic of the X Window System in which windows can look and act any way the software developers want. This idea is the converse of the idea that, if all the windows on your screen look and act in a similar way, they will be easier for you to use (see Chapter 10).

**portable software.** Software (programs) that can be run on a number of different kinds of computers. UNIX is portable because it runs on an amazing number of different types of computers.

**POSIX.** The IEEE *p*ortable *o*perating *s*ystem *i*nterface. (Aren't you glad you asked?) POSIX defines a family of definitions of how parts of computer systems work with each other and, incidentally, with users. POSIX is intended to look just like UNIX but to be independent of any specific vendor. There are about a dozen members of the POSIX family; the one you care about is 1003.2 (known as "dot two") and the related *u*ser *p*ortability *e*xtension (UPE). Together, they define the way the commands and shells work. A system that complies with 1003.2 and UPE looks enough like UNIX that everything in this book applies to it.

**PostScript.** A computer language spoken by printers and the programs that communicate with these printers. PostScript enables printers to print a wonderful array of characters in all kinds of sizes and shapes, as well as pictures. When a program wants to print something on a PostScript printer, rather than just send the characters to print, it has to send a PostScript program that tells the printer how to print the stuff. See Chapter 9 for more than you want to know.

**printer.** A machine that makes marks on paper, preferably representing the letters or pictures you requested. There are many kinds of printers. The printer may be connected to your computer; if you are on a network, it may be connected to a computer elsewhere in your office. To find it, just listen for the sound of printing or follow people around for a while. See Chapter 9.

**process.** A running program (see Chapter 23).

`.profile`. A hidden file that contains shell commands. If you use the Bourne or Korn Shell, this file runs automatically every time you log in.

**program.** See *software*.

**prompt.** The character or characters displayed whenever UNIX (or some other program) is waiting for you to type something. The two common UNIX prompts are $ (if you use the Bourne or Korn Shell) or % (if you use the C Shell).

**pushpin.** A cute, little gizmo in the upper left corner of an OPEN LOOK window. If you push in the pushpin, it pins the window so that it stays open. Cute, no?

**queue.** A waiting line, just as in real life. The most common queue is the print queue, in

which the output of `lp` or `lpr` commands waits in line to get printed (see Chapter 9).

**RAM.** *R*andom-*access* memory. See *memory*.

**read-only.** A file that can be read (copied, and so on) but not written (changed). UNIX has a system of permissions that enables the owner of the file, the owner's group, or all users to have or not have permission to read, write, or execute the file. See the section "Mother, May I?" in Chapter 28.

**real-time.** Right now, as opposed to whenever the computer gets around to it.

**redirection.** To hijack the output of a command, which is usually on-screen, and put it somewhere else (this process is called *output redirection*). Alternatively, you can use information from somewhere else as the input for a command (called *input redirection*) rather than take the input from the keyboard. To redirect the output of a command to a file, use the > character. To redirect the input of a command from a file, use the < character. To redirect the output of one command to become the input to another command, use the pipe (|) character. See Chapter 6 for information about how this works.

**remote login.** Logging in to another computer from your own computer. This process requires that your computer be on a network or have a phone connection (see Chapter 20).

**remote mount.** Using NFS to connect directories from disk drives on other machines so that they appear as part of your file system (see Chapter 19).

**request ID.** The ID number of a print job as it waits in the print queue for the printer daemon to get around to printing it. See Chapter 9. You need to know the request ID if you want to cancel printing when, for example, the output is horribly fouled up and wasting lots of paper.

**Return key.** When you use a UNIX shell, pressing Return means that you have just typed a command and you want UNIX to do it. When you use a text editor, pressing Return means that you want to begin a new line. The Enter key and the Return key usually do the same thing (your keyboard may have one, the other, or both).

**RFS.** Remote File Sharing. Like NFS, a program that lets you treat files on another computer in more or less the same way as you treat files on your own computer (see Chapter 19).

**RISC.** Reduced Instruction Set Computer. A type of CPU chip. Different from CISC, but not in a way you care about.

**root.** See *superuser.*

**root directory.** The main, top-level directory on a disk. All the files on the disk are in either the root directory or a subdirectory of the root directory (or a sub-subdirectory, and so on). See Chapter 5.

**rotating backups.** Not using the same tapes or floppy disks every time you make a backup. By rotating among two, three, or more backup sets, you have a longer history and a more reliable system. See the sidebar "Backup strategies" in Chapter 22.

**screen.** The TV-type thing that shows you what's going on in your computer. Also called a *monitor,* CRT, and VDU. Some screens can display many colors; others can do only one, usually green. Some screens can display pictures (graphics); others can do only characters. See Chapter 8 for descriptions of the types of screens.

**screen editor.** A text editor that deals with text an entire screen at a time. The vi and emacs programs are screen editors (see Chapter 12).

**script.** See *shell script.*

**SCSI.** Small Computer Systems Interface. A way to connect a disk drive to a computer. A SCSI disk (pronounced "scuzzy," except in some parts of California, where — typical — they say "sexy") can connect to any SCSI-compatible connector, used by many workstations, PCs, and Macs.

**search path.** A list of directories in which UNIX looks for programs (see Chapter 14).

**server.** See *X server.*

**shar message.** An electronic-mail message that contains a shell script, which, when you run it, re-creates one or more files. This is a clever way to send files through electronic mail (see Chapter 14).

**shell.** A UNIX program that listens for commands you type and tries to execute them. There are several UNIX shells, including the Bourne Shell, Korn Shell, and C Shell. See Chapter 2 to figure out which shell you have.

**shell script.** A file that contains a list of UNIX shell commands. You can *run* a shell script, thereby telling UNIX to execute every command in the list (see Chapter 14).

**slash.** The / character UNIX uses in pathnames. A / by itself, or at the beginning of a pathname, means the root directory of the file system. Slashes are used also between one directory name and the next, and between the directory name and the filename in long path names (see Chapter 5).

**snail-mail.** A mail system in which you print the message you want to send to another person, address a paper envelope of the correct size to fit the paper, insert the paper in the envelope, close the envelope, find a postage stamp, and place the entire thing in a U.S. mail box. Many UNIX users find electronic mail simpler, faster, and more convenient (see Chapter 18).

**soft link.** A link that contains the name of another file, which may be on another file system. A soft link makes it look as though the file that might be on another file system is in a directory on your own file system. Also called a symbolic link. See the section "When You Want To Find Files on Other Machines" in Chapter 26. See also *link*.

**software.** A set of instructions (also called programs) that tell a computer to do something. In contrast to hardware, which includes the physical components of your computer, software is composed of information on a disk (or tape, or whatever).

**Solaris.** A version of UNIX, based initially on BSD UNIX and later on System V Release 4, distributed by Sun for use on Sun workstations and 486 PCs.

**subdirectory.** See *directory*.

**superuser.** The user name (known also as root) with which you can do all sorts of dangerous things to the system, including creating new user names and installing new hardware and software. With luck, you don't know the password for the superuser. If you do, *use it carefully*. The system administrator really should be the only person who logs in as the superuser.

**SVR4.** Release 4 (the latest major version) of UNIX System V. Contains more features than any six people would ever want to use. The latest release of SVR4 is SVR4.2 which is even more feature-packed than the original version of SVR4.

**switch.** See *option*.

**symbolic link.** See *soft link*.

**system administrator.** The person whose job it is to keep the computer, and possibly the network, running.

**System V.** A version of UNIX developed and distributed originally by AT&T and later by UNIX System Labs, which is now part of Novell.

**tape.** A computer tape stores vast amounts of information but is not convenient to use. Tapes are used primarily for making backup copies of information, for which they are terrific. With luck, your system administrator backs up your files to tape regularly. See Chapter 7 for more information about tapes.

`telnet`. A program that enables you to log in to another computer from your computer. See the section "Logging In and Logging Out" in Chapter 20.

**terminal.** A screen and keyboard connected to a computer somewhere else. The terminal doesn't run UNIX and all those neat programs itself, it just lets you use the computer that does. See Chapter 1.

**terminal emulator.** A program that enables a big, powerful computer to act like a dumb, cheap terminal. Commonly, a PC can run a terminal emulator so that you can use another computer running UNIX (see Chapter 1). UNIX includes a simple terminal emulator called `cu` (see Chapter 20).

**terminal output stop mode.** A terminal setting in which a background job stops if it tries to send anything to your screen. See Chapter 15 and 28.

**text editor.** A program that lets you create files of text and edit (or change) them. The most common UNIX text editors are ed, vi, and emacs (see Chapter 12).

**text file.** A file that contains lines of text. All the stuff in a text file must be ASCII characters — no bizarre control codes, data, programs, or the like. You can use the cat command to look at a text file on-screen. If a file looks like it was written by Martians when you use the cat command to view it, it's not a text file.

**text formatter.** A program that reads text files and creates nice-looking formatted output. The most common UNIX text formatters are troff, nroff, and TeX (see Chapter 12).

**trackball.** A pointing device, equivalent to a mouse lying on its back, that lets you move the cursor on the screen (see Chapter 10).

**UNIX.** An operating system written by a couple of people at Bell Laboratories in 1972. They also wrote the C programming language. Since then, several variants of UNIX have appeared, including BSD UNIX, System V UNIX, and Xenix.

**UNIX International (UI).** A consortium of computer vendors that supports System V and gives guidance to USL.

**UNIX System Laboratories (USL).** The organization that develops and maintains UNIX System V. Originally owned primarily by AT&T, it is now part of Novell.

**usenet.** A very large, very informal, very disorganized network through which many megabytes of news, rumor, and gossip are distributed every day. See the section "How To Read So Much Electronic Gossip That You Have No Time Left To Work" in Chapter 28.

**user name.** The name by which UNIX knows you. You enter this name when you log in. Also known as your *user ID* or *login ID* (see Chapter 1).

**utility.** A small, useful program. UNIX comes with some utilities like diff and sort.

**uucp.** The UNIX-to-UNIX copy program. One of the ways that mail, usenet news, and random files can be sent between computers. See the section "A Really Gross Old Network" in Chapter 28.

**uuencoded file.** An electronic-mail message format that contains a binary file disguised as text. When you run the message through uudecode, the binary file is reconstituted. This is a clever way to send binary files through electronic mail (see Chapter 14).

**virtual memory.** A sneaky trick by which UNIX pretends to have more memory than it really does. When you are not looking, UNIX copies information from memory to the disk to free up space in memory. When you need the information on disk, UNIX copies it from the disk back into memory. Virtual memory is generally invisible, except when a program uses it too enthusiastically; then the computer spends all its time copying stuff back and forth to the disk and no time doing useful work, a condition called *thrashing*.

**wildcard.** A special character that acts like a joker when it is used in filenames or pathnames. UNIX shells have two: * and ? (see Chapter 6).

**WIMP.** *W*indows, *i*cons, and *m*ouse *p*ointing. See *GUI* or Chapter 10.

**window.** A rectangular area of the screen in which a program displays something. If you use a GUI, you can have several windows on-screen at a time, each displaying a different program (see Chapter 10).

**window manager.** The program (like OPEN LOOK or Motif) that gives the screen the overall look of a GUI (see Chapter 10).

**wizard.** A person who knows more about UNIX than is really healthy. Encourage wizards to get outside once in a while. (A typical wizard figures that turning up the brightness on the screen is equivalent to going out in the sunshine.)

**word processor.** A program that lets you create documents — files that contain text, pictures, and formatting codes (see Chapter 12). UNIX word processors include WordPerfect and Microsoft Word.

**working directory.** The directory you are working in. The pwd command tells you your working directory.

**workstation.** A computer with a big screen, a keyboard, and a mouse. If it runs UNIX, it's called a workstation; if it runs DOS, it's called a PC. And, if it runs Macintosh Finder (or whatever that system is called), it's called a Mac. (If a train stops at a train station, what happens at a workstation?)

**X server.** A program that draws the pictures and displays the text on-screen if you use the X Window System or a GUI based on X (see Chapter 11).

**X terminal.** A terminal that can act as an X server so that you can use the X Windows System, Motif, or OPEN LOOK. It has a little computer in it to do the X-specific stuff (see Chapters 1 and 10).

**X Window System, or just X.** A GUI designed at MIT. Two other major GUIs, Motif and OPEN LOOK, are based on X (see Chapter 10).

**XENIX.** A version of UNIX developed by Microsoft, of all people, and now maintained and distributed by SCO (Santa Cruz Organization).

**Yellow Pages.** See *NIS*.

# Index